CHANEL

CHANEL

LOUIS VUITTON

LOUIS VUITTON

GUCCI
SIGMUND FREU
Three Contributions
to the
Theory of Sex

GUCCI

FEELS LI

E PRADA

#FEELSLIKEPRADA

FEELS LII

KE PRADA

#FEELSLIKEPRADA

FEELS LI

#FEELSLIKEPRADA

SAINT LAURENT

SIHANA
FALL 21 COLLECTION
YSL.COM

SAINT LAURENT

SIHANA
FALL 21 COLLECTION
YSL.COM

See the films on miumiu.com

See the films on miumiu.com

FENDI

ROMA

FENDI

ROMA

LOEWE

Gillian Anderson with the Amazona
by Juergen Teller in London

loewe.com

LOEWE

Anthea Hamilton with the Amazona
by Juergen Teller in London

loewe.com

MEANTIME FALL — WINTER 2021

DSQUARED2

WE WERE ALWAYS WAITING FOR SOMETHING TO HAPPEN...

MEANTIME FALL — WINTER 2021

DSQUARED2

WE WERE WAITING FOR OUR LIVES TO REALLY BEGIN, BUT THE THING IS, THEY ALREADY HAD— I HAD MET YOU.

GUESS

CLASH [UN]LIMITED

Cartier

Loro Piana

BURBERRY

LONDON ENGLAND

ANDREAS VIVIENNE
KRONTHALER WESTWOOD

Alexander
McQUEEN

DUNHILL.COM

dunhill

Zegna

(RESET)
WHAT MAKES A MAN

ZEGNA.COM

SPORTMAX FALL / WINTER 21

LOOK 09/50 BLACK LEATHER ENSEMBLE

SPORTMAX

FILA 110th Anniversary Collection

FILA 110th Anniversary Collection

NER

bogner.com

FENDI

ANOTHER MAGAZINE
ISSUE 41 — *Autumn / Winter 2021*

EDITORIAL DIRECTOR Jefferson Hack   EDITOR-IN-CHIEF Susannah Frankel   CREATIVE DIRECTOR Marc Ascoli
FASHION DIRECTORS Katie Shillingford (womenswear), Ellie Grace Cumming (menswear)
EDITOR Sophie Bew   MANAGING EDITOR Hannah Lack
FASHION FEATURES DIRECTOR Alexander Fury

FASHION   SENIOR FASHION EDITORS-AT-LARGE Katy England, Alister Mackie, Agata Belcen, Nell Kalonji
CONTRIBUTING FASHION EDITORS Rae Boxer, Marie Chaix, Marcus Cuffie, Reuben Esser, Avena Gallagher,
Samia Giobellina, Raphael Hirsch, Ai Kamoshita, Karen Langley, Olivier Rizzo, Isabelle Sayer,
Robbie Spencer, Emma Wyman

CASTING DIRECTOR Noah Shelley at Streeters
FASHION AND MARKET COORDINATORS Rebecca Perlmutar (womenswear), Jordan Duddy (menswear)
FASHION ASSISTANTS Isabella Kavanagh, George Pistachio

PHOTOGRAPHY   PHOTOGRAPHIC EDITOR Helena Whelan
ACTING PHOTOGRAPHIC EDITOR Ellie Robertson
PHOTOGRAPHIC PRODUCER Beth Mingay

DESIGN   ART DIRECTORS Marc Ascoli
Diego Fellay at Atelier 32
DESIGNER Boris Meister with Atelier 32
COORDINATOR Alexia Cayre at Atelier 32

FEATURES   DEPUTY EDITOR Ted Stansfield
BOOKINGS EDITOR Greg Krelenstein
SUB-EDITOR Sam Thackray
PRODUCTION EDITOR Laura Allsop
EDITORIAL ASSISTANTS Gilda Bruno, Emily Dinsdale

PRODUCTION   GROUP PRODUCTION MANAGER Emily Moore
PRINT AND REPROGRAPHICS MANAGER Steve Savigear
PRODUCTION CONTROLLER Valeria Della Valle

PICTURES   Marili Andre, Korakrit Arunanondchai, Halil Atasever, BFRND, Mel Bles, Janicza Bravo, Cosima, Enrico Chico
De Luigi, Nicolas Di Felice, Leah Dou, Estileras, Jenna Fletcher, Regina José Galindo, Paula Garcia, Oliver
Hadlee Pearch, Misan Harriman, Jamie Hawkesworth, Paris Hilton, Larissa Hofmann, Toyin Ibidapo, Wesley
Joseph, KangHee Kim, Paul Kooiker, Arnaud Lajeunie, Matthieu Lavanchy, Ilya Lipkin, Carlos Martiel, Taro
Mizutani, Fumi Nagasaka, Maggie Nelson, Jackie Nickerson, Thue Nørgaard, Sharna Osborne, Yiannis Pappas,
Thurstan Redding, Ola Rindal, Liberty Ross, Antwaun Sargent, Bianca Saunders, Collier Schorr, Casper
Sejersen, Tony Shanahan, Patti Smith, Maria Stamenković Herranz, Jet Swan, Willy Vanderperre, William
Waterworth, Vivienne Westwood, Joshua Woods

TEXT   Marina Abramović, Emma Hope Allwood, Halil Atasever, Sophie Bew, Selim Bulut, Anna Cafolla, Emma Davidson,
Estileras, Susannah Frankel, Alexander Fury, Coco Fusco, Regina José Galindo, Paula Garcia, Jefferson Hack,
Claire Marie Healy, Belle Hutton, Ashleigh Kane, Katie Kitamura, Hannah Lack, Sagal Mohammed, Lynette
Nylander, Yiannis Pappas, Patti Smith, Maria Stamenković Herranz, Ted Stansfield, Vivienne Westwood

ANOTHERMAG.COM   EDITOR Ted Stansfield
SOCIAL MEDIA EDITOR Orla Brennan
CONTRIBUTING EDITORS Claire Marie Healy, Belle Hutton, Sagal Mohammed, Lucy Kumara Moore, Jack Moss,
Dominique Sisley, Hannah Tindle

PUBLISHING   PUBLISHERS Jefferson Hack, Rankin Waddell
PUBLISHING DIRECTOR Susanne Waddell
GLOBAL PUBLISHING AND COMMERCIAL DIRECTOR Luke Robins
PR & EVENTS pr@dazedmedia.com
DAZED STUDIO dazedstudio@dazedmedia.com
FINANCE finance@dazedmedia.com
ADVERTISING commercialprojects@dazedmedia.com
ITALIAN AGENTS advertising@jbmedia.com

DISTRIBUTION   CIRCULATION MANAGER Stuart White, stuart.white@dazedmedia.com
SUBSCRIPTION ENQUIRIES info@boutiquemags.com

COLOUR AND REPROGRAPHICS Tapestry
AnOther Magazine is printed by YM Group using paper supplied by Denmaur Media made from FSC® certified
forestry sources, which have been carbon offset through the World Land Trust's Carbon Balanced Paper scheme.
Printed and published in the UK - available online at boutiquemags.com

ISSN 1355-5901 © 2021. Published twice a year by AnOther Publishing Ltd,
2 Arundel Street, London WC2R 3DA, +44 0 20 7336 0766

Objects connect.

CONTENTS

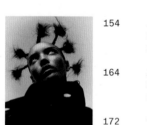

Zendaya by David Sims at the Palace Theater in Los Angeles, 17th April 2021

Editor's Letter

We live and learn. It's not only impossible but inconceivable to disregard the events of the past 18 months – shifts in the minutiae of the everyday accompanied by societal structures reassessed, re-evaluated and even torn down to be rebuilt. We have lived through, and continue to live through, moments of profound change. And fashion, always a mirror of the world, reflects that.

While considering this issue of AnOther Magazine, we thought of different ideas that felt tied to the moment. The most pertinent seemed to be 'hindsight' – namely, the knowledge to be drawn from a situation after its occurrence, the reasoning why, and the importance not just of lived experience but learnt experience. Such lessons are applicable not only to the fashion industry but also a wider cultural context. The word and definition returned, again and again, like a heartbeat.

More than merely looking back, hindsight draws on history to move forward into the future. Looking back at Zoë Kravitz's heritage it now seems inevitable that she would become a star – although it remains difficult to predict her future trajectory as she simultaneously embraces her bold-face parentage and forges her own path. With hindsight, maybe we wouldn't have scheduled her shoot with Collier Schorr in June, when New York experienced a heatwave and the temperature reached 37C on set. We cannot thank Kravitz enough for persevering, nor Schorr for these extraordinary images of an icon in the making. Kravitz speaks openly here with Lynette Nylander.

Travis Scott's deep-rooted, far-reaching collaboration with Kim Jones and the house of Dior on its Spring/Summer 2022 menswear collection guarantees his presence in fashion's history books. As Scott samples and remixes sounds, so he and Jones rework the heritage of Dior, captured here in an interview with them both and an exclusive preview shoot on the set of the show by Ellie Grace Cumming and Joshua Woods.

"Our ideas come from what we saw, what we heard, what we read. We are our past. How can we pretend it doesn't exist?" These are the words of Miuccia Prada, one of fashion's foremost thinkers, who pinpoints the entire industry's continual reinvention of the past as a catalyst for the future. Prada embraces the history of her family's label but, under the imprint of Miu Miu, offers a fundamentally personal vision, inspired by her own tastes, attitudes and attire. For this issue she has, for the first time, pulled from the Miu Miu archive to dress a cast of powerfully individual young people. They are styled by Katie Shillingford and photographed by Jamie Hawkesworth, who travelled back to the location in Milan where he photographed the designer herself four years ago. Prada talks about her experience of the recent past, and of the importance of bravery – fitting for a designer who always epitomises that.

So too does Vivienne Westwood. She is also, at heart, an educator who has always believed in the power and relevance of history – the root of a creative bond forged with her husband Andreas Kronthaler more than three decades ago. Here, his latest collection under her name is joined by the clothes and words of a new generation of talent inspired by her approach. And Westwood herself expands on the subject she is most passionate about, climate crisis, weeks before the COP26 summit in Glasgow.

The past of Gucci is near-legendary – the family's complex saga, worthy of Medicis and Borgias, has just been transformed into a motion picture. Its century-long aesthetic identity is equally complex, allowing creative director Alessandro Michele the freedom to toy with the brand's history – to hack, meaning to violently cut and reshape, as well as to gain unauthorised access. For the new season, Michele hacked away at Gucci's equestrian roots, but also into the modern heritage of stablemate Balenciaga, stamping its silhouettes with Gucci's identity. In return, Willy Vanderperre and Olivier Rizzo hack Gucci right back, re-contextualising this collection in the fairy-tale landscape of their northern European world.

Demna Gvasalia's revival of Balenciaga's couture operation was always going to be exciting. However, few might have anticipated the delicate reverence and respect that accompanied his couture debut, which drew on the house's archives to create something new. In a series of interviews through the spring of 2021, Alexander Fury explored the past with Gvasalia, while Marie Chaix and Ola Rindal celebrate the future: Balenciaga's rekindled couture and its first collection since 1968.

Looking back perhaps makes it simpler to see what really matters, what will remain for posterity. Legacy is the theme highlighted by Marina Abramović, often described as the godmother of performance art, who guest-edits our Document section. She devotes its pages to the performance artists of the future – all of whom have learnt from her processes and, inevitably, drawn from her legacy. And for our Art Project we examine the life and work of the Japanese-American sculptor Isamu Noguchi, to coincide with the Barbican's 2021 retrospective. Alongside a photographic essay of his sculpture at his eponymous New York museum, the acclaimed novelist Katie Kitamura breathes life into his legacy through 12 fragments, encapsulating the artist's humane essence.

A preternaturally gifted polymath, Patti Smith shaped so many of our pasts and continues to inform our futures. In an intimate conversation with this magazine's founder, Jefferson Hack, and in partnership with RIMOWA, Smith talks about travel: physical travel but also travel of the mind. Their dialogue is thought-provoking, Smith's observations both timely and timeless.

This letter is always a space to celebrate the passionate creatives who make each issue of AnOther Magazine possible – the photographers, stylists, journalists, beauty teams and models. At a time when the entire fashion system, including the very notion of a fashion season, is challenged like never before, we uphold its endlessly inventive and protean ability to capture the now – through Jackie Nickerson's wild distillation of some of the moment's boldest, bravest looks, Robbie Spencer and Oliver Hadlee Pearch's bravado and pile-it-on excess and the raw grace of Peter Philips's Dior beauty story with Thue Nørgaard. This will be a time to remember – frightening and difficult, perhaps, yet also exciting, energising and filled with promise. And I hope, with hindsight, our magazine captures this moment.

SUSANNAH FRANKEL, editor-in-chief

VERSACE

La Greca • [grè-ca] 1. A decorative pattern constructed from one continuous line. 2. An iconic code of the Versace brand. 3. A new Versace print and accessories line worn by Dua Lipa.

LIFE IN COLOURS

AVENA GALLAGHER
styles
ZOË KRAVITZ

p284

What did you and Collier Schorr want to capture in the shoot with Zoë? *We wanted to capture a very 'raw' image of her ... something intimate, but more than that – something unproduced somehow.* What piece of advice would you give your younger self? *I would tell teen me to throw out any expectations that were imposed upon me. I tried too hard to meet the expectations of the adults in my life to a point where their expectations usurped my own hopes and it got really confusing. I had no compass. I would advise myself to follow every inner attraction or intuition and let that lead.*

LYNETTE NYLANDER
interviews
ZOË KRAVITZ

p284

Describe Zoë in one word. *Alluring.* What was the most memorable moment of your interview with her? *Zoë giving me dating advice and her thoughts on savouring being young and enjoying the moment. She's a wise one.* What makes her a great actor? *She's a shapeshifter. And although she's impossibly beautiful and cool, she somehow makes her roles relatable.* Can you give us a lesson you've learnt from hindsight? *Appreciate every moment. It could all be over tomorrow!*

JAMIE HAWKESWORTH
photographs
MIU MIU

p342

What was the best moment of your Miu Miu shoot? *Watching England v Denmark in an Italian bar and England winning.* If you could relive any part of your life, which would it be? *I don't think I would.* What piece of advice would you give your younger self? *Always make time to exercise!*

MARIE CHAIX
styles
BALENCIAGA COUTURE

p318

What excited you about the shoot with Ola Rindal? *Shooting the Balenciaga Couture collection in Paris by the Palais de Tokyo and the Trocadéro, which is magical to me – the tall architecture and the scale, all of this through the stillness and calm of Ola's lens.* What was the most memorable moment? *The bride alone at the top of the stairs. And the black couture hat being blown away by the wind, which was quite scary.* What is a lesson you've learnt from hindsight? *Trust your instincts.* What would you like your legacy to be? *Genderless long nails with square tips.*

TOM FORD

EYEWEAR

KATIE KITAMURA
writes
ISAMU NOGUCHI

p482

What drew you to write about Isamu Noguchi? *Above all, the work. He led an extraordinary life, but it's the work that is endlessly mysterious and captivating.* What's the most interesting thing you discovered about him? *I wasn't aware of the texts Noguchi wrote while incarcerated in an internment camp during the second world war. They are fascinating, deeply ambiguous documents.* What piece of advice would you give your younger self? *There's a certain amount of wisdom in withholding judgment.* If you could relive any part of your life, which would you choose? *I don't think I would! Even the thought fills me with mild horror.*

LARISSA HOFMANN
photographs
THE THINGS DIVINE

p232

How did you set about creating a mood for the shoot? *'Raw opulence' were the first words we discussed. We wanted our character to feel in control and strong, and soft and emotional at the same time. Step by step our idea formed, and when Meadow came into the picture everything just fell into place.* What was Meadow Walker like to work with? *She was great! As well as being very easy-going and pleasant to work with, she was the perfect fit for our story.*

JET SWAN
photographs
ONLY IN SLEEP

p264

Looking back, what was the best moment of your shoot? *Right at the beginning, just before taking the first picture is the most exhilarating ... You can forget everything else and get into your own head with it.* What piece of advice would you give your younger self? *The things you feel self-conscious about are your greatest strengths.* If you could relive any part of your life, which would you choose and why? *I wouldn't relive anything. The best moments are the best because you can't have them again.*

JOSHUA WOODS
photographs
TRAVIS SCOTT

p308

What interested you about shooting Travis? *It was Days Before Rodeo for me. It was summertime in New York in 2014 and it was ringing in the streets, and then Skyfall was the music to the HBA show that September and I just remember the energy at the show – it was electric. It was a moment.* What piece of advice would you give your younger self? *What's meant for you is already aligning. Don't save any money. Spend your money on experiences. Get a passport and go learn a language. Take your time and make all the mistakes you need to. Open up more, take more risks and address any fears, don't internalise things.*

ISABEL MARANT

Jun *Takahashi*

Paris *Hilton*

Bianca *Saunders*

Maggie *Nelson*

Liberty *Ross*

Cosima

Antwaun *Sargent*

Janicza *Bravo*

Korakrit

Arunanondchai

Nicolas *Di Felice*

Wesley *Joseph*

Leah *Dou*

Jenna *Fletcher*

Manolo *Blahnik*

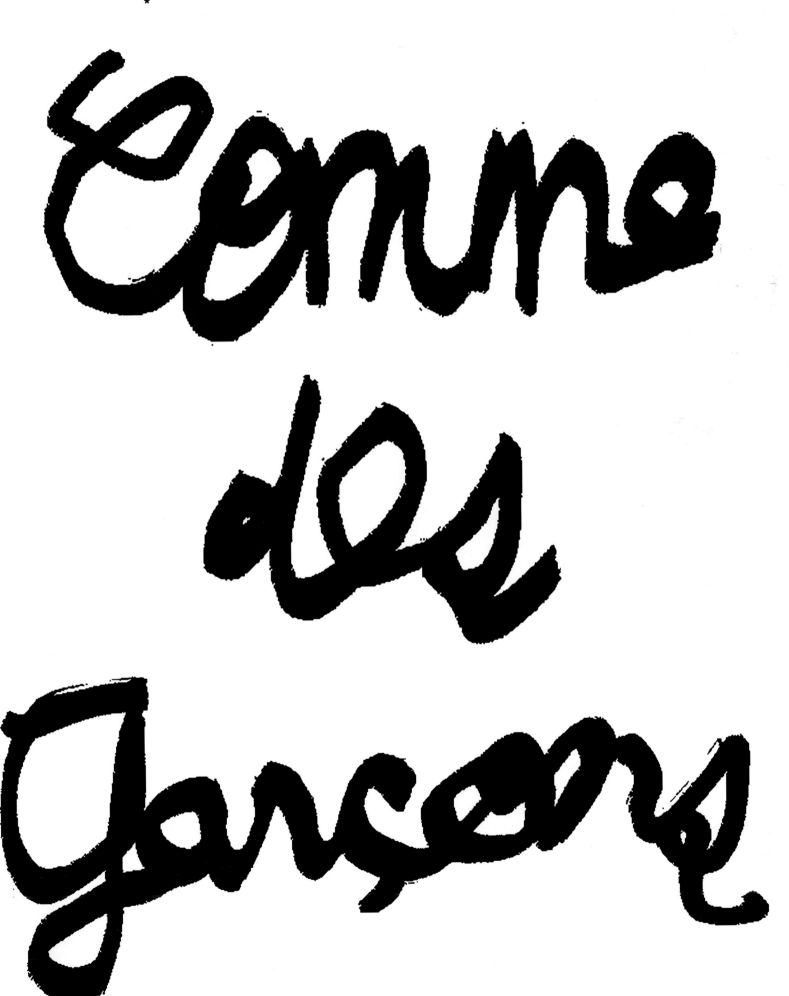

JUN TAKAHASHI,

designer,

on

anarchy

❝To me, anarchy means to be mentally free. Important is not the right word – this is the basic principle of my life. I've rebelled against almost everything. I first encountered the anarchy symbol in music and movies – as a kid, I loved media with strong characteristics. I felt digging into those arts was anarchic and liberating. People who seek spiritual liberation are anarchists. This philosophy is deeply rooted within me, so it's difficult for me to explain in words. It is not about my design in particular, it is more about my perspective of the world and how I come up with designs. Something invisible. Recently I applied a circle-A, the anarchy symbol and an iconic emblem of punk culture, to the back of a simple chair [as part of a collaboration with interior designer Kazuya Sasaki]. It expresses the idea of punk spirit settled into daily life. There is controversy of some sort in any time or age – questioning and rebelling are essential. Anarchists exist in every era.❞

Jun Takahashi is an avowed design anarchist, with an affinity for punk that goes beyond sentiment: he was the lead singer of a cover band named the Tokyo Sex Pistols, and his fashion label Undercover continues a spirit of rebellion and nonconformity that stems straight from the culture-shattering creations Vivienne Westwood and Malcolm McLaren filled their King's Road shop with in the 70s. His earliest pieces, shortly after he established his brand in 1990 while a student at the Bunka Fashion College in Tokyo, were collaged T-shirts in the Seditionaries mould; his move to showing in Paris from 2002 marked not only a new sophistication of technique but a continued and continual rebellion in aesthetic. It's not post punk, because for him punk never stopped. Words ALEXANDER FURY

Portrait by Taro Mizutani

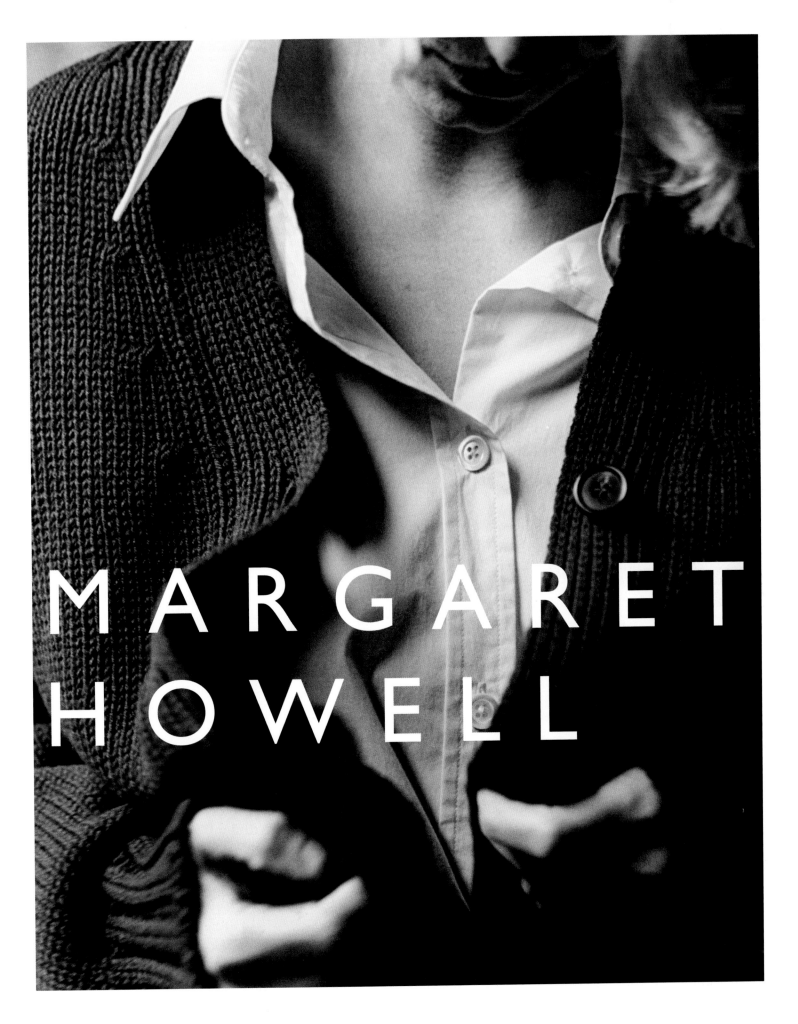

PARIS HILTON,

entrepreneur & DJ,

on

NFTs

We are living in a new era of Paris Hilton. Last year, the original, pastel-pink influencer and heiress embarked on a campaign to protect a new generation of students from the institutionalised abuse she says she suffered while attending a Utah boarding school for 'troubled teens'. She then took a chameleonic turn in Lanvin's Spring/Summer 2021 campaign, and now she has turned her hand to digital art, creating a series of mesmerising, colour-drenched NFTs (an acronym that stands for non-fungible tokens – unique, collectible digital assets) that depict life in the virtual space of her metaverse. Created in collaboration with rising Los Angeles-based artist Blake Kathryn, Hilton's works feature subjects – herself, her bedroom, a beloved pet – that are transported into candyfloss-like clouds. Meanwhile she is also the star of a new Netflix show entitled Cooking with Paris, which she likens to her defining reality series The Simple Life, only with more food, celebrity guests and full-on high-fashion looks.

Words EMMA DAVIDSON

❚❚ As an Aquarius, I've always been a very creative person and I've loved art my whole life. Ever since I was a little girl I've been obsessed with pop art and Andy Warhol, and how he's painted so many icons of our time. My favourite Warhol pieces are of Marilyn Monroe and Elizabeth Taylor. Marilyn is one of the most iconic women ever born and has always been such a huge inspiration to me.

I've always loved to draw and paint, and I love to collage. I'm very into cabochons, as well as resin and glitter. I love making pop art and digital art too. A friend who was working with [the blockchain-based digital-collectible auction site] Cryptograph approached me in early 2020 about making my first NFT for charity, so I decided to make one of my cat. I knew there was something really special about this medium, but I didn't realise [the artworks created through it] would blow up in the way they have. I love the way they give power back to the creator – it's amazing that all these talented digital artists are finally getting the respect they deserve.

Everything is going digital, so it's not surprising art is moving in that direction. I now own more than 150 NFTs, and I love collecting pieces that I have a connection with – usually created by friends or people who I have a lot of respect for. Some of my favourites are by Pak, Mad Dog Jones, Josh Pierce, and Blake Kathryn, who I collaborated with on my most recent pieces. I really wanted to work with a female artist because I feel like there are not enough women in the industry – I love breaking glass ceilings and uplifting other female creatives. Her style and aesthetic are so perfect and reflect me so well, right down to the colours.

One of my favourite pieces that I've created is of a hummingbird in the metaverse, which is dedicated to my grandmother. She was a huge inspiration to me throughout my life, and we were so close. She painted every single day and was the first person I ever painted with, when I was three. Every time I stayed with her for a weekend, or when I lived with her when I was in ninth grade, we would paint all the time. We started off with animals, like cats and dogs, and then we moved on to people. She was a very talented artist and really encouraged me to be creative – I owe a lot of my love of art to her.

She passed away in 2002 from breast cancer, but before she died she told me she would always be there for me as a hummingbird. Ever since she passed, particularly when I'm in Palm Springs, which is where she lived, there's a hummingbird that follows me around, or even comes up to the window. I'll go outside and it'll be flying around me, and I feel like it's her because hummingbirds are usually scared of people and fly right away. I have NFTs all over my house now, and every time I walk into my dining room, I can see her flying. It feels so good that she's there with me.

All the pieces we created have a story. As well as my grandmother and the hummingbird, there's also Bedroom Bliss, a visual depiction of what my bedroom would be like in the metaverse. It's this kind of safe space that I built after going through a lot of things when I was a teenager. Another features Tinkerbell, my chihuahua, who was my best friend, my sister, my other half. I miss her so much and I wanted to honour her like I did my grandmother. And I'm obsessed with avatars, so there's a futuristic version of me in the line-up, too. It makes me so happy to know people will own these deeply personal works of art. It's beautiful to think that my friends or fans or people who love art will have a piece of me and my story. **❚❚**

BIANCA SAUNDERS,

designer,

on

Lynette Yiadom-Boakye

" I first discovered Lynette Yiadom-Boakye when I was applying to the Royal College of Art. My sister and I came across an exhibition of hers at the Serpentine Gallery and I remember thinking, 'Wow, this is the best thing I've ever seen in my life.' I immediately went home to study her work and fell in love with it even more. I was most interested in the idea of creating a character by combining different forms of imaginary people – which is something I like doing in my own work. I'm fascinated by the way multiple people are able to identify with the figures in her art. She paints her fictitious subjects with certain movements and gestures, and you can imagine that person's scars. It's so interesting – I often use her work on my research boards for inspiration. Her ability to create something dark that still holds elements of joy within it is so important, especially during the time we're in right now. **"**

Bianca Saunders has established herself as one of the most exciting names in British fashion. After graduating from the Royal College of Art in the summer of 2017, she debuted at London Fashion Week Men's the following June and was named by the British Fashion Council as One to Watch. The southeast London-born talent is currently at the forefront of a new generation of designers,

reshaping the idea of masculinity and harnessing its nuances to shift ideas about menswear. Her chosen tools include a gender-fluid authenticity and cultural inspirations sparked by her Caribbean roots; they have won her international plaudits (most recently the Andam Fashion Awards Grand Prize) and an ever-increasing circle of fans and clients.

Words SAGAL MOHAMMED

MAGGIE NELSON,

author,

on

Tala Madani

❝ The Womb [2019] by Tala Madani is a very short piece of video art – 3 minutes, 26 seconds. I first saw it at Madani's mind-blowing show Shit Moms, at David Kordansky Gallery in Los Angeles in the fall of 2019, when we had no idea of the 2020 awaiting us around the bend. Even then, I had the strong feeling that The Womb was a necessary – urgent, even – preparation: for the foetus, most obviously, who here gets a crash course on the history of the world, with all its absurdity, technology and violence – but also for the mother, who houses the projection, and the viewer, who is made aware of her own entrapment in the nightmare of history. Like much of Madani's work, the triumph of The Womb lies in its tone – it is alarming, funny, profound and cathartic all at once. I've thought of it often over the past year, as its jaunty, morbid and dauntless vision has heartened me at moments when I felt most gripped by a 'I can't go on/I'll go on' state, which was, let's be honest, nearly constant. **❞**

LA-based author, poet and thinker Maggie Nelson navigates the messiness of life in clear-eyed prose, untangling knots in our language and finding breathing spaces in ideas that seem sewn up and impenetrable. Her genre-defying books include Bluets, a freewheeling paean to the colour blue, The Argonauts, a luminous meditation on love and identity, and The Red Parts, a haunting account of the 1969 murder of her aunt and its fallout – all works that draw on a vast library of critical thought, pop culture and the minutiae of daily experience to make their investigations. Nelson's new book, On Freedom, puts that weighted and unwieldy concept under the microscope, exploring its many meanings, ambiguities and possibilities in the four realms of art, sex, drugs and climate. Words HANNAH LACK

MOOSE KNUCKLES

LIBERTY ROSS,

creative
director,

on

Flipper's Roller Boogie Palace

It was in 2013 that Liberty Ross first delved into the history of the famed LA venue that also holds the key to her own family history: Flipper's roller rink, which from 1979 to 1981, at the corner of La Cienega and Santa Monica boulevards, was the after-dark destination of choice for a huge cross section of LA cultures. Presided over by her father, Ian "Flipper" Ross, and mother, Bunty Ross, with several small children in tow, the roller rink was where you'd find people from all surrounding neighbourhoods and backgrounds under a single, glorious roof: from a young Laura Dern to Jane Fonda and Nile Rodgers, skating to live performances by the likes of Black Flag, the Go-Go's and Prince. Now, as the pandemic lends outdoor activities a new cultural significance, there has been a noticeable roller resurgence, which makes the forthcoming release of Ross's new book, Flipper's Roller Boogie Palace, feel joyfully meant to be. Under her creative direction, the book will be published by Idea this autumn.

Words CLAIRE MARIE HEALY

❝ I was 24 when I first moved back to LA and I would tell people how, when I was a little girl, my parents owned a roller disco called Flipper's in the city. I can't have been more than about three when it closed but, even 20 years later, I kept meeting people with incredible stories about their experience there. That's what led me to want to know more. The process of putting this book together – digging through photos, seeing how people dressed at that time, how they behaved – has been amazing. We found dedicated Facebook pages and Instagram accounts I was able to tap into. I met people online who were so happy to share their memories – 'I had my first kiss there,' 'I had my 13th birthday party there,' 'I met Cher there.'

It's a family story – it comes from something very real and truthful. Without really knowing anyone, my parents shacked up in LA and opened Flipper's in 1979. I was a baby. I have five siblings and our childhood was bohemian, I suppose – unconventional. Making this book has been very meaningful for us all. Connecting with my brothers and sisters, asking them about their memories, has brought us closer. And it has been incredible for my parents. They had no idea of the impact they had. When I think about my dad specifically, about Flipper's but also the fact that he gave rock'n'roll a voice in England from his ship in the Sixties, it makes me realise that a passionate motivation to merge different cultures has always been part of who he is. [Ian 'Flipper' Ross ran the pioneering pirate station Radio Caroline, designed to skirt the record companies' monopoly over regular music broadcasting.]

Flipper's was a place where everybody felt safe – everybody was family and everybody was included, no matter where they were from. There's something about roller skating. You can be really bad at it or really good at it, but no matter what, you're smiling when you put your skates on. If nothing else, roller skating forces you to put your phone away for a few hours, to get into your body and have some fun. It's all about being present and connecting with yourself and those around you. Still today, all the rinks are community driven, which makes it even sadder that they're slowly closing down.

I have been going to this one remaining rink, in Long Beach, with my husband. We go three times a week. One of the guys there is 73 and he's been skating his entire life. When I told him about Flipper's he was like, 'Oh my God, *that* place.' He remembers the sound system, he remembers how you would hear music there that you'd never heard anywhere else – you'd hear and experience things there for the first time. A few weeks later, he'd put two and two together – he said, 'Wait a second. Are you Lettice Lark?' Those are my two middle names. Apparently he had met me when I was a baby, when my dad used to carry me around the rink at Flipper's in his arms. ❞

COSIMA,

musician,

on

Simone Bittencourt de Oliveira

"Brazilian music has always been very important to me – there's so much expression in the melodies and Brazilian singers have incredible, distinct vocal tones. When I was younger I read a Quincy Jones quote that described Simone as one of the world's greatest singers, and I had to find out who she was and why her voice was so special. When I was growing up, my voice didn't really fit with other people's around me, and listening to Simone gave me confidence in that. There's one song of hers called Jura Secreta, which is just her and an electric piano. I was sold from then on – I love production but vocals are really what move me, and her voice is the emotional anchor of the song. Whenever I need to really sit with my feelings, that's the track I put on. It made me think about what I could do with my voice and unlocked the possibility of letting my vocals do the work. It's something I always think about. Every time I make new music, I listen to that song at some point in the process."

Cosima launched South of Heaven Records in 2019. Through her label, the Peckham-born and based musician makes art on her own terms, and hopes other young artists can take note. "It's realising that you can come from a normal, working-class background and still retain ownership," she says. Previously signed to a major label, she cherishes this freedom. She has had a busy year: in February she released the EP The Fun Is Here? In July she performed at Valentino's Autumn/Winter 2021 haute couture show in Venice, and her EP What Kind of Summer Are You Having Without Me? is newly out. The musician mines life's complexities in her emotion-led writing process, her soulful, bittersweet tracks making for a striking listening experience. Much like the artists she admires – women such as Janis Ian, Cindy Sherman, Nina Simone, Anaïs Nin – Cosima is writing her own rules.   Words BELLE HUTTON

shop at tela9.com

ANTWAUN SARGENT,

curator & critic,

on artists with social practices

66 We're in a moment of profound change and that has called for us to rethink the role of artists. I'm interested in artists who are taking social concerns and thinking them through creatively. Like Linda Goode Bryant, who thinks about space with real-life consequences and created an urban farm initiative. She uses farming like a painter uses a brush. Or the photographer Tyler Mitchell, who imagines a new type of figure. Or Amy Sherald, who asks what a new American image might look like in her paintings. Then you have Mark Bradford, who is exploring how to rebound as a community. And Kehinde Wiley, who is translating his painting practice into a space that allows younger artists to have the opportunities that he's had. These are artists who are not painting a rosy picture of what the future should be, but putting their art on the line to establish that future. Like the Black arts movement of the 1960s and the Harlem Renaissance, these artists are rethinking their relationships with culture and society and what they want their art to do. I find that incredibly exciting. 99

Originally from Chicago, Antwaun Sargent moved to New York City in 2011, where he worked as a kindergarten teacher before pivoting to art writing – for which he is now widely celebrated. Having initially written about his artist friends, in 2019 the budding curator and critic published his best-selling first book, The New Black Vanguard: Photography Between Art and Fashion, which spotlights 15 young Black artists currently setting the agenda in fashion photography – an accompanying exhibition has been staged at several art institutions around the world. At the beginning of this year, Sargent joined Gagosian as a director and curator, and this summer curated his first exhibition there, Social Works, a group show that considers the relationship between space – personal, public, institutional, psychic – and Black social practice. "For me," Sargent says, "art is a profound medium that not only records our time in history, but also allows us to propose new possibilities of being."

Words TED STANSFIELD

Self-portrait by Antwaun Sargent

TORINO

JANICZA BRAVO,

director,

on

Bill Gunn

"Stressful comedy is my sweet spot," says Janicza Bravo, the acclaimed director of multiple shorts and the Sundance-feted dramedy Lemon. Her newest film, Zola, is a case in point: based on a viral, 148-tweet thread, it details the true story of an impulsive road trip from Detroit to Florida taken by a Hooters waitress, an exotic dancer, her boyfriend and her pimp – a journey that veers spectacularly sideways. Zola masterfully captures the scrappy energy of Twitter and the queasy seepage between the digital and real world, finding absurdist humour in the worst of circumstances and beauty in the neon, tropical underworld of the Sunshine State. The New York-born, LA-based filmmaker will follow it up with another slippery, stranger-than-fiction tale, A Suspense Novelist's Trail of Deceptions. Starring Jake Gyllenhaal, the series is based on the tangled life of bestselling author AJ Finn, real name Dan Mallory. Words HANNAH LACK

" Three years ago a friend and fellow filmmaker suggested I read the book Rhinestone Sharecropping by Bill Gunn, because I had written a film called The Dead Pay No Rent, about the experience of trying to make my first movie. Rhinestone Sharecropping is based on Gunn's experiences as a Black director in Hollywood and it's really funny – it's a tragicomedy, both humorous and incredibly distressing. The book was published in 1981 and wasn't available anywhere – in the end, I had to borrow this friend's very delicate first edition. I kid you not, I held on to the last 40 pages for a full year because I didn't want it to be over. There was some kind of soothing I was getting from this book, knowing there had been another artist who had walked in my shoes, who had experienced the conversations I had been experiencing for innumerable years. Knowing that the road has been walked before just makes you feel less alone and less crazy. I had seen movies about making movies – my favourite is Day for Night by François Truffaut – but I hadn't encountered a director who felt like a stand-in for me.

There were a couple of things that particularly struck me about Rhinestone Sharecropping. Firstly, I love work about the artistic process. I like to know how the sausage gets made – the art sausage, as it were. I love the conversations in the back room. The book felt especially radical because I hadn't read anything about how an artist navigates their home life and work life before, and Gunn explores the experience of being in a relationship with a partner who is also a maker – how crunchy it can get around the pitfalls and frustrations of just trying to get the work done.

Another thing that resonated with me was a meeting in the book where you notice that the reason a white executive invites Gunn's character in has less to do with what he offers as an individual as it has to do with him being Black. In my own experience, I would sometimes wonder about that. I don't want to be there to check certain boxes, I want to be there for my brain. It's getting better, but Hollywood is a business that has made room for a multitude of white, cisgender men to succeed and it has not yet made the room for women and non-white people to do the same.

Bill Gunn was also an actor, and there's a performance by him in Kathleen Collins's 1982 film Losing Ground that I love. Someone had told me to watch this movie, they said it would be seminal for me. I finally found it on DVD and he is fantastic – you get a sense of who he was in his body and how he moved. After that I sought out a movie directed by Gunn, [the 1973 avant-garde horror] Ganja & Hess – again, it's very hard to find. It's a movie that might play at a festival, that exists in this underground world of hard-to-access Black art films. Gunn wrote an article in the New York Times in 1973, To Be a Black Artist, directly addressing white criticism of Ganja & Hess.

There's now a reprint of Rhinestone Sharecropping and a series of Bill Gunn's films was recently on the Criterion Channel – he is beginning to achieve recognition. But I'm sad I didn't discover him until my late thirties. I can't help but think, if I had had access to him when I was younger, what doors in my mind would have opened up? What places would I have travelled to in my head? "

KORAKRIT ARUNANONDCHAI,

artist,

on

freediving

" With freediving you take one breath and swim down to the depths of the ocean. I've been doing it for a little over a year and it's really influenced my relationship with my body and my mortality. There's a place in Koh Tao, Thailand, called New Heaven Dive School that teaches ocean conservation and a course linking yoga with freediving. It's quite primordial and scary to begin with, but when you bring it back to yoga practices it's all about the breath. My teacher talks about freediving as a wedge with a threshold – a boundary you don't cross, like running out of air and passing out. But metaphorically, in life there are boundaries and the wedge opens more space for you to exist without crossing that boundary. It's not like freediving extends your mortality, but it gives you a certain faith in the ability of your body. You realise the human body possesses powers and abilities that you're not really aware of until you put them into practice. **"**

Korakrit Arunanondchai creates hypnotic work that transcends time and space. A multidisciplinary research-based artist working across video, painting, performance and installation, he is revered for his Painting With History series. Based in both Thailand and Brooklyn, Arunanondchai experienced an upbringing that profoundly informs his practice, and he often explores the role that spirituality and belief systems play in forming cultures. He draws on pop culture, memory, technology and globalisation to immerse audiences in thought, mediation and, at times, frightening foresight that connects east with west, and the past with both the present and our increasingly uncertain future. This autumn he debuts newly commissioned works, including video installations, paintings and sculptures, at both the Migros Museum für Gegenwartskunst in Zurich and Kunstverein, Hamburg – marking his first solo exhibitions in these cities – with a jointly produced show titled Songs for dying / Songs for living. Words ASHLEIGH KANE

Self-portrait by Korakrit Arunanondchai

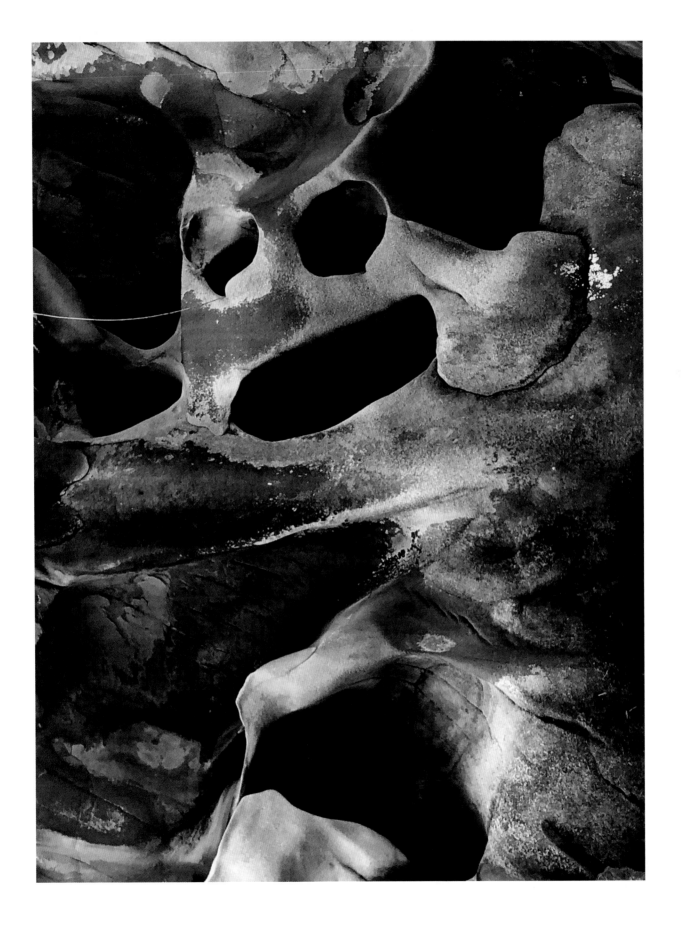

marsèll

NICOLAS DI FELICE,

designer,

on

The Sound of Belgium

" There is this documentary that I love, from 2012 – The Sound of Belgium, about the Belgian clubs that had a huge influence on music between 1985 and 1995. It became mainstream, the Benelux techno sound, the new beats. I really lived it. What I love is that it shows lots of passionate people and how they made this new sound – disco arrived, then punk. In the documentary, you see how it develops, this music with a cold wave, punk attitude but with a disco sound. The bass was more rounded, more heavy. The first club dedicated to this was called Boccaccio – it was like a temple. It was mirrored, like Studio 54, but playing this dark, heavy sound inside. All this, in the Belgian countryside – my friend lived a kilometre away from one of the biggest clubs and every weekend there would be strangers in her garden, it was all a bit surreal. Music, lights, in the middle of nowhere – at night, there were these lasers coming from huge clubs. It was like Batman. And it inspires me – in my work, I always think something is more powerful when you decontextualise it. "

Thirty-seven-year-old Nicolas Di Felice has come a long way from the Belgian countryside outside Charleroi where he grew up and began clubbing at the age of 13. Having studied at La Cambre, he worked alongside Raf Simons and Pieter Mulier at Dior and then Nicolas Ghesquière at Louis Vuitton before receiving the call inviting him to helm the storied house of Courrèges – a long-term inspiration. Working at a brand with one of fashion's most influential and well-known aesthetics makes Di Felice's task doubly difficult, requiring him to satisfy fanatics while evolving a new, 21st-century identity. Three collections in, his offerings include gentle tailoring and sportswear, alongside the painstakingly precise, Persil-white space race futurism that still defines the label. He's also been diving into the archives – learning about the man behind the name. "André Courrèges was obsessed, even more than walking on the moon, with dressing people on the street," he says. "That talks to me a lot." Words ALEXANDER FURY

WESLEY JOSEPH,

musician,

on   Kahlil Joseph

The DIY spirit has always burned bright in the Walsall-raised, London-based musician, filmmaker and producer Wesley Joseph. The 25-year-old started out as a founding member of the radical rap and production collective OG Horse in his hometown before heading to London to study film in 2016, all while crafting music in a make-shift home studio. With sinewy, elastic beats that hop between genres and sensual lyricism, his self-produced debut album, Ultramarine, dives deep into romance and infatuations, nostalgia, loss and thrill. While his self-directed visuals flirt with neo-noir and the surreal, Joseph's sound oscillates between R&B and future funk, delivering vocals with the ice-cold flow of André 3000 and the textured aesthetics of Jai Paul. It's in this bombastic affinity between screen and sound that the artist's world-expanding storytelling comes to life. Words ANNA CAFOLLA

" When other kids wanted to be fire-fighters or astronauts, I wanted to be a filmmaker. It even came before music for me. All my favourite pieces of art, music and film come from a dark place that looks towards a brighter one – it's the work of Kahlil Joseph that really encapsulates that perspective and gets to that emotional, human mission I want to be at the centre of.

Kahlil's visuals uplift the music of the artists he works with. I felt this first when I saw his short film for Flying Lotus's [2012] album Until the Quiet Comes. When you're young and making your way through Tumblr and all the small internet communities, stumbling on a piece of work like that is life-altering. He has what I see as a deep understanding of tone, time and the importance of a truly emotional journey. His world-building is so fantastical and yet so real. The landscapes can feel chilling and faraway, but he injects his work with such warmth. It always moves me in a completely different way. Creative work should feel like a tapestry that you can revisit again and again and come away from with new thoughts and feelings each time.

The film for Sampha, Process, was just sick. It has this beautiful way of subtly but powerfully demonstrating culture and heritage. You get what that dense, hot air feels like in his streets, the energy from his grandmother's voice. It is all-encompassing, and in partnership with Sampha, gives the music more depth and another perspective. I was totally floored when I went to see The Infinite Mix exhibition in London [in 2016], where they showed his film for Kendrick Lamar, MAAD – seeing it with the surround sound and the multiple screens really added to the multisensory experience you get from a Kahlil film. He just understands how to elevate the story of a musician with his own interpretation – he can bring you headfirst into Compton, diving deeper into that ridiculous Kendrick

album and its themes. I push myself to find that detail and truth in my own work – I'm really working on it.

He makes me think of the power that music videos have today, too – you can condense so much emotion and complexity into a short space of time and create a piece of work that really stays with people. I go into my projects with these hopes in mind – like my recent film Patience, with Jorja [Smith]. I always want to appeal to people on an abstract level rather than in a traditional way with characters and a plot and backstories. I wrote, directed, scored and edited my own short film, Pandomony, and I went into it intent on displaying human emotion in sync with the music, on going into those vast relationships and differing experiences people have of grief. This was very much inspired by his touch.

It's easy to get lost in the ocean of meaninglessness at the moment, especially in this field of work, and even more so in a pandemic, when you have to seek out inspiration. BLKNWS [Kahlil's installation/news channel] has continued to feel like an innovative, relevant moment – even last year, amid it all. It had such a strong sense of purpose that we all needed to feel.

The power of collaboration is also integral to his work – when you work with another person who just gets you, it's spiritual. You feed off each other and intertwine perspectives to create something that's vast and layered. On my own record [Ultramarine], I got to bring people together who want to push boundaries like me – Leon Vynehall, Lexxx, Jorja, Dave Okumu, Mike Bozzi. It makes me feel like a supervillain when you hit on that magic point collectively – you flex these creative muscles together in the studio and create a more powerful thing. When I engage with work like this, work with people who have these ideals, I feel my purpose. **"**

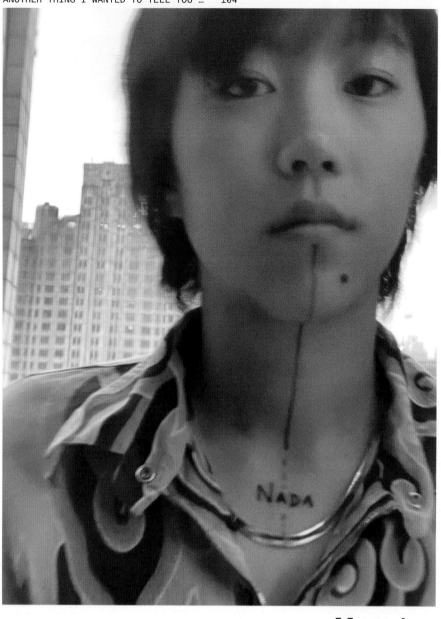

LEAH DOU,

singer-songwriter,

on Mother Earth's Plantasia

❝Plantasia was written by Mort Garson in the Seventies. I believe the album was made for plants, to help them grow. I remember being in Los Angeles a couple of years back with a friend who was like, 'Let me play you a record you're gonna love.' I swear I was blown away. It was a mind-blowing experience for me. Plantasia oozes sugariness. I don't know much about Mort Garson but listening to this record gives me a very vivid picture of him, even if it's just my projection of what he would have been like. In my mind he's a very kind figure, someone who probably acts quite childlike sometimes and is very playful. That's a quality that I really look up to when it comes to making music. It's something I strive to achieve. It takes a certain sense of honesty to let yourself be like that, whether you're playing a character while you're making music or you're being completely open. Music like this is rare. It's so pure, really – I can't think of any other word.**❞**

It should come as no surprise that Leah Dou was drawn to an album as unusual as Mother Earth's Plantasia. Born into Chinese pop royalty (her mother is pop star Faye Wong, her father rock musician Dou Wei), Dou has never been too interested in conforming to mainstream expectations. With her unconventional, androgynous style and distinctive face tattoo, she creates left-field, experimental and genre-averse music. Recently, the 24-year-old has also stepped into acting. When we speak, she's on the bullet train from Beijing to Shanghai to promote her friend Queena Li's episodic, oddball film Bipolar – in which she has the lead role – and which follows an appearance in Jianbin Chen's dark comedy The Eleventh Chapter, for which she won a best supporting actress award at Beijing International Film Festival. Dou is also at the "beginning stages, making sketches in the studio" for her next album.　　Words SELIM BULUT

BIANCA SAUNDERS

JENNA FLETCHER,

design consultant,

on

Willi Smith

Self-portrait by Jenna Fletcher

❝ The WilliWear universe was very free, and free from the confines of the fashion industry – both how it was then and still is now. In Willi Smith, I see someone who was creating what they wanted to create, despite the invisible obstacles – or *visible* obstacles – you hit as a Black queer person. I relate to his being in the fashion sphere and not giving a shit about the establishment. When he was designing his studios with rule-breaking architectural practice Site, Willi said that he wanted his spaces to be the exact opposite of what a Ralph Lauren studio looked like. That's how I feel about where Oswalde sits in the design world. I think Smith was one of the forefathers of fashion culture as we know it – he should be so much better known than he is. And he should still be here with us. **❞**

"I do not want to sit in any kind of system that will box me in," says Jenna Fletcher, founder of category-defying furniture store, archive, design incubator and interiors consultancy Oswalde. Whether selling colourful 1970s Italian plastic or contemporary design from Lagos, Fletcher keeps a desire to rethink the stuffy, staid, and elitist world of interiors at the heart of her approach. This spirit of making your own space in a world dominated by outdated conventions is one she shares with the late American designer Willi Smith, whose pioneering yet unsung 'street couture' label WilliWear defined cutting-edge New York fashion in the late 70s and 80s. The brand turned over sales of more than $25 million a year and Smith was considered the most commercially successful Black American designer of his era before he tragically died of Aids-related illness in 1987, at the age of 39. Words EMMA HOPE ALLWOOD

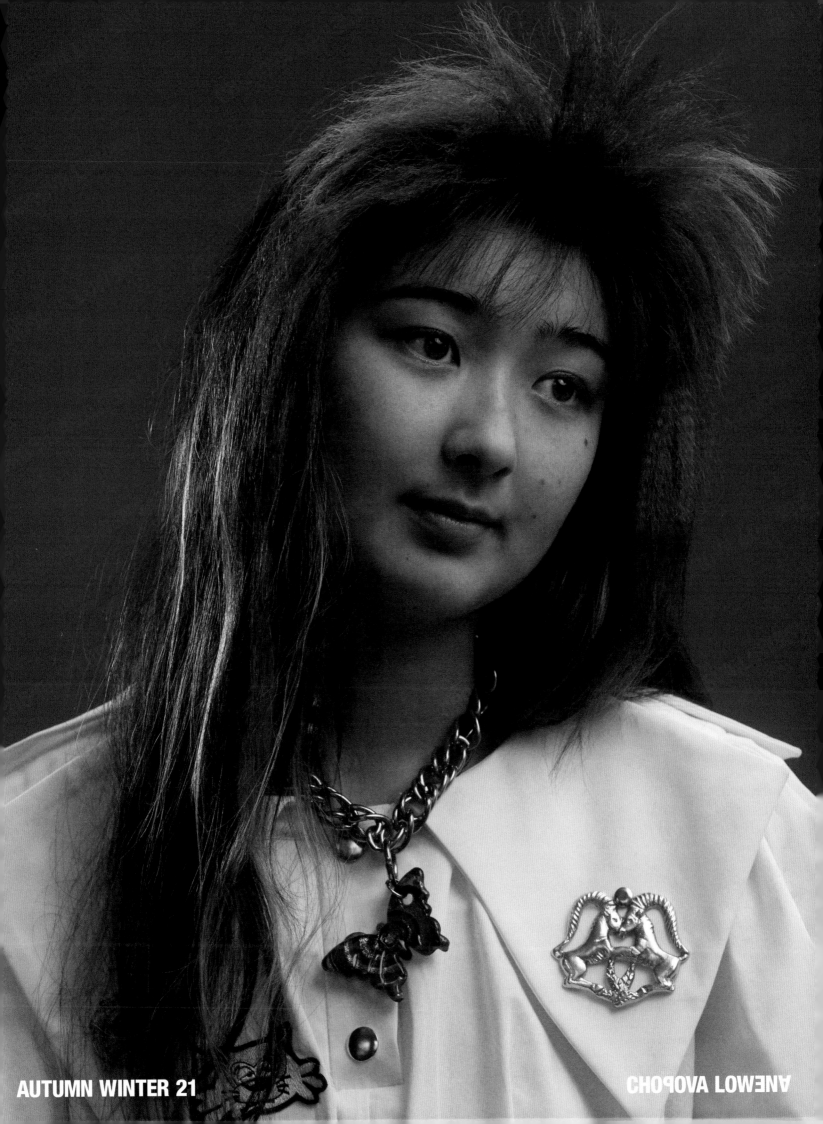

AUTUMN WINTER 21

CHOPOVA LOWENA

MANOLO
BLAHNIK,

shoe
designer,

on

Francisco
de
Zurbarán

Manolo Blahnik celebrates the 50th anniversary of his business this year. The most feted shoe designer of our time, his work has been exhibited in major international museums and purchased by discerning women for half a century. After growing up in Santa Cruz de la Palma in the Canary Islands, he studied law and literature in Geneva, before moving to Paris in 1968 and then to London, intending to pursue a career in set design. In New York in 1969, he met Diana Vreeland and showed her his portfolio – she told him to make shoes, which he did. Vreeland went on to wear paper-flat pumps that he designed especially for her for most of her life. Between then and now, Blahnik has made shoes for everyone from Ossie Clark and John Galliano to Vetements, and has dressed the famous feet of Bianca Jagger, Tina Chow, Madonna, and Rihanna, with whom he has also collaborated. In 2005, he designed the shoes for Sofia Coppola's Marie Antoinette. A true – and truly refined – aesthete, he shifts effortlessly between languages and trains of thought, staccato, at great speed. "I am a victim of culture, I was born like that," Blahnik says. "When I see a painting it's like I am that painting. When I'm reading a page, I am the page."

Words SUSANNAH FRANKEL

Portrait by Misan Harriman

    " Zurbarán has been my obsession since I was a little boy living in the Canary Islands. You know, when you're small they take you to church on Sundays and, in Spain, they love Murillo, which is camp – horrible, tacky. But I kept with me my postcards of Zurbarán's Saint Bartholomew almost in agony [1632]. I had about ten of them.

We used to travel by boat to get to school in Geneva or to get my sister to school in Germany. And we always stopped in Cádiz, where there's the wonderful Museo de Cádiz, which has an incredible collection of Zurbaráns. I must have been about 13 by then, or even 15, and what a revelation it was. Every time I passed by Cádiz for whatever reason, I went there. It was wonderful – Zurbarán seemed like second nature to me by then.

Later on, my mother took me to the Prado in Madrid, and I always wanted to stop when I saw a monk by Zurbarán, with his eyes looking up to the heavens and his mouth open, almost as if light were coming out of it. The light is like Josef von Sternberg's light. In retrospect I realise that von Sternberg was totally copying the light of all the old masters and copying Zurbarán especially. It was that light that attracted me – the light but also the hands, the sandals with the dirty feet. So beautiful. There's one beautiful Christ on the cross too, which is in Chicago. I sometimes do these personal appearances and for one I went to the Art Institute of Chicago and saw it there. I thought, 'My God.' I returned the next day and took photographs of the painting with my phone. That Christ is fantastic. The top of the body, nailed to the cross, looks dead, but the hands, the legs, the feet are alive. In Spain that painting is not very well known. I always get surprises with Zurbarán and I have been following him, and have been followed by him, for ever somehow.

He influences my work. Not all the time, but often. The stiff materials I use sometimes, religious materials, heavy wools, tweeds – I love the austerity of those things. Then there's my interest in the 18th century, which I have also always been very receptive to – those manners. You can read Saint-Simon and on each page you can imagine a shoe. Zurbarán is very pure, very austere. The 18th century is not very practical but I love that too. I am kind of deranged in a funny way.

When I had an exhibition in London with Mr Conran, at the Design Museum in 2003, the National Gallery lent me Saint Margaret of Antioch [1630–34] by Zurbarán. Can you imagine they gave that to us? And in 2017 we did this exhibition at the Hermitage in St Petersburg. It was the first time a man of shoes opened a show at the Hermitage and it was divine. I saw written on the front of that building from far away, 'Manolo Blahnik' – huge – and I thought, 'Oh my God.' There was a room there with shoes influenced by Zurbarán and also by Goya, Picasso, Matisse, Mondrian. I'm talking about Zurbarán because he's my favourite but I love all the tenebristic painters and the modern masters too.

I love the exaggeration, the theatrical part of the people in Spain. And, you know, they're unreliable, completely out of their minds, totally living a fantasy. I am a mixture, a cross, a bastard. My father was Czech, my mother super-Spanish. As I get older I see myself very much as a Spaniard. Still, England has a kind of exotica for me that I think I was always pursuing. Zurbarán is totally Spanish. Balenciaga was really, really influenced by him. Zurbarán was like a peasant – in his paintings you can feel Seville, southern Spain, that is what he captures so well. The earthiness, the colours – nobody can touch that colour. And the beauty of the human soul. **"**

Golden
Years

Photography
MATTHIEU LAVANCHY

Styling
SAMIA GIOBELLINA

Gilding the lily: celebrating a half-century
of creativity, Manolo Blahnik devises an all-gold
capsule collection reimagining a cache of his
classic silhouettes

All footwear from the MANOLO BLAHNIK 50th anniversary capsule collection

Anissa is wearing a technical satin coat by COMMISSION.
Straight-leg leather trousers by CORMIO

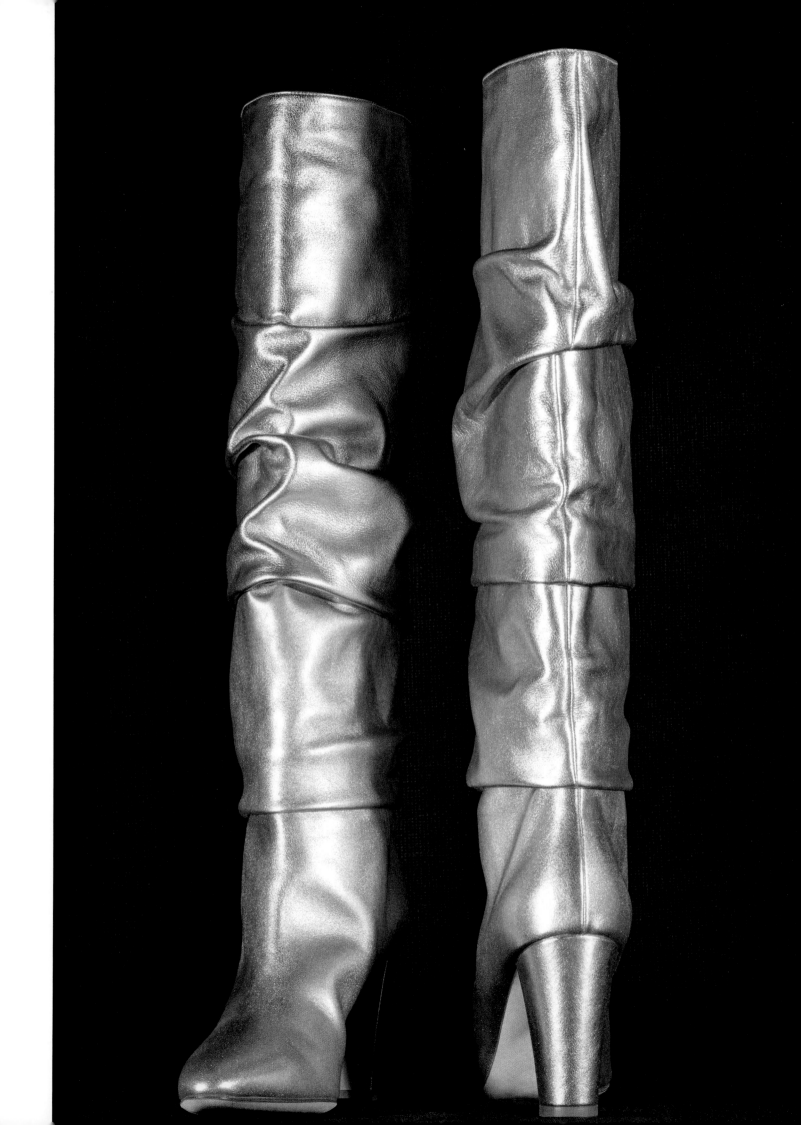

Leather dress by 1017 ALYX 9SM

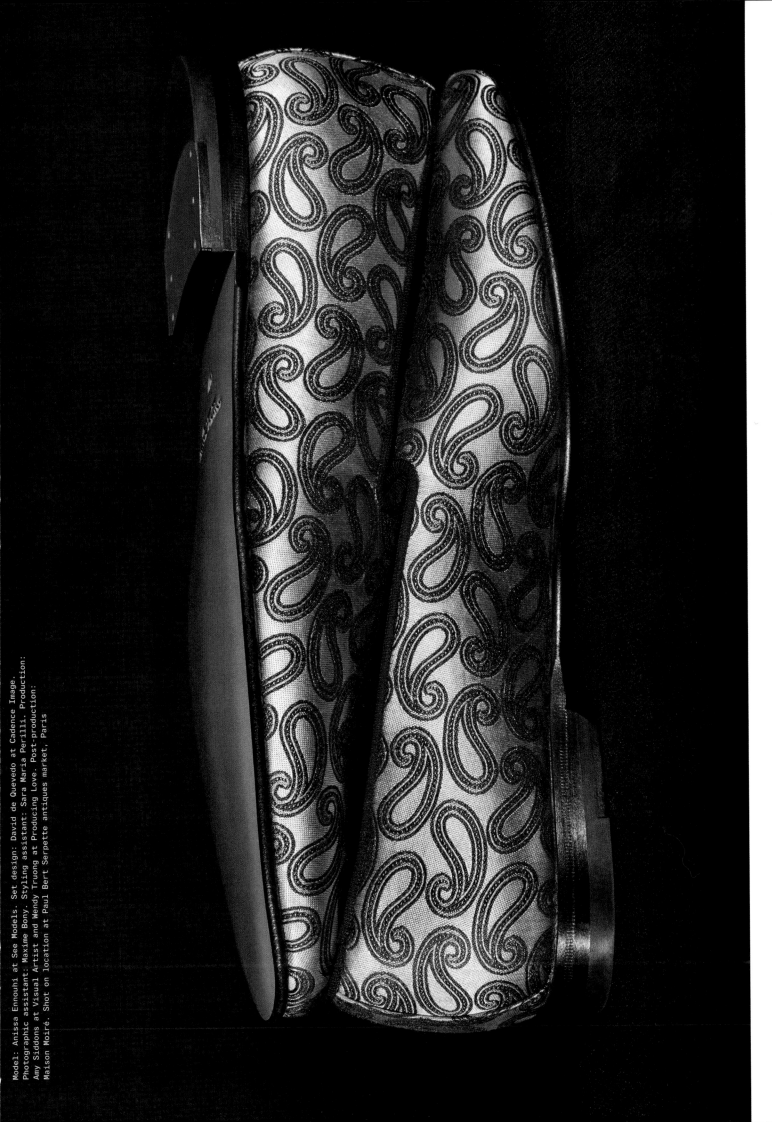

Model: Anissa Ennouhi at See Models. Set design: David de Quevedo at Cadence Image.
Photographic assistant: Maxime Bony. Styling assistant: Sara Maria Perilli. Production:
Amy Siddons at Visual Artist and Wendy Truong at Producing Love. Post-production:
Maison Moiré. Shot on location at Paul Bert Serpette antiques market, Paris

MARTE AT A GAS STATION DOCUMENTED BY JOEL MEYEROWITZ, CASTIGLIONE D'ORCIA, TUSCANY
APRIL 2021

TWILIGHT DOCUMENTED BY JOEL MEYEROWITZ, BIBBIANO, BUONCONVENTO, TUSCANY
APRIL 2021

TEXTURED WALL DOCUMENTED BY JOEL MEYEROWITZ, BONNIEUX, PROVENCE
APRIL 2021

JIL SANDER

MALICK SLEEPING DOCUMENTED BY JOEL MEYEROWITZ, CASTELNUOVO TANCREDI, BUONCONVENTO, TUSCANY
APRIL 2021

AnOther *loves*

Skin
Metal
Love
Letters

Photography   Styling
ARNAUD LAJEUNIE   AGATA BELCEN

Janet is wearing a padded leather jacket with oversized collar,
brushed mohair jumper and oversized acetate sunglasses by TOM FORD

This page: Metal ring with crystals by GUCCI. Opposite: Sacha is wearing a technical
jacquard anorak and jumpsuit with printed Peter Doig motif, brass earring with lion
charm and resin pearl necklaces with tulle and brass rose charms by DIOR

This page: Bella is wearing a seersucker nylon bikini by
HUNZA G. Leather ski glove and steel signet ring with gold
logo by MIU MIU. Opposite: Oregano soap bar by LOEWE

This page: Sacha is wearing a mesh and Aran knit jumper with
cross embroidery by SAINT LAURENT BY ANTHONY VACCARELLO.
Nylon swimming briefs by SPEEDO. And rimless sunglasses by
ERMENEGILDO ZEGNA XXX. Opposite: Printed enamel bangles
with gold-plated hardware by HERMÈS

This page: Sterling silver logo hoop earring and stud earring by PRADA.
Opposite: Janet is wearing a cut-out one-shouldered Lycra body by
FANTABODY. Leather belt with LV logo metal buckle and leather gladiator
boots with bows by LOUIS VUITTON. And leather Pochette Tête bag
by LOUIS VUITTON X FORNASETTI

This page: Janet is wearing a double high-neck cotton T-shirt, nylon trousers and polyester
hat by ERL. Smooth satin leather Sesia bags by LORO PIANA. Stylist's own socks. And leather
and suede squash trainers with rubber soles by HI-TEC. Opposite: Kim is wearing a tulle
dress with sequin embroidery and oversized wool beanie by DSQUARED2. High-waisted briefs by
LES GIRLS LES BOYS. Sterling silver and resin earrings with crystal detail by BOTTEGA
VENETA. And leather bracelet clutches by LOEWE

This page: Sacha is wearing tailored silk and wool trousers and
leather GT Lock bags by DUNHILL. Leather belt with oversized
logo buckle by LOUIS VUITTON. Opposite: Tailored silk and wool
trousers by DUNHILL. Silver chain necklace and silver Heirloom
necklace by JIL SANDER BY LUCIE AND LUKE MEIER

This page: Janet is wearing a shearling patch jacket by ERL. Zip-up bomber jacket by ATLEIN. And earrings in 18-carat white gold with onyx and diamonds by CARTIER. Opposite: Cashmere body with silk trim, beaded metal necklace, coneflower chain metal belt, sheer nylon tights and leather slingback heels with metallic toecaps by SAINT LAURENT BY ANTHONY VACCARELLO

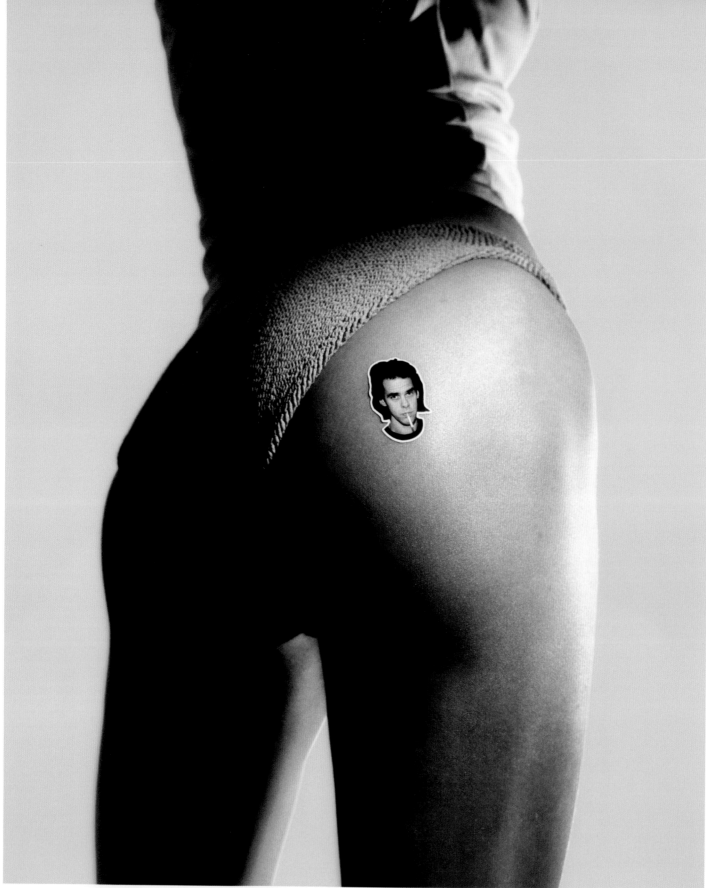

This page: Bella is wearing an organic cotton T-shirt and World's Best sticker by CAVE THINGS. Seersucker nylon bikini bottoms by HUNZA G. Opposite: Sacha is wearing a double-breasted belted wool jacket, knitted wool rollneck and shorts and leather duffel bag by FENDI. Ribbed cotton socks by PANTHERELLA from UK TIGHTS. And printed nylon and leather snow boots with rubber soles by DIOR

This page: Bella is wearing a fur-printed V-neck wool trench coat, reconstructed
wool fleece gilet, stretch tulle turtleneck body and leather Olympia bag by
BURBERRY. Seersucker nylon bikini bottoms by HUNZA G. Opposite: Kim is wearing
18-carat yellow gold hoop earrings and rings by TIFFANY & CO

This page: Michelle is wearing a wool tweed cropped jacket with contrast lining, silk jacquard
top, knitted cashmere beanie, resin and strass brooches (on her beanie), metal, strass and
resin earrings and metal, strass and leather necklaces by CHANEL. Opposite: Long-sleeved stretch
macramé dress, ribbed cashmere dress (worn underneath), sterling silver and resin earrings
and necklace with crystal detail, leather Mount bag with chain detail and thigh-high leather
boots by BOTTEGA VENETA

Telfar

Words SAGAL MOHAMMED

When Telfar Clemens went to sign the contract for his new home in Bedford-Stuyvesant, Brooklyn, he spotted a woman walking into the house next door carrying a box-shaped, medium-sized orange shopping tote with double shoulder straps, top handles and an embossed TC logo. She looked at him, pointed at the bag and realised her new neighbour was the designer behind her Bushwick Birkin, a nickname coined by multimedia artist Xya Rachel for the faux-leather Bloomingdale's-inspired shopping bag. "It's everywhere, I see it on people all day," says Clemens. "Whenever we meet someone with it, we're immediately connected because they get us," adds Babak Radboy, the artistic director of Clemens's label Telfar. "That's what makes our customers so special."

Radboy has known Clemens, now 36, since the two were teenagers. "We don't know where we met because we were just in the same spaces with the same friends, as kids in New York who look like us are," says Radboy, who was born in the Iranian capital, Tehran, in the midst of the country's revolution in 1978. Like Clemens, who was born and raised in LeFrak City, Queens, Radboy spent his adolescent years in New York, where they crossed paths while growing up. But it wasn't until 2013, when he started dating Telfar stylist Avena Gallagher (now his partner and the mother of their six-year-old son, Malcolm Rae), that Radboy – who is also known for his creative direction on Kanye West's video for Power, the Middle East-focused arts publication Bidoun and the art and fashion line Shanzhai Biennial – officially began working with Clemens. "When Avena and I moved in together, Telfar would always be having fittings at our house and I just slowly started to get involved in the business. I'd always wanted to work with him but I also needed to pay my rent," he says with a laugh. "So I got a big job in 2013, designing stuff for a video game and, after that, I decided to take three months out and work with Telfar, and I just got hooked. Out of all the people I knew, I saw what he was doing as the most forward thinking."

Despite its popular moniker, the Telfar shopping bag is worlds apart from the rarefied, much-fetishised Birkin by Hermès – its leather is fake, its price point markedly accessible and its availability egalitarian, shattering traditional expectations of cult items and It bags. When Clemens won the CFDA award for American Accessories Designer of the Year in 2020, he used his prize fund to scale-up production, offering an unlimited number of bags available for pre-order over a 24-hour period. The now-signature staple had gone viral a year earlier – everyone from Oprah to Alexandria Ocasio-Cortez to people travelling to and from work on the streets of Brooklyn had it, each new drop selling out almost before its arrival had been announced. Perception of Clemens's namesake label, already successful and acclaimed, changed palpably.

That bag is big – actually, it comes in three sizes – but Telfar is about far more. Since its inception in 2005, the brand has spearheaded the celebration of gender fluidity and inclusivity. Its debut at Paris Fashion Week for Spring/Summer 2020 was inspired by the archetype of a newly arrived immigrant in the western world, known in the West African diasporic community as Johnny Just Come. Described by Clemens as "you've-just-come-to-this-country kind of style", the looks combined new and second-hand clothes in the form of running shorts over fishnets, hoodies with starched collars underneath and his most recognisable design to date: a sporty tank top with straps askew. Clemens hybridises unexpected fabrics and cuts – his cargo-blended jean shorts are a prime example – to not only subvert traditional clothing but also ideas of sexuality, reimagining Americana and celebrating Black queerness. Catering to all is what Telfar is about.

"I'm creating something bigger than fashion," he says. Moments before we talk, he is announced as the official designer of Liberia's 2020 Olympic kit (Clemens is Liberian-American, with both parents hailing from the West African country; the kit is made up of flag-print tights, unitards and thigh-split joggers, true to the Telfar touch). A few days later, he unveils a new drop for his long-standing Converse collaboration – he's a busy man. Then there's the alliance with Ugg, a brand Clemens dreamt of partnering with as soon as he laid eyes on the much-maligned shearling boots. Just as the Telfar bag is the must-have today, Uggs were the boot du jour of the Noughties. Kate Moss and Paris Hilton wore them regularly, as did teenage schoolgirls on the local high street. The fuzzy pieces of footwear, most popular in their chestnut shade, were adored for how ugly they were.

Clemens has designed a range of cosy loungewear-cum-underwear and shearling-trimmed accessories, seamlessly blending his own logo with Ugg's newly retro aesthetic. "With Telfar, we don't follow a specific fashion diet when it comes to images and inspiration," Radboy says. "We follow a daily-life diet – when Ugg boots were a huge phenomenon, the whole thing was that they looked horrible yet we all had them. That's the fashion dream. They were so weird and yet still the most normal thing. What's cool is that fashion had nothing to do with dictating that."

Prioritising this sense of punter power fits Telfar's direct-to-consumer business model and the brand's slogan

Michelle is wearing a shearling-lined hoodie and bucket hat, cotton boxers and leather and shearling shopping bags and boots by TELFAR x UGG

"Not For You – For Everyone". Culture and accessibility have been key from the start. Clemens launched his label while studying at Pace University, when his designs were worn by like-minded friends and an intimate cohort of queer people of colour immersed in the New York party scene. Inspired by the visual and cultural essences of local neighbourhoods in the city, and combined with his genderless objective and attainable price points, Clemens's clothes offered something new. "We've always been very much about the real world," he says. "You're going to see it around you in your day-to-day life before it gets in the magazines. We're turned on by entertainment, TV and what's actually going on in the culture sphere globally, on a mass level where every single person sees it, not just a select few who are part of an exclusive group."

For both Clemens and Radboy, following their own vision is of utmost importance – a vision that has, ironically, inspired numerous imitators. Some of these have caused outrage on social media, stirring up conversations about copycat culture and the notion of major fashion companies 'borrowing' ideas from smaller, independent and Black-owned brands. "What I've been making, I've been making since the early 2000s. People 'borrow' that constantly and then forget where it came from," says Clemens. "If you're making a thing and you're known for it, keep making it. How many people are trying to make a version of our bag? But it doesn't come with me in it, so it won't ever work." As for those claiming that they're merely paying homage, he has one question: "Aren't you a little embarrassed? Just make your own thing instead of trying to pay homage to someone who is literally still here doing theirs."

Genderless garments and viral bags aside, Telfar's 'thing' is giving back. The brand uses fashion as a social act, most notably through its collaboration with American fast-food chain White Castle. Their relationship began in 2015, when the chain agreed to sponsor the Telfar Spring/Summer 2016 show. He has recently designed unisex uniforms for White Castle's 100th anniversary – royal blue and black logo-printed T-shirts, wide-collared polos, aprons, visors and durags, in the label's typical slouchy-slinky shapes – and has made pieces available as a limited-edition collection for his clientele. Proceeds from this range are being donated to Robert F Kennedy Human Rights, an organisation whose work has included contributing to bail funds to help those who are unable to pay bail themselves. Similarly, Telfar's partnership with the Liberian Olympics team marks another move with significance: in the biggest external investment the company has made, it also paid for the team, plus its officials and sports staff, to attend the

Games. Clemens himself was even invited to travel to Tokyo with the Liberian delegation. "It's really funny because my entire life, I hated the idea of a uniform. I purposely failed any entry exam for high schools where you had to wear a uniform because the only freedom I had in my childhood was how I was able to dress," Clemens says. "The idea of making uniforms now and dressing everybody has a sense of ubiquity, but it's also about having a thing that's new and that you remember from that year."

Clemens built his reputation in the New York City creative scene when he was a teenager, doubling as a DJ and designer. He created a circle of friends in the same space, including Hood By Air designer Shayne Oliver, who became his partner in crime on the New York nightlife scene. Together they were regulars at underground events such as GHE20G0TH1K and hosted the kind of fashion week after-parties that catapulted them into socialite status. This fun-loving nature is reflected in Telfar's campaigns – a recent Ugg campaign featured cast members of Bravo's The Real Housewives of Potomac, with the statement "Fuck the Police" at the end of it. Why? Because they can. "It's who we are. We do what we want, when we want," Clemens says. Adds Radboy: "One of our rules when collaborating with brands is that they get no say in what we decide to do with our campaigns. They're not even invited to the shoot." This principle of freedom will no doubt be its recipe for a long-standing legacy. "I've been doing this for 20 years, not for anyone else but for myself and the people around me," Clemens says. "Right now, that number is growing and it's great. But one thing I'll never do is seek validation from anyone. I'm just trying to keep things as me as possible."

Alighieri

Words SOPHIE BEW

The jewellery designer Rosh Mahtani has strong feelings about the nuances of translation. Over Zoom, with piles of chunky gold chain bracelets jangling, she reels off the first terzina of Dante Alighieri's Commedia – The Divine Comedy – in Italian, before sharing her own interpretation of the text. She knows the quote by rote: "In the middle of the journey of life, I found myself in a dark wood where the right path was obscured." It's her own interpretation, sort of – a mishmash of all her favourite variations. "Some people translate it as, 'the correct way was unclear'. I'm like, 'No, it needs to be obscure. It says *oscura*.'" Obscure, meaning unclear but also dark or dim, is preferable to Mahtani for its complexity. The finer details are important to her. The canonical text has inspired her entire livelihood, after all. Alighieri, an award-winning, seven-year-old jewellery brand, comprises a constellation of intricately worked gold pieces – like gilded fragments from former civilisations, they correspond to the 100 cantos of Dante's epic poem.

Melted sovereigns, rugged coins, jagged shards of shields, barnacled bones and oversized asymmetric pearls come plated with, or set in, 24-carat gold and in the form of pendants or earring drops. Sometimes they are twisted into thick rings or hoops. Precious pieces, they evoke a certain sanctity – a sense of heirlooms passed down through generations; of keepsakes that were somehow here before the wearer and will outlive them too. That's where Dante comes in. Mahtani studied his 14th-century masterpiece intensely, canto by canto, week by week, during her fourth undergraduate year studying French and Italian at New College, Oxford. "Dante created something that is still so present without us even knowing," she says. "He's present in so many parts of culture, in so many references in the arts, in literature, in film. It's as if the echoes of the past are constantly drawn through the fabric of the present day."

Seven years ago, when Mahtani sat at her kitchen table with a wax candle and some of her mother's cutlery, she began carving and melting her first jewellery prototype – a silver metal crab claw that was somewhat liquefied in appearance. It was a distraction, she says now, from her uncertainty over her future path. That very lack of clarity took her back to her past: she was reminded, she explains, of her maternal grandmother's gold sovereign. A small medallion, it was the one treasure this much-loved matriarch carried with her when she and her husband fled India following the partition in August 1947. The couple moved, along with their best friends – Mahtani's paternal grandparents – to Zambia, where they raised their five children. Mahtani's parents hated one another growing up, their daughter says today, but ended up marrying happily after they reunited in their twenties and initially brought up their own two children in Zambia, too. When Mahtani was eight the family moved to London, accompanied by that same sovereign. Evading bloodshed and fear, oblivious to time and space, it had by then attained near-mythical stature, tucked away in Mahtani's mother's jewellery box.

London had a less desirable lustre, Mahtani explains. "I went from living this barefoot life, playing with leaves and rocks, to this all-girls school in Hampstead, where it was freezing cold and I wore a beret, a skirt with braces and a duffel coat," she says. "I had a little green hymn book and said the Lord's Prayer – I was so out of my depth. I hated it, I cried so much. I felt like an alien. It's weird to think it was the Nineties, but I was the only non-white person in my school – I just felt so innately different, with this sense of not belonging that always plagued me." The aforementioned crab claw, in all its molten, roughly hewn glory, hails in its own way from this sense of otherness. Mahtani had attended half of a one-day wax-carving course earlier on in the day of the piece's inception and decided that the precise nature of the technique being taught there was not for her – she walked out of the Hatton Garden class where fellow students were hand-sawing a tube of wax following exact measurements, then matching the finished cast, millimetre by millimetre, to the original design. That evening she "went free form", watching the wax melt over a flame and sculpting it with her bare hands; she was invigorated by the spontaneity and freedom of the finished result. She loved every warp and air bubble and embraced the claw's singular strangeness. It looked old, as if dug up from the earth. At that time Mahtani was, by her own admission, bored by a job in fashion merchandising, where every day they asked, "What's new?" This object, paradoxically ancient in appearance, felt like it invited new kinds of questions.

When Mahtani took her claw, and an accompanying six-legged crab, to Just Castings, a family-run business in Hatton Garden, they were far from impressed. "What is this?" they asked of the object in question. "It needs to go to the hospital. It's missing two legs – it's broken." Nonetheless, Mahtani begged them to cast it in bronze, the cheapest metal on offer, and to leave it unpolished before plating it. The exchange horrified the artisans, but that is where the Alighieri texture – and brand – was born. That same workshop has since produced more than 900,000 pieces for Mahtani.

Alighieri began as a business with a 48-unit order from a major fashion e-tailer five years ago. That quickly expanded to a second order, for 200 pieces, after the

Michelle is wearing a ribbed coated jersey dress by BOTTEGA VENETA. The Meteor in Free Fall and The Sorcerer's Theory necklaces in 24-carat gold-plated bronze by ALIGHIERI

first sold out within a month. Two seasons later, a 1,000-piece order came in. Meanwhile, founded in the Sixties and furnished with a Royal Warrant of Appointment, Just Castings has had to upscale and build infrastructure as fast as Mahtani, whose production team is now 25 strong. Yet only one member of the design team continues to mould each and every prototype with candle, flame, scalpel and, of course, hand – Mahtani.

She is focused and prolific. She has diversified her range, designing two jewel-embellished capsule shoe collections, and including items such as hand-linked chain bridal veils and gilded bookmarks resembling tiny, smelted puddles of gold, which appear in her biannual collections alongside the jewellery. Then there are atelier pieces such as the Calliope Camisole – a slip made entirely from freshwater-farmed cornflake pearls and gold-filled wire that took 40 hours and 900 pearls to create. References to The Divine Comedy range from literal – an oversized rain-droplet-covered chain-link bracelet inspired by the tears of the sinner Buonconte da Montefeltro in Dante's purgatory – to lateral, seen in the exploration of the redemptive nature of storytelling more broadly. Mahtani has named pendant necklaces (the Silencio or the Night Cap, for example) after fragments of her childhood – the jingling sound of her mother's gold bangles at bedtime being a formative memory. As a body of work, Alighieri represents an epic journey all of the designer's own.

The newest chapter of that journey is the arrival of Alighieri Man, although this is by no means the first time Alighieri has attracted male customers. "A lot of guys bought into it in the beginning – especially my friends – and seeing how they wore it was so inspiring. Over the past two years especially there have been amazing male customers who feel really confident and able to delve into the main site and adopt the pearls into their wardrobe, and they don't really mind whether it's labelled as men's or women's. A lot of couples would buy pieces and then steal them from each other's nightstands, which I love."

The resulting formalised men's collection riffs on many of the themes Mahtani has visited before – battered rings, chunky hand-linked chains (though this time in smoother, woven Celtic shapes) and a lion, the label's signature talisman, whose appearance in Dante's dark wood was so terrifying that the air around its mane trembled; a crude, cross-like medieval sword named The Torch of the Night joins the roster, too. Those motifs appear largely in sterling silver or with the black lustre of rhodium-plated bronze; red cornelian and black onyx stones lend signet rings a mystical magic. Scabrous baroque pearls bring a new edge to these typically masculine metal tones – dangling from single earrings, attached to chain chokers, or threaded into full-on pearl necklaces. It's an inclusive and inviting offering, one that feels modern and eternal.

And that is as it should be. Because for Mahtani there's a heart-warming and heartfelt continuity present in both jewellery and literature. "There are some things that never degrade," she says. "When you enter Dante's dark wood at the beginning of the poem, you remember that whatever your problem is today, whatever you are worrying about, your ancestors almost certainly worried about it as well."

Lady Dior

Introduced 26 years ago, the Lady Dior bag is an
emblem composed of emblems – quilted with cannage
patterns taken from the Napoleon III-style chairs of
Christian Dior's own salon and hung with charms shaped
in the maison's neoclassical logotype. It has been
reinvented by Maria Grazia Chiuri for the 21st century
– a timeless icon, now newly timely

Janet is wearing a wool and silk dress, cannage leather Lady Dior bags, printed silk scarves (wrapped around the handles), woven cotton bracelets, wool socks and D-Chess heart-motif neoprene trainers by DIOR

This page: Michelle is wearing a wool and silk dress, cannage leather Lady Dior bags, printed silk scarves (wrapped around the handles), woven cotton bracelets, wool socks and quilted nylon trainers by DIOR. Opposite: Janet is wearing a wool and silk dress, logo earrings with gold finish, cannage leather Lady Dior bag, woven cotton bracelets, wool socks and D-Chess heart-motif neoprene trainers by DIOR

Hair: Benjamin Muller at MA and Talent using DYSON. Make-up: Vassilis Theotokis at MA and Talent using BYREDO. Models: Sacha Dahdouh at The Claw, Janet Jumbo at IMG Paris, Michelle Laff at Next, Bella Michlo at Digital Icon Agency and Kim Schell at Viva. Casting: Noah Shelley at Streeters. Movement director: Ryan Chappell. Set design: César Sebastien at Swan Management. Manicure: Béatrice Eni at Saint Germain using BYREDO. Digital tech: Daniele Sedda at Sheriff Project. Photographic assistants: Clément Dauvent, Aurélien Hatt and Jeanne Le Louarn. Styling assistants: Nicola Neri and Sara Maria Perilli. Hair assistant: Alexandra Adams. Make-up assistant: Clara Barban-Dangerfield. Set-design assistant: Enzo Selvatici. Production: Kitten Paris

Pragmatic yet dramatic, Moncler's
latest collaboration brings together
the signature volumes and technical
prowess of the beloved Italian
luxury brand with the finely honed
purity of Japanese minimalists Hyke

All clothing and accessories from the 4 MONCLER
HYKE Autumn/Winter 2021 collection

A Hazy
Shade
of
Winter

Photography
MEL BLES

Styling
AI KAMOSHITA

hair: Kiyoko Odo at Bryant Artists using AMIKA. Make-up: Laura Dominique at Streeters using MAC. Model: Georgia Palmer at IMG. Casting: Noah Shelley at Streeters. Digital tech: Tim Grant. Photographic assistants: Edward Boumier, Sebastian McCluskey and Hayleigh Longman. Styling assistant: Charlotte Harney. Hair assistant: Kyosuke Tanzawa. Production: Thea Charlesworth at TheArcade Production. Production assistants: Ash Thomas at TheArcade Production and Poppy Thorpe at Webber

Another Time, Another Place

Photography
TOYIN IBIDAPO

Styling
JORDAN DUDDY

Channelling the energy of the Tokyo underground,
Yoon Ahn's Ambush collection echoes a multitude of
subcultures, creating a new wardrobe that encompasses
elegance, luxury and rebellion
All clothing and accessories from the AMBUSH Autumn/Winter 2021 collection

This page, from left: Clorey and Dries are wearing stylist's own cotton vests

Hair: Ryan Mitchell at Streeters using DYSON. Make-up: Laura Dominique at Streeters using Autumn/Winter 2021 Tone on Tone, Sublimage Le Baume and La Crème Corps et Décolleté by CHANEL. Models: Dries Haseldonckx at Tomorrow Is Another Day, Fien Maes at Rebel Management and Clorey at Menace Models. Casting: Noah Shelley at Streeters. Set design: Julia Dias at The Wall Group. Photographic assistant: Jimmy Mould. Styling assistant: Fergus O. Hair assistant: Kirsten Bassett. Make-up assistant: Katrina McLeod. Set-design assistants: Sam Edyn and Kettivy Hor

These Days

Photography
FUMI NAGASAKA

Styling
MARCUS CUFFIE

Blurring day and night, formal and casual, men's and women's, Dami Kwon and Jessica Jung's We11done explores the contradictions and juxtapositions inherent in the way we dress

All clothing and accessories from the WE11DONE Autumn/Winter 2021 collection

Hair: Tsuki at Streeters using BUMBLE AND BUMBLE. Make-up: Kuma using NARS. Models: Nasana Banepali at Dora Project, Wenhao Hu at Crawford Models, Joyce Keokham at Anti-Agency, Wonhee Lee, Jiashan Liu at Identity Hop Nguyen at Offshore, Kei Tsuruta at Ricky Michiels, Jaychelle Yamanoha at Supreme and Zi Yi at Barbara Pfister Casting. Casting: Barbara Pfister Casting assistant: Ti Nguyen. Set design: Lian Calvo Serrano at We Are the Valiants. Photographic assistants: Justin Mulroy and Ben Kasun. Styling assistant: Sebastian Aceto. Hair assistant: Kazu Katahira. Make-up assistant: Wakana Ichikawa. Production: Dirty Pretty Productions

Editions
of
You

Photography
THURSTAN REDDING

Styling
KAREN LANGLEY

Dream-home panoramas frame the showgirl glitz and
hardy glamour of Dean and Dan Caten's Autumn/Winter
2021 Dsquared2 collection

All clothing and accessories from the DSQUARED2 Autumn/Winter 2021 collection

Hair: Shon Hyungsun Ju at The Wall Group. Make-up: Morgane Martini at The Wall Group. Model: Lola Nicon at Rebel Management. Casting: Noah Shelley at Streeters. Digital tech: Matias Brigidano. Photographic assistants: Yves Mourtada, Anthony Karayan and Rémi Procureur. Styling assistant: Thomas Santos. Hair assistant: Romain Durand. Make-up assistant: Yin Lu. Production: Ashley Dansey and Olivia Campbell at Parent. On-set production: Mona Perron at White Dot. On-set production assistants: Merlin, Alex Gimenez, Remi Amuah, Thibaut Virolan and Mathieu Berrou

Reflections

Photography
ILYA LIPKIN

Styling
ISABELLE SAYER

Tweeds and pearls, camellias and ciphers.
Virginie Viard's Autumn/Winter 2021
collection for Chanel holds a mirror up
to the house's eternal aesthetic codes,
reinvigorated for the now

All clothing and accessories from the CHANEL
Autumn/Winter 2021 collection

Fiona is wearing stylist's own vest (throughout)

Vest as before. Rouge Coco Flash lipstick in 60 Beat by CHANEL

Stylist's own string shopping bag

Hair and make-up: Ana Buvinic at Basics Berlin. Model: Fiona Reventlow-Grinling. Casting: Mollie Dendle at Mini Title. Photographic assistants: Chaemus Leonard Mac, Esme Thompson-Turcotte and Laura Zepp. Styling assistant: Jil Gielessen. Production: Philip Bode and Yfke Ossentjuk at RCP Berlin. Production assistant: Hermann Sobe. Post-production: MCD Creative

Music, When Soft Voices Die

Photography
SHARNA OSBORNE

Styling
AGATA BELCEN

Vibrates
in
the memory

This page: Lauren is wearing an oversized knitted mixed wool jumper with logo patch and polka-dot
sleeve, oversized padded polyester and nylon shirt and viscose roll-neck jumper with logo detail
(just seen) by RAF SIMONS. Cotton trousers with side slits by SPORTMAX. And vintage leather trainers
(throughout) by KIKO KOSTADINOV X ADIDAS. Opposite: Moire cropped top with strass embroidery by
GUCCI. Belted geometric leather trousers by JW ANDERSON. And trainers as before

This page: Xue is wearing an organic cotton and recycled polyester corset dress with printed detachable front panel and leather string belt by ANDREAS KRONTHALER FOR VIVIENNE WESTWOOD. Leather boots by MARSÈLL. Opposite, from left: Akuol is wearing a cut-out leather dress with poppers by COURRÈGES. Sterling silver disc earrings and bangle with ball charm by BOTTEGA VENETA. And argyle wool leggings with stirrups by ANDREAS KRONTHALER FOR VIVIENNE WESTWOOD. Xue is wearing a metal and polyester chainmail dress by SPORTMAX. Metal necklace with whistle charm by COURRÈGES. Stylist's own zebra-printed nylon tights. And zebra-printed suede carpet mules by BOTTEGA VENETA

This page: Tumi is wearing a padded nylon jacket with shearling lining and padded
nylon satin trousers by MIU MIU. Asymmetric Lycra bra top by FILA. Opposite: Akuol
is wearing a ruched leather dress by DSQUARED2. Cubic zirconia, sterling silver and
glass earrings by BOTTEGA VENETA. And nylon tights by TRASPARENZE

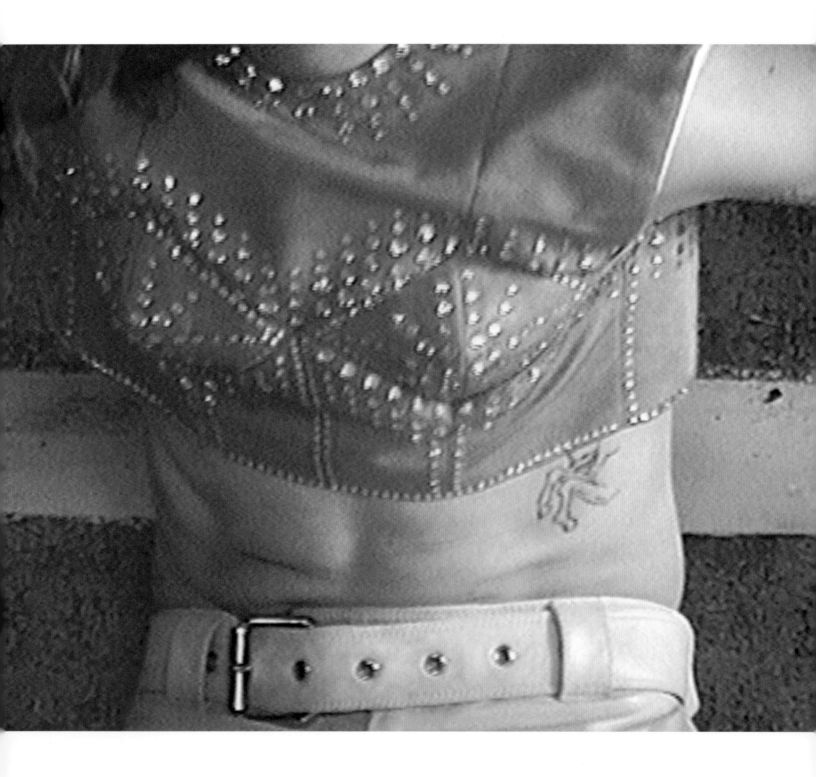

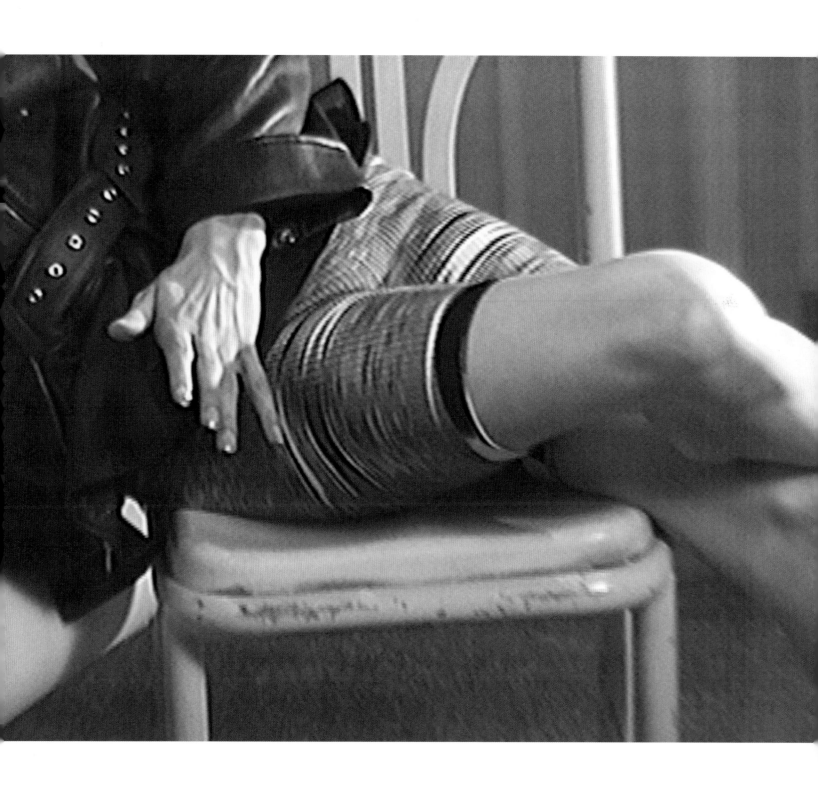

This page: Lauren is wearing a belted leather biker jacket with
ruffle hem by SUPRIYA LELE. Knitted cotton cycling shorts by MISSONI.
Opposite: Moire cropped top with strass embroidery by GUCCI. Belted
geometric leather trousers by JW ANDERSON

This page: Xue is wearing a padded polyester gilet by GUESS ACTIVEWEAR.
Denim trousers with chevron detail by PETER DO. Modal opera gloves
by SPORTMAX. And sterling silver bangle with ball charm and rubber
ankle boots by BOTTEGA VENETA. Opposite: Lauren is wearing a sleeveless
wool top by JW ANDERSON. Cotton workwear trousers by RAF SIMONS

This page: Lauren is wearing an oversized knitted wool jumper with logo patch and polka-dot sleeve, oversized padded polyester and nylon shirt and viscose roll-neck jumper with logo detail (just seen) by RAF SIMONS. Cotton trousers with side slits by SPORTMAX. And trainers as before. Opposite: Tumi is wearing an oversized wool jumper with checked scarf collar, viscose roll-neck jumper with logo detail (just seen) and workwear cotton trousers by RAF SIMONS. Rubber ankle boots by BOTTEGA VENETA

This page: Akuol is wearing a pleated silk satin dress and
patterned silk and cotton tights by VERSACE. Sterling silver disc
earrings and zebra-printed suede carpet mules by BOTTEGA VENETA.
Opposite: Lauren is wearing a leather and shearling moto jacket
and ribbed elastane leggings by STEFAN COOKE

Hair: Franziska Presche at Together using ORIBE. Make-up: Vassilis Theotokis at MA and Talent using Autumn/Winter 2021 Tone on Tone and Sublimage Le Baume by CHANEL. Models: Akuol Deng at Milk Management, Lauren Auder, Tumi at Select and Xue Huizi at IMG. Casting: Midland Agency. Choreographer: Eric Christison at Parent. Set design: Hella Keck at Webber. Manicure: Chisato Yamamoto at Caren. Photographic assistants: Jodie Herbage and Rory Cole. Styling assistants: Nicola Neri and Douglas Miller. Hair assistant: Shinnosuke Nakashimo. Make-up assistant: Kimie Yashiro. Set-design assistant: Mo Adams. Manicure assistant: Maria McKenna. Producer: Abi Bickley at 360PM. Production assistant: Rachel Travers at 360PM

To
Yesterday

Photography
MARILI ANDRE

Styling
NELL KALONJI

**Remind you
of
a glance,
a word,
a touch**

This page: Gloria is wearing a polyamide, mohair and nylon jumper by MARTINE ROSE. Opposite: Chloe is wearing a ruched viscose top by STELLA MCCARTNEY

This page: Gloria is wearing a polyester jacket, knitted wool vest
and knitted mesh turtleneck by VALENTINO. Opposite: Josephine is
wearing a polyester top and trousers by ISABEL MARANT

Josephine is wearing a laminated satin
dress with ruffles by MARNI

This page: Destiny is wearing a sequined dress by BOTTEGA VENETA. Opposite, from
top: Nyibol is wearing a metallised leather trench coat by CHANEL. Stylist's own
cotton turtleneck. And leather gladiator boots with bows by LOUIS VUITTON. Iggy
is wearing a sequined bomber jacket by MISSONI. Stylist's own ribbed cotton vest.
And denim jeans by GUESS JEANS

From left: Iggy is wearing a polyester-mix tube dress by OFF-WHITE C/O VIRGIL
ABLOH. Stylist's own nylon socks. Rosalind is wearing a Lycra body by KATZ
DANCEWEAR. Stretch velvet miniskirt by GUESS JEANS. And stylist's own nylon socks

This page: Iggy is wearing a stretch crepe minidress
by DSQUARED2. Opposite: Natasha is wearing a leather
dress with zip and eyelet details by ALEXANDER MCQUEEN

Natasha is wearing a re-nylon faux-fur coat by PRADA. Lycra body by
KATZ DANCEWEAR. Stylist's own nylon socks. And leather boots by MARSÈLL

Chloe is wearing an unravelled wool jumper and tulle skirt by DIOR. Lycra body
(as underwear) by KATZ DANCEWEAR. And chain link necklace and wrap bracelet
(as a necklace) in 18-carat yellow gold by TIFFANY & CO

This page: Bibi is wearing a studded velvet shirt by LOUIS VUITTON. Her own jewellery. Opposite, from top: Sequin tabard by MARC JACOBS. Stylist's own bandeau and underwear. And her own jewellery. Destiny is wearing a double-breasted leather coat and biodegradable PVC trousers by SALVATORE FERRAGAMO. Leather shoes by MARSÈLL

Hair: Kiyoko Odo at Bryant Artists using AMIKA. Make-up: Vassilis Theotokis at MA and Talent using NARS. Models: Destiny Boka Batesa, Gloria Fior Harcourt, Rosalind Jana and Josephine at People-file, Bibi Isako Bisala at Select London, Iggy at Premier, Nyibol at Titanium Management, Natasha at Casting Real and Chloe Tang at Models 1. Casting: Gabrielle Lawrence at People-file. Set design: Hella Keck at Webber. Manicure: Loui-Marie Ebanks at CLM. Digital tech: Thomas Carlà. Lighting: Simon Wellington and Victor de Halleux. Styling assistants: Rebecca Perlmutar and Rosie Borgerhoff Mulder. Hair assistants: Kyosuke Tanzawa and Katsuya Kachi. Make-up assistants: Sunao Takahashi and Maiko Iwashita. Set build: Konstrukt Creative. Set-design assistants: Mo Adams, Kai Ohlsen and Mike del Forno

The Things
Divine

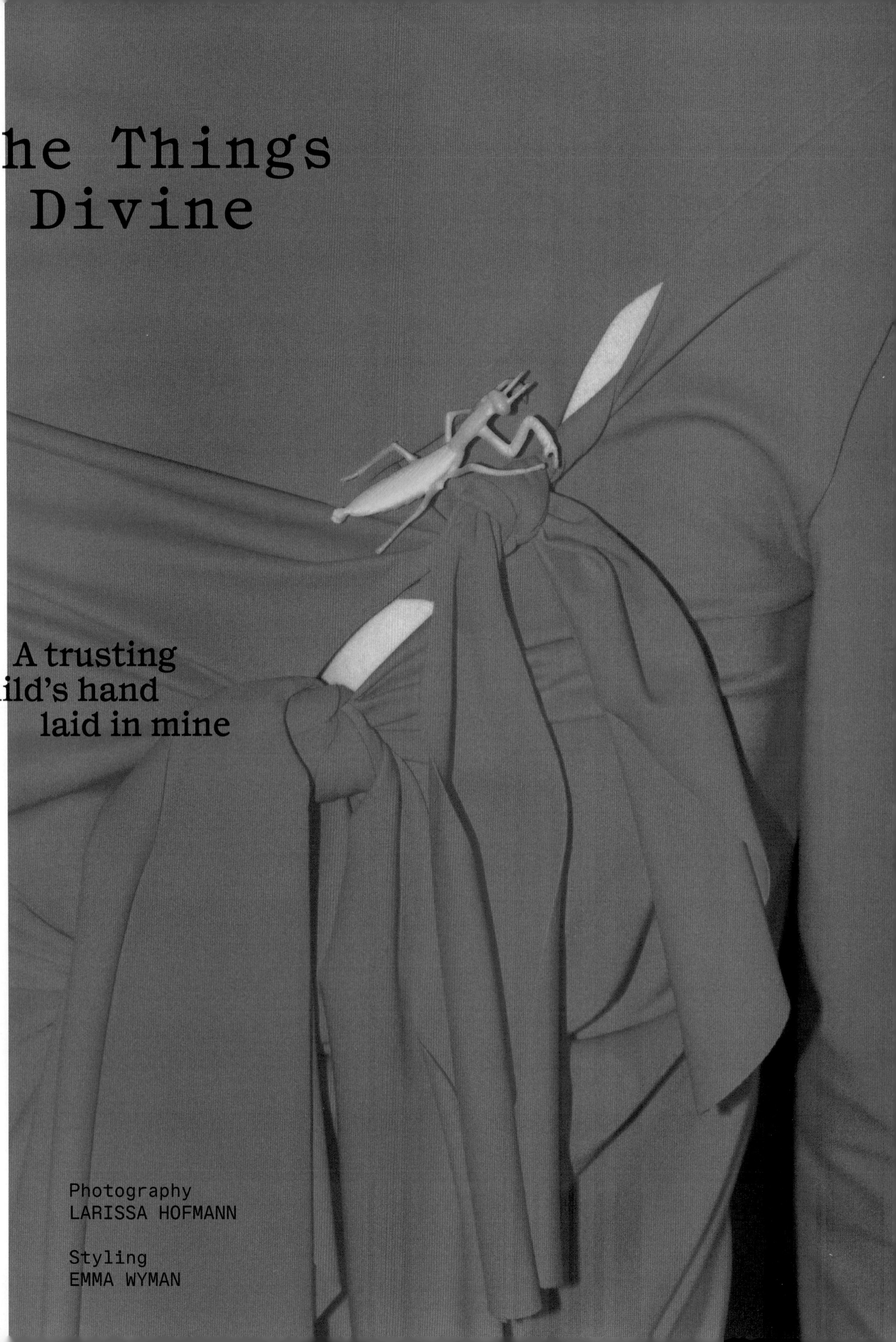

A trusting
child's hand
laid in mine

Photography
LARISSA HOFMANN

Styling
EMMA WYMAN

This page: Meadow is wearing a wool dress by FENDI. Mohair bonnet (throughout) by MIU MIU. And bead and crystal necklaces (throughout) by THE ATTICO. Opposite: Knotted nylon and spandex top by VAQUERA

This page: Crocheted recycled polyester halterneck bra by SUPRIYA LELE. Shearling skirt and boots by CHANEL.
Opposite: Wraparound leather belt (worn as a top) by BOTTEGA VENETA. Knitted wool cashmere underwear by SALVATORE FERRAGAMO

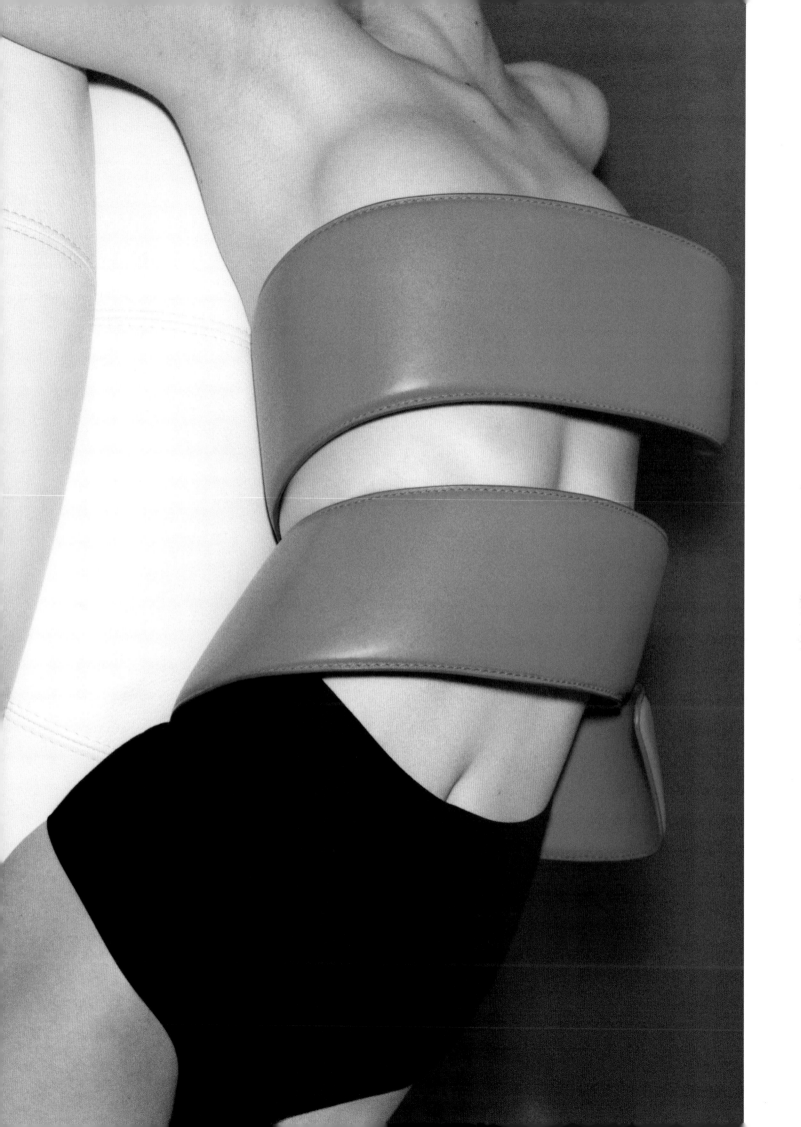

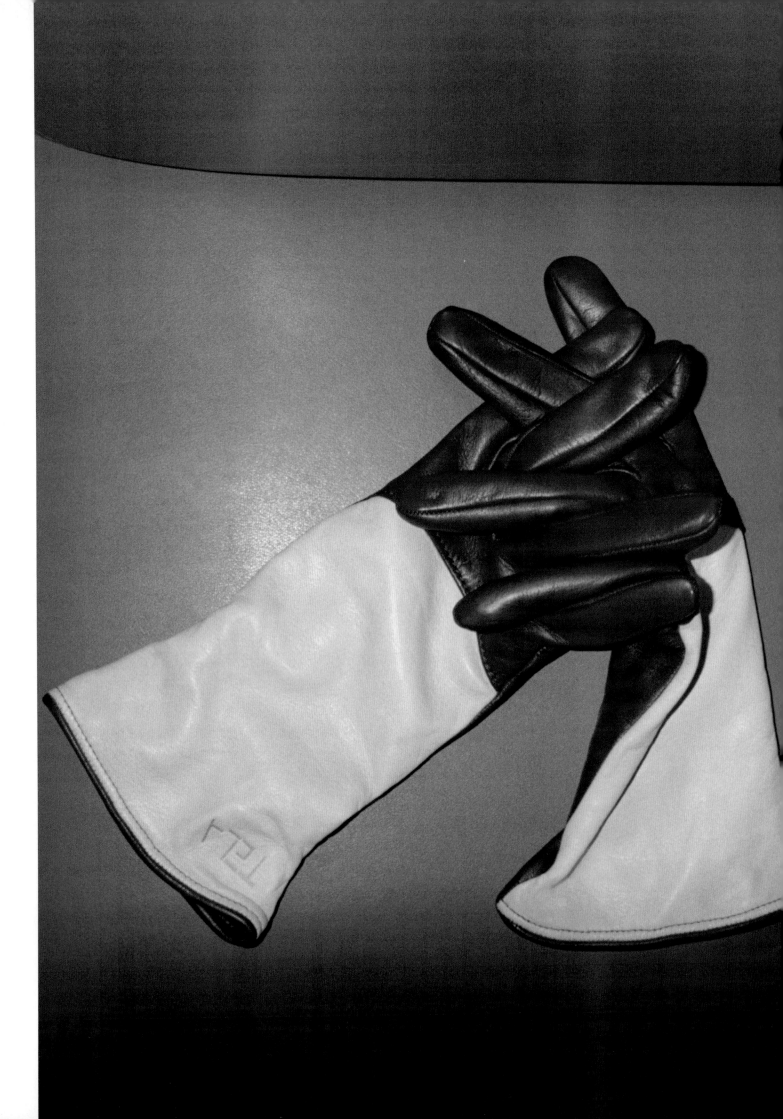

This page: Knitted wool body by JIL SANDER BY LUCIE AND LUKE MEIER. Bonded latex miniskirt by ATSUKO KUDO. T pendant in 18-carat rose gold with diamonds and turquoise and T pendant in 18-carat rose gold with diamonds and pink opal by TIFFANY & CO. Necklace (worn as a belt) as before. And padded nylon boots (throughout) by MIU MIU. Opposite: Leather gloves by TELA

This page: Leather and shearling aviator jacket by DIOR. Tulle body with crystal embroidery by BLUMARINE. Oxidised metal, enamel and crystal rhinestone choker by SAINT LAURENT BY ANTHONY VACCARELLO. And necklace (worn as a belt) and boots as before. Opposite: Patent leather boot by VIC MATIÉ

This page: Velvet, silk and wool jacquard leggings and viscose snood by KENZO. Necklace (worn as a belt) and boots as before. Opposite: Crocheted cotton minidress (worn as a top) by DE PINO. Shearling-lined skirt by DSQUARED2. And necklaces as before

This page: Viscose top with buckle embellishment by LOEWE. Hand-blown glass
rings by EYLAND JEWELLERY. Opposite: Knitted wool, viscose and mohair
catsuit by SALVATORE FERRAGAMO. Hand-blown glass rings by EYLAND JEWELLERY

This page: Recycled polyester bodysuit by GUESS ACTIVEWEAR. Bonnet and boots as before. Oxidised metal and rhinestone belt by SAINT LAURENT BY ANTHONY VACCARELLO. And cotton gloves by ACNE STUDIOS. Opposite: Laminated jersey body, cropped tweed miniskirt with faux-fur band and oxidised metal, enamel and rhinestone choker by SAINT LAURENT BY ANTHONY VACCARELLO

This page: Cropped cashmere turtleneck with buckle detail by GUCCI. Eco-leather skirt by TELA. And vintage plastic beaded necklace (worn as a belt) from THE CONTEMPORARY WARDROBE COLLECTION. Opposite: High-neck elastic viscose body with cut-out waist and embroidered tulle underwear by GUCCI. Scrunched PVC trousers by VAQUERA. Bonnet and necklace (worn as a belt) as before. And velvet platform Mary Janes by MARC JACOBS

Set design: Louis Simonon at The Magnet Agency. Manicure: Saffron Goddard at Saint Luke using Le Vernis in Ballerina and La Crème Main by CHANEL. Photographic assistant: Pierre Lequeux. Styling assistants: Giulia Bandioli, Emma Bundy, Kristina Agynayeva and Imaan Sayed. Set-design assistants: Macy Trieu Dingle and Tomomi Kishimoto. Production: Ayesha Arefin at Together and Susannah Phillips at Truro Productions. Post-production: Lever Post. Location: Eaton House Studio

Mouhameth is wearing a felted wool flannel blazer by HERMÈS. Cotton poplin
shirt by CHATO LUFSEN. Wool and silk blend tie by PAUL SMITH. Pleat-front wool
trousers by DRIES VAN NOTEN. And leather driving gloves by ERNEST W BAKER

Piano

To the old Sunday evenings at home, with winter outside

Photography
PAUL KOOIKER

Styling
RAPHAEL HIRSCH

This page: Abdou is wearing a cotton poplin shirt and silver cufflinks by CHATO LUFSEN. Wide-leg cotton drill trousers by RICK OWENS. Elasticated braces by CHARVET. And leather Oxford shoes by JOHN LOBB. Opposite: Mouhameth is wearing a cotton jersey tank top by GMBH. Tailored wool trousers by JIL SANDER BY LUCIE AND LUKE MEIER. Leather belt by LEMAIRE. Cotton socks (throughout) by FALKE. And leather Oxford shoes by BERLUTI

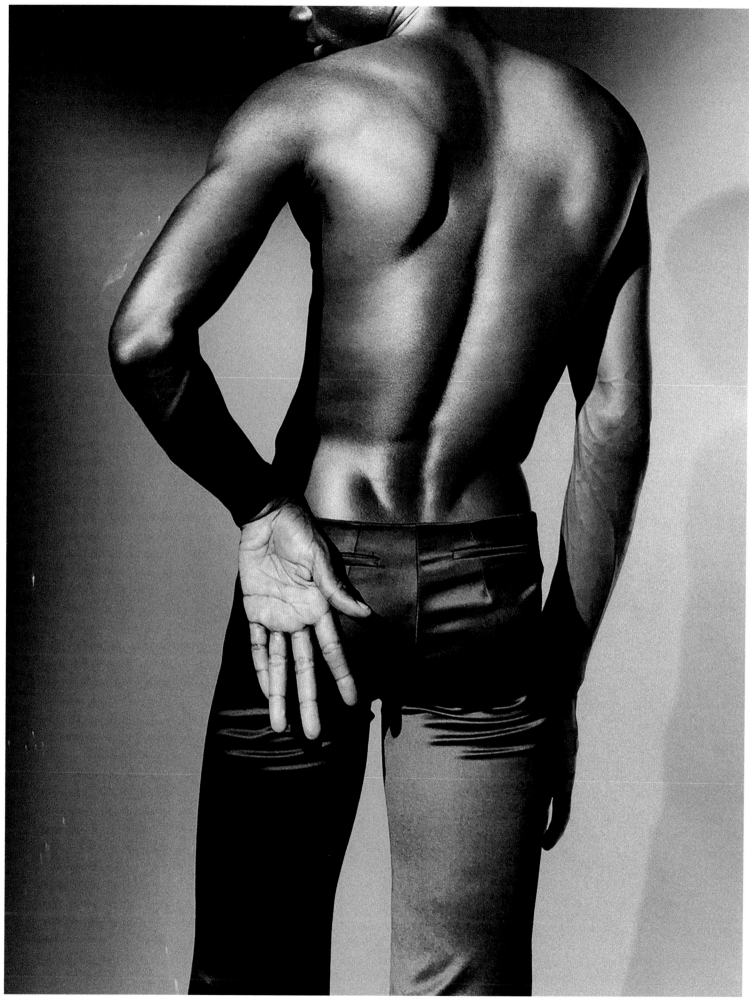

This page: Mouhameth is wearing tailored satin trousers by PALOMO SPAIN. Opposite: Abdou is wearing a leather vest from LES MAUVAIS GARÇONS. Cotton poplin shirt, leather aviator trousers and square-toed leather boots by DSQUARED2. Satin tie by CINABRE. And socks as before

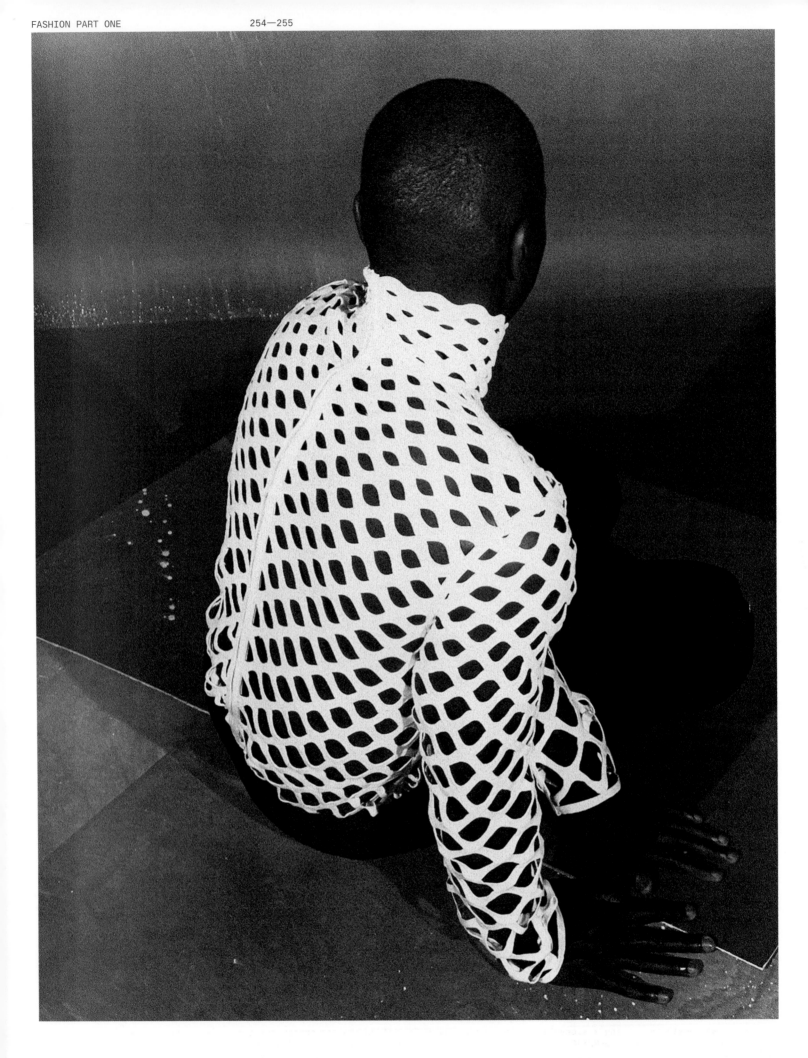

This page: Mouhameth is wearing a sleeveless padded nylon jacket by AMBUSH. Cotton poplin shirt by JIL SANDER BY LUCIE AND LUKE MEIER. Satin tie by CHARVET. Tailored wool trousers by MARGARET HOWELL. Stylist's own silver tie clip. And leather boots by MARSÈLL. Opposite: Abdou is wearing a mesh knit rollneck by VALENTINO. Wide-leg wool trousers by JUUN J

Mouhameth is wearing a cotton jersey vest and
tailored wool trousers with zip detail by GIVENCHY

This page: Abdou is wearing an oversized leather trench coat by KENZO. Tailored stretch velvet shorts by GUCCI. Opposite: Double-breasted cotton corduroy overcoat, padded pinstriped wool waistcoat and tailored wool trousers by LOUIS VUITTON. Cotton poplin shirt by JIL SANDER BY LUCIE AND LUKE MEIER. Wool tie by LUDOVIC DE SAINT SERNIN. And leather monk strap shoes by JOHN LOBB

This page: Abdou is wearing an oversized leather trench coat by KENZO.
Tailored stretch velvet shorts by GUCCI. Opposite: Wool bodysuit and
brushed leather Derby shoes by PRADA. Socks as before

Hair: Ramona Eschbach at Total. Models: Abdou Diop at Rock Men and Mouhameth N'diaye at Hakim Model Management. Casting: Piotr Chamier at Streeters. Photographic assistants: Django Tetteroo and Salomé Perroton. Styling assistants: Andra-Amelia Buhai, Cosima Menier and Agustina Chuliver Perez. Grooming assistant: Isabelle Lefebvre. Casting assistant: Benedikt Hetz. Production: Mini Title. Producer: Thomas Darnal.

This page: Abdou is wearing an oversized barathea wool suit and armoured metal shoes by BALENCIAGA. Cotton poplin shirt, silk satin cummerbund and silver cufflinks by CHATO LUFSEN. And club striped satin tie by CHARVET.
Opposite: Mouhameth is wearing pinstriped dégradé wool trousers by Y/PROJECT. Leather Oxford shoes by BERLUTI

This page: Jip is wearing nylon track
pants by FILA. Opposite: Leather trapper
hat with shearling lining by DIOR

Only in Sleep

Photography
JET SWAN

Styling
REBECCA PERLMUTAR

I met their eyes and found them mild

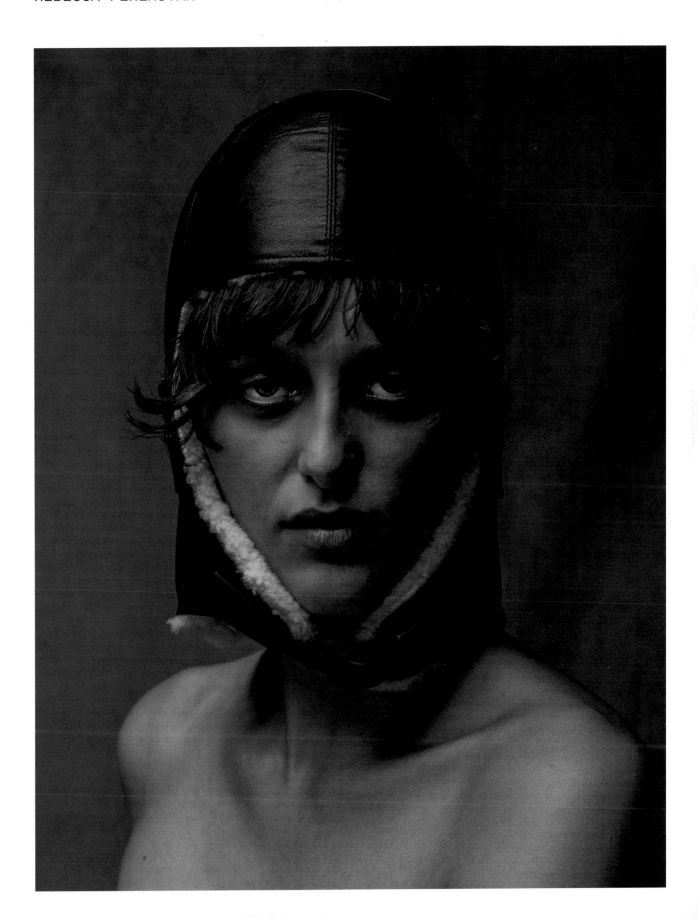

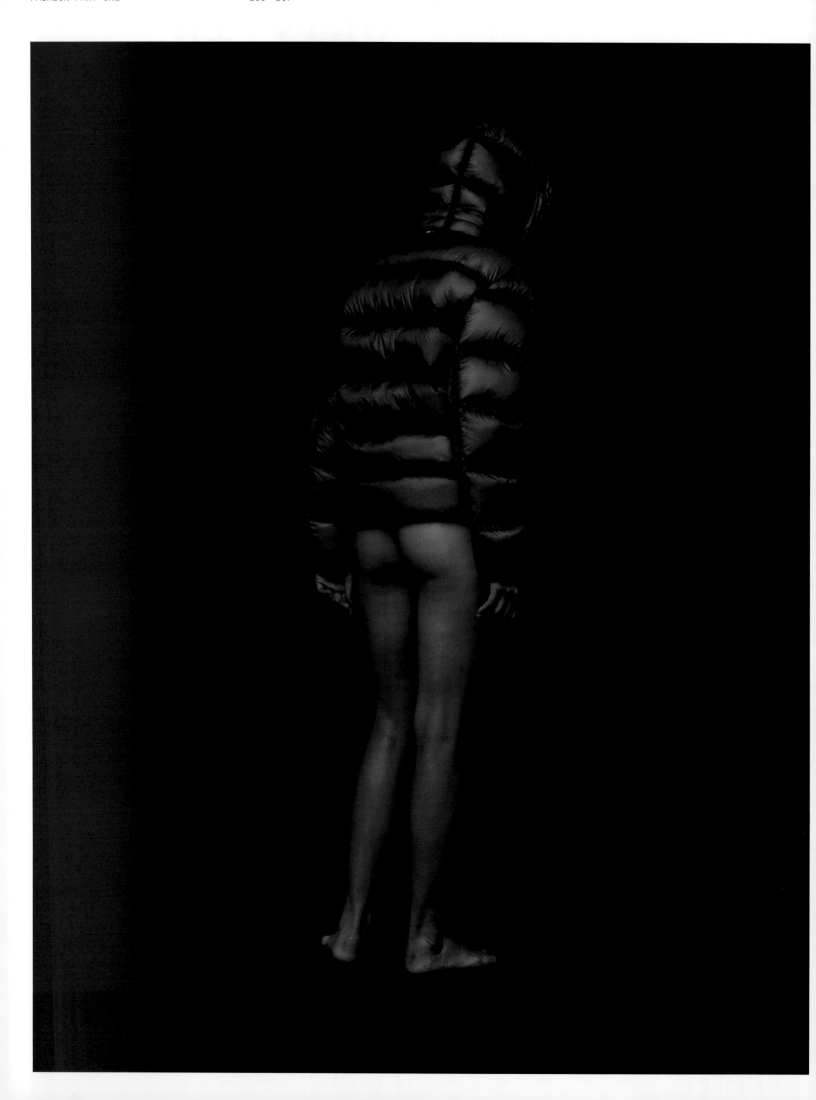

This page: Jip is wearing thigh-high leather boots by BOTTEGA VENETA.
Opposite: Padded nylon micro rip stop jacket by MOOSE KNUCKLES

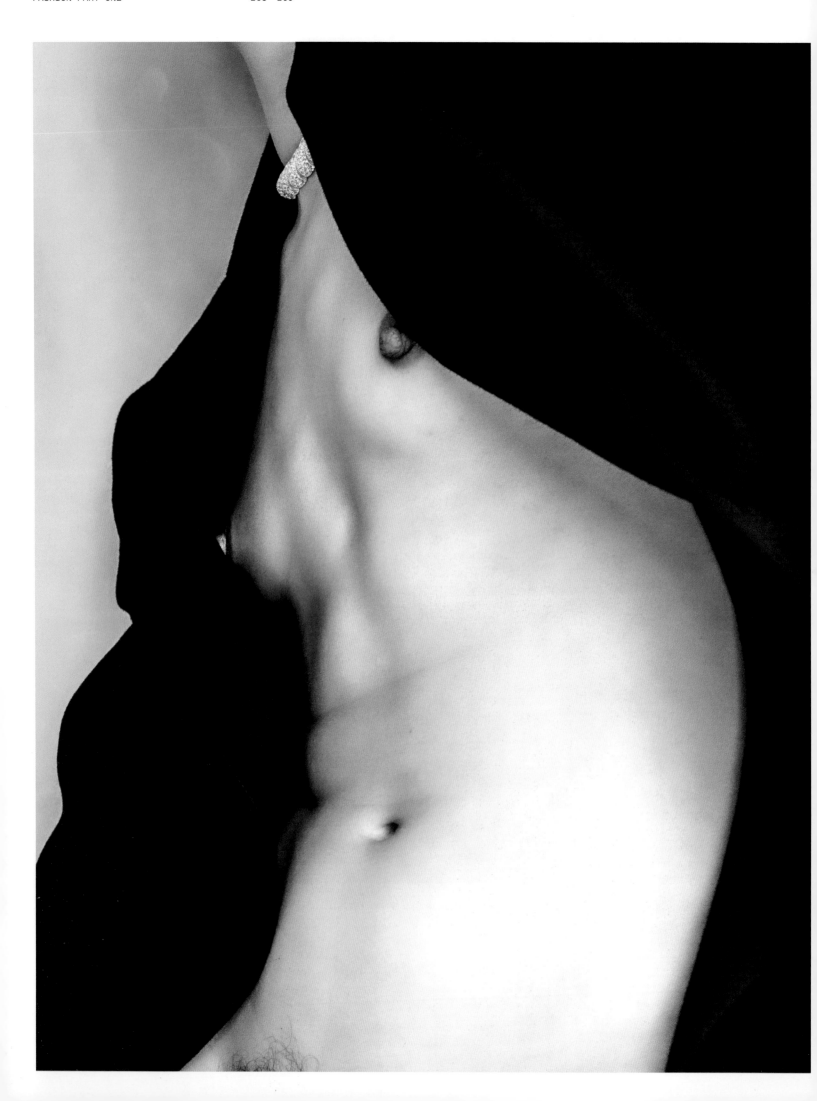

This page: Jip is wearing a viscose shirt by JIL SANDER BY LUCIE AND
LUKE MEIER. Opposite: Lilith is wearing a double wool coat by VALENTINO.
Sterling silver and zirconia necklace by BOTTEGA VENETA

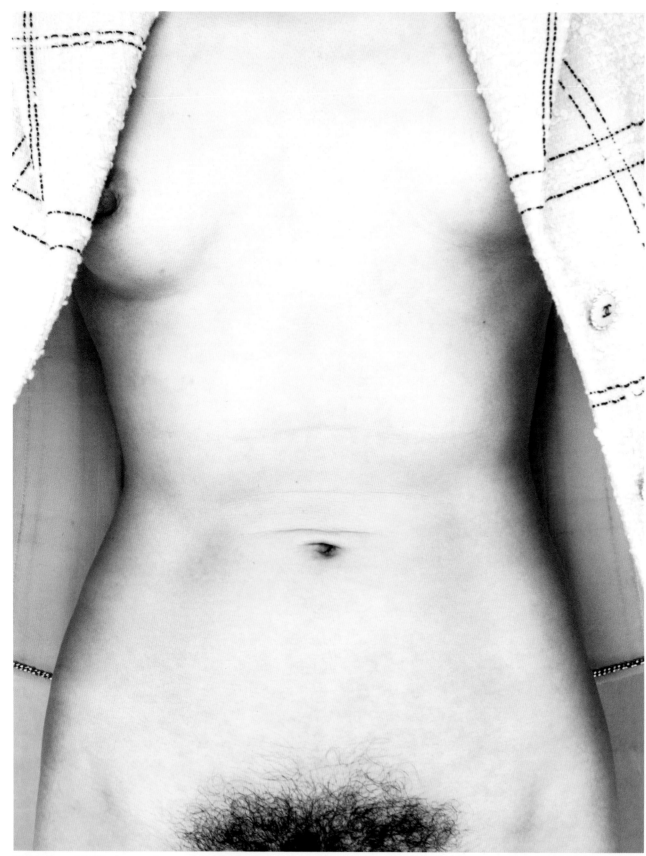

This page: Lilith is wearing a wool tweed jacket by CHANEL.
Opposite: Jip is wearing a high-waisted wool pencil skirt by FENDI

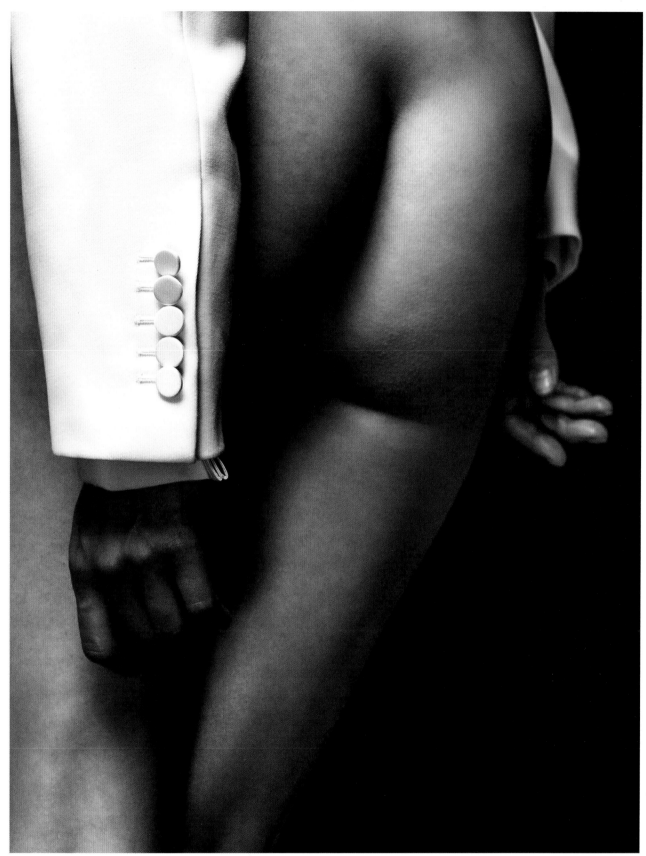

This page: Jip is wearing a fluid barathea wool blazer with satin details
and silk crepe shirt by GUCCI. Opposite: Embroidered Lady D-Lite bag by DIOR

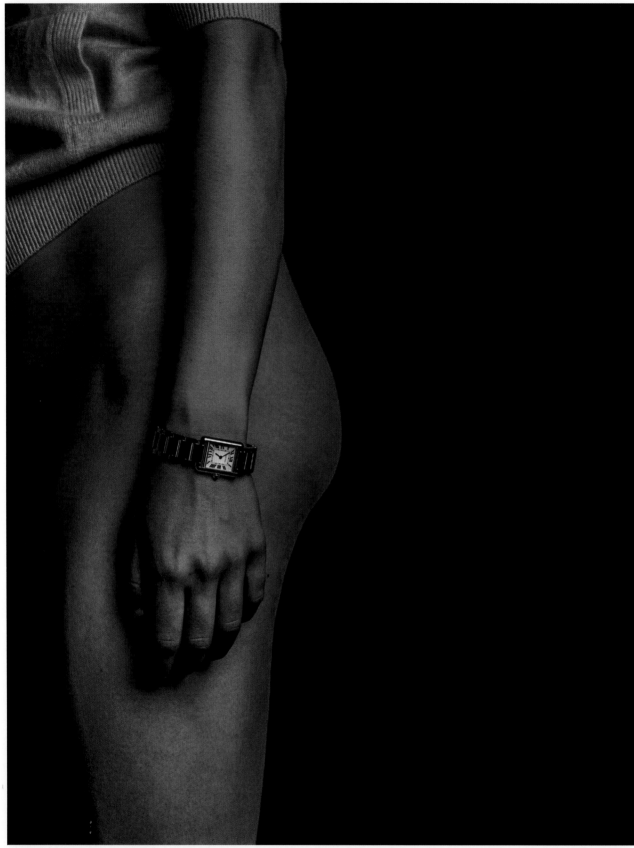

This page: Lilith is wearing a hooded zip-up cashmere jumper by LORO PIANA.
Steel Tank Must watch with beaded crown set, silvered dial and blued-steel
hands by CARTIER. Opposite: Jip is wearing a checked wool skirt by DIOR

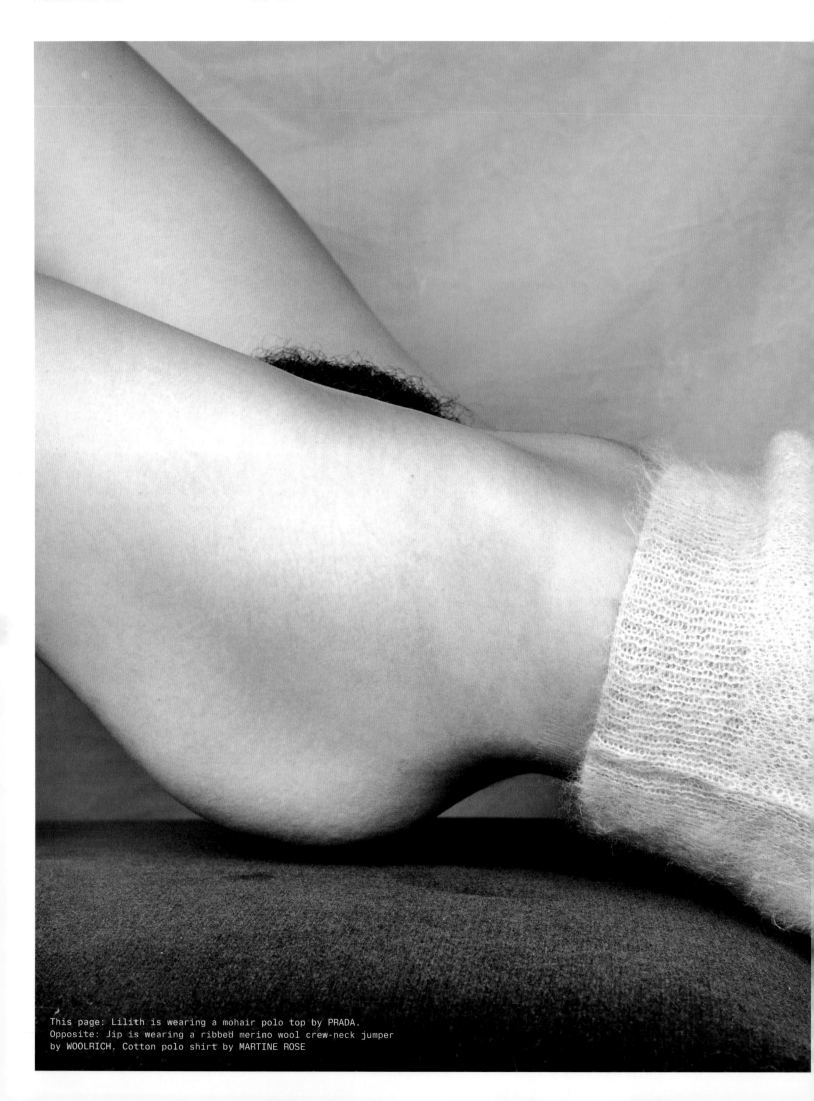

This page: Lilith is wearing a mohair polo top by PRADA.
Opposite: Jip is wearing a ribbed merino wool crew-neck jumper
by WOOLRICH. Cotton polo shirt by MARTINE ROSE

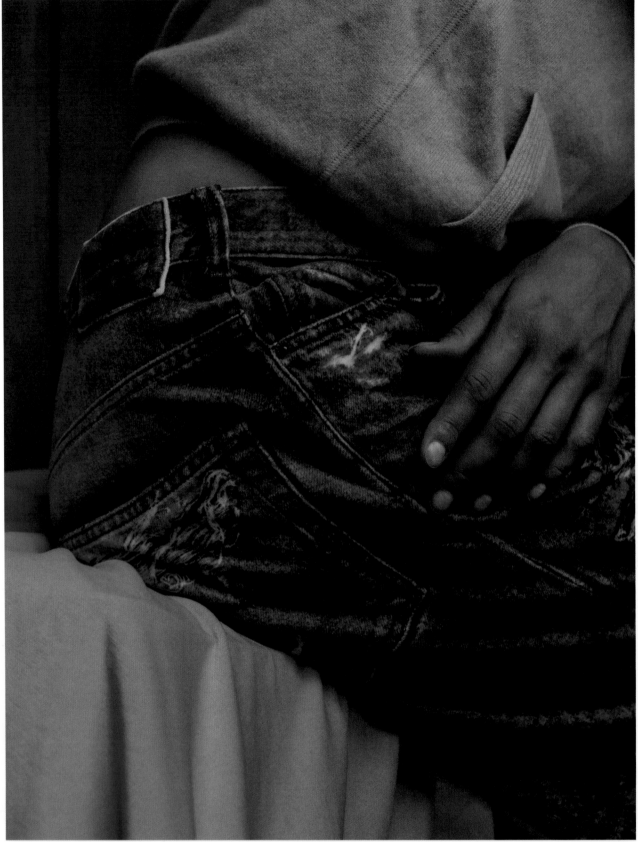

This page: Jip is wearing a hooded zip-up cashmere jumper by LORO PIANA. Trompe l'oeil denim velvet jeans by BALENCIAGA. Opposite: Cashmere roll-neck bib by LORO PIANA

Hair: Chi Wong at MA and Talent using ORIBE. Make-up: Siobhan Furlong at LGA Management
using MAC. Model: Jip Boxstart at Matt Models. Body model: Lilith Newson. Casting:
Gabrielle Lawrence at People-file. Set design: Staci-Lee Hindley. Photographic assistant:
Bradley Polkinghorne. Styling assistant: Julia Veitch. Production: Mini Title

Hind

sight

Zoë Kravitz

Photography COLLIER SCHORR
Styling AVENA GALLAGHER

This page: Laminated jersey body and leather over-the-knee boots by SAINT LAURENT BY ANTHONY VACCARELLO. Earrings as before. Opposite: Lurex and fur body, metal bracelet and coneflower chain metal belt by SAINT LAURENT BY ANTHONY VACCARELLO. Earrings as before

This page: Organic crepe muslin dress and knot-chain metal choker by SAINT LAURENT
BY ANTHONY VACCARELLO. Opposite: Laminated jersey shorts, metal bracelet and patent
leather slingback heels by SAINT LAURENT BY ANTHONY VACCARELLO. Earrings as before

This page: Her own cotton T-shirt. Vintage denim shorts by LEVI'S from RAGGEDY
THREADS. And metal pendant necklace and metal bracelet by SAINT LAURENT BY
ANTHONY VACCARELLO. Opposite: Organic crepe muslin dress and metal bracelet
by SAINT LAURENT BY ANTHONY VACCARELLO. Cotton briefs by HANES

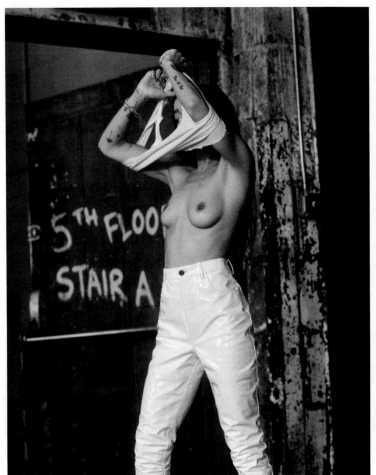

This page: Vest as before. Patent leather pantaboots and metal bracelet
by SAINT LAURENT BY ANTHONY VACCARELLO. Opposite: Laminated jersey body
by SAINT LAURENT BY ANTHONY VACCARELLO. Earrings as before

Faux-fur coat, laminated jersey shorts and patent leather slingback
heels by SAINT LAURENT BY ANTHONY VACCARELLO. Earrings as before

This page: Vest as before. Laminated jersey shorts by SAINT LAURENT
BY ANTHONY VACCARELLO. Opposite: Vintage cotton hoodie from RAGGEDY
THREADS. Tweed briefs with trim detail by SAINT LAURENT BY ANTHONY
VACCARELLO. And stylist's own vintage gym socks and trainers

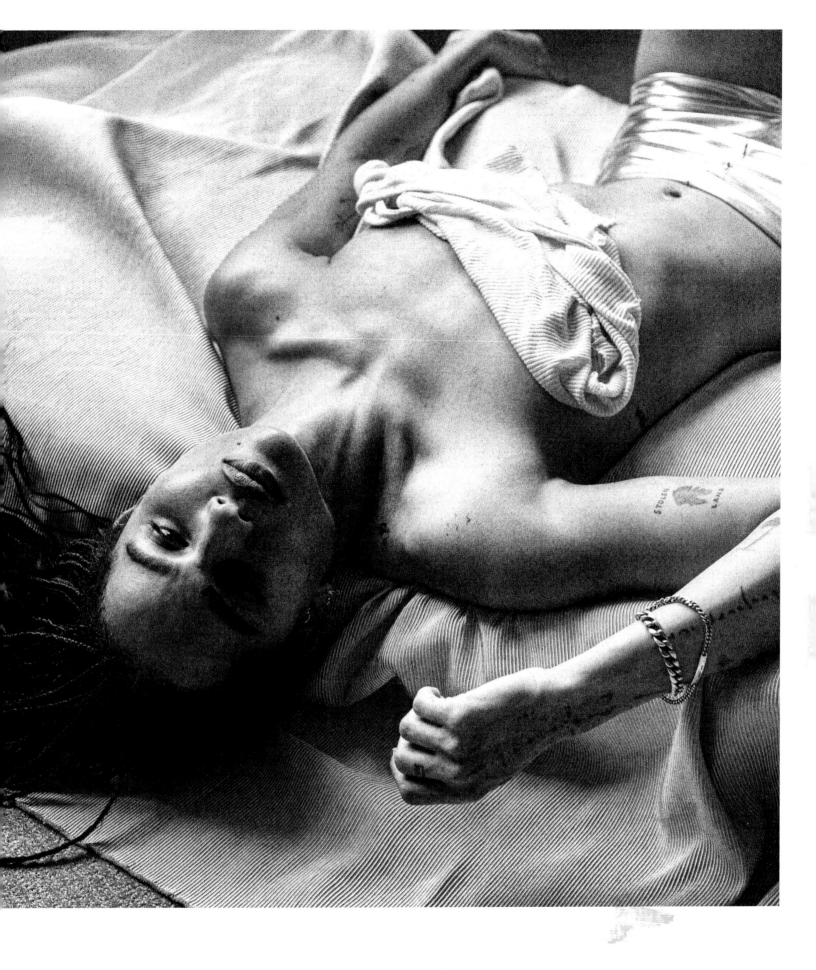

This page and opposite: Vest as before. Laminated jersey shorts and metal
bracelet by SAINT LAURENT BY ANTHONY VACCARELLO. And earrings as before

Faux-fur coat and laminated jersey shorts by SAINT LAURENT BY ANTHONY VACCARELLO. Earrings as before

Hair: Nikki Nelms at Ice Studios using MAUI MOISTURE. Make-up: Nina Park at Kalpana using YSL BEAUTY. Manicure: Aki Hirayama at Tracey Mattingly using YSL BEAUTY. Set design: Maxim Jezek at Walter Schupfer. Digital tech: Jarrod Turner. Lighting: Ari Sadok. Photographic assistants: KT Tucker and Rob Orlowski. Styling assistant: Taryn Bensky. Set-design assistants: Odin J Grina and Natalia Janul. Executive producer: Shea Spencer at Artists Commissions. Production: Jemma Hinkly at Artist Commissions and Alana Amram at Hen's Tooth Productions. Production assistant: Donovan Powell. Post-production: Two Three Two

No one can resist the allure of Zoë Kravitz. Not the waifish model-cum-waitress serving us at Greenpoint's premier hangout Five Leaves, where we're meeting for our interview. Between taking our order she reports back to her colleagues in hushed tones that she is serving "Zoë's table". Not the archetypal Brooklynite couple reclining in the park on the overwhelmingly humid mid-July day, who only break from gazing at each other to stare as we stroll past post-lunch. Not the two hipster bros who whip their heads around at breakneck speed on Williamsburg's Bedford Avenue as she walks back to her home nearby.

Although Kravitz herself seems unaware of the attention, one thing is clear: she is the cool kids' cool kid. She arrives for our interview straight from Pilates, dewy from the midday heat and dressed down in a white tank and heather-grey yoga shorts, her signature wavy braids framing her delicate features. Her mix of good looks and down-to-earth energy (she's happy to offer counsel on my dating life) goes to prove that some people really do have it all. She's genuinely nice too. She greets me with a hearty grin, graciously pours us both water every time we run low, and takes breaks from her kale and steak salad to ask with genuine concern if the sound from the busy Brooklyn street where we are sitting will interfere with my recording.

Arguably set up for life with Eighties (and enduring) style icon and actress Lisa Bonet as her mother and perennial rock god Lenny Kravitz for a father, Zoë Kravitz could easily have had her head turned by the inevitable interest this was going to generate in her and her life and assumed vapid It-girl status. A fashion favourite, she has been the face of Saint Laurent across beauty, fragrance and fashion for four years – "It's simple and beautiful clothing," she says. "I feel like me and Anthony inspire each other. We talk about inspiration pictures and send things back and forth. Me and Anthony are tight." She has also fronted campaigns for Calvin Klein, Tiffany and Balenciaga. Yet Kravitz has taken that undeniable head start in life and written her own story.

Beginning her acting career with appearances in films such as 2011's X-Men: First Class and 2014's Divergent garnered her big-screen time, albeit in supporting roles. A kick into high gear came with parts in George Miller's Mad Max: Fury Road and the Fantastic Beasts film series. But it was her performance in HBO's Big Little Lies that led to Kravitz breaking through. Holding court as the bohemian yoga instructor Bonnie Carlson (a part originally written for a white woman, and for which Kravitz adroitly handles the nuanced racial power dynamics in the shifting of the story), she stars alongside an assemblage of Hollywood's finest actors: Meryl Streep, Nicole Kidman, Reese Witherspoon and Divergent co-star Shailene Woodley.

An ability to flit seamlessly between indie flicks and mega-budget franchises is Kravitz's superpower. Her turn as Robyn "Rob" Brooks in the 2020 TV adaptation of Nick Hornby's 1995 novel, High Fidelity, may have been short-lived (it was cancelled after one series), but she cleverly reinvented it with millennials in mind. Her character, a female record store owner living in Brooklyn's Crown Heights, who has flashbacks to and laments her ill-fated relationships with both men and women, ensures this is a far cry from the Stephen Frears movie of the same name, which John Cusack and her mother starred in 20 years earlier. Kravitz, here, plays the Cusack role.

In addition to the lead character, Kravitz was an executive producer on the project and her command was seen everywhere from the freewheeling, globe-trekking soundtrack to the directing decisions. "I don't think the network understood the importance of that story," she says, "but I am still touched by how many women, especially women of colour, come up to me saying they loved it."

In the midst of the Covid-19 pandemic, she left her Williamsburg home for London to take on her biggest role yet, starring alongside Robert Pattinson's Batman as Selina Kyle – aka Catwoman. She had already played the role, after a fashion, in 2017's The Lego Batman Movie, but now she can get her teeth into a character that has already been portrayed by Michelle Pfeiffer, Halle Berry and, most recently, Anne Hathaway. It was the biracial Eartha Kitt's 1960s Catwoman – coming as it did in an era of racial tensions even more heightened and politicised than our own – that has remained in memory, immortalised. Today the role comes with its own legacy and feverishly passionate fanbase. The weight of that didn't go unnoticed by Kravitz, but it didn't deter her either. "It was different. It was scary. It was unexpected for me. And that was what was exciting."

With megastardom on the cards, her rise hasn't come without setbacks. After marrying actor Karl Glusman in an intimate ceremony at her father's Paris home in 2019, she filed for divorce 18 months later – a dark spot on an otherwise bright few years but the start of an invigorating new chapter. She feels affirmed – unafraid. Her feature directorial debut Pussy Island was recently acquired by MGM. Kravitz herself is reluctant to divulge much but she's already hard at work on the project, off to scout for locations after we meet. "I am 32 and it's fucking fantastic," she says. "I am happy about all the experiences. If you don't learn and grow, what's the point?"

Lynette Nylander
How have you been spending your time in these strange circumstances we find ourselves in? What's been your reality in the pandemic?

Zoë Kravitz
It's been so many things. I never had to worry about my job or where I was going to live – how I was going to pay rent or for food. In that respect, I'm very lucky. I also worked a lot through it. We had already started shooting The Batman when it happened. It was crazy because we were shooting this big movie and then everything stopped. The movie was shut down for six months. I stayed in London for three months, in a house in Notting Hill, this dark, funny house in London. It was very weird being away from home and my family being in other places.

LN   Whereabouts are your family?

ZK   My dad's in the Bahamas. My mom's in California. Eventually I ended up coming back here to New York for a couple of months and living upstate, which was good for me. I think it was important to take the time to feel all the things that we were all feeling. I realised how I was personally using the fast-paced life as a way of not doing and dealing with a lot of things. I'm very thankful for that time to really sit and look at, "Who am I? What do I want to be doing? How do I want to spend my time? How am I connecting with my friends and family when I talk to them?" All of those things, I had to look at.

LN   I am interested in your childhood from your perspective and the allure of your family. Everyone says you've got the coolest parents in the world. Though to you they're simply Mum and Dad. That photo of you at a fashion event sitting next to Donatella Versace springs to mind.

ZK   Yeah, if you look closely at that picture, I'm looking at my nails. I'm bored. I want to hang out with my friends. You know what I mean? Yes, that stuff is very cool from the outside, but when you're a kid you don't know what that means. It doesn't feel the same. It was all very normal to me and then alienating in a lot of ways because when you're a kid you're just trying to fit in with other kids. Standing out was the worst thing in the world.

LN   How old were you when your parents separated?

ZK   Two. I don't even remember them together but they were very friendly. I lived with my mom in LA primarily until I was 10 or 11. My dad was on tour then, so I didn't see him very often. He'd be in town for a month or a couple of days. It was the schedule. He was around, but it wasn't one week on, one week off, or anything like that. When I was 11, I moved in with him for a couple of years in Miami, near the Bahamas, where his family is from. I moved out when I was 18 and came to New York.

LN   It's natural to put you in an indie-role category – how do you navigate your career and choose the breadth of roles that you do?

ZK   I don't put a lot of thought into it in terms of, "I have to do something different so I don't get boxed in and put into a corner." We have many layers. I'm very lucky to be able to be creative for a living. I simply want to have fun and explore and challenge different sides of myself. If I read something that I feel that I've seen or done before, it doesn't spark that thing inside me. When I read something unexpected for me, it's exciting and scary. It makes me feel alive.

LN   I love that you changed your Instagram bio to Black Lives Matter.

ZK   There's nothing else to say. If you disagree with that you should leave.

LN   I remember that it used to read "Trying not to be a TOTAL asshole since 1988".

ZK   That's the point, we're all quite an asshole sometimes, and that needs to be OK.

LN   You are not afraid to put yourself out there. LGBTQ+ advocacy, Black Lives Matter – political conversations.

ZK   I feel like we're living in a very odd time, where people confuse posting something with activism, which is not the same thing. There are people who dedicate their lives and their time and their physical bodies to being at rallies and meetings and being on the front lines.

I always want to make it very clear that I am not that person. I'm not saving the world.

That's been a really difficult thing, emotionally, for me, where I've felt pressure to post something that I wasn't ready to post about or didn't know enough about. It affected me. It can feel like if you don't post about something that means you don't care about it. That's conflicting for me because sometimes I don't have enough information and need to learn more, or I don't want to be on my phone today and something's going on in the world. I'll get a lot of hate for not talking about something, and I'm like, "I'm not a fucking news anchor." Also, just because I don't post on this thing it does not mean that I'm not feeling it or learning about it. My silence doesn't mean I'm taking a side. The internet is not the real world.

LN   How did the Catwoman role come about?

ZK   My agent called me and was like, "They're making a Batman movie and there's a Catwoman role. You're on the list of actors they are looking at." I think the first thing that happened was I went to LA and met with Matt Reeves, the director, who also wrote the script, and just talked to him.

I read the script. Then he talked with me again to hear my thoughts, to see if we were on the same page. I didn't know him well and it was a bit of a process. When these big opportunities come up, these big roles, and you really want them, it's heartbreaking when you don't get them. You put a lot of energy into it.

The thing that I tried to keep in check throughout, though, was just wanting to be agreeable and likeable to get the role. To read the script and say, "I love it. I love everything about it." Then I go to the audition and I have this puppy dog energy.

It was important to give him an idea of what it's really like to work with me. To say what I really think and, if we're on set together, to ask the questions I want to ask. I tried to come at it from the angle where I am showing him what I see and feel about this character. I believe that's why it happened and I got the role. Matt's a fantastic director, and he's really into talking about the character. We had some really good conversations. I had some thoughts about the character once I'd read the script too and they were welcomed.

LN   Have you seen all the other Batman movies?

ZK   I've seen all the movies, yeah. I've read some of the comics now, but I wasn't a comic head or anything. I also tried to think about it not as Catwoman, but as a woman, how does this make me feel? How are we approaching this and how are we making sure we're not fetishising or creating a stereotype? I knew it needed to be a real person.

LN   How do you feel about the importance of that massive comics universe? It's different from what you've previously done. Those fans are hardcore.

ZK   They are, and because I respect them so much I chose not to think about them when making the movie. If I'm thinking about wanting everyone to like it and wanting all the fans to like it, I'm not going to actually bring a real person to life. Matt wrote a really interesting story with a complex character, and the relationships are really interesting. All I wanted to do was honour that story.

Sometimes with really big movies, it can feel like you're just a puppet and part of this big machine. This felt like an independent movie in the way that there was real heart and soul and thought being put into the process and into every scene. It was incredibly collaborative. Matt's very specific. It took him a year to make this because of Covid. We were in this bubble, really in this world, and it was an incredible experience. To spend a year of your life, and it's very physically demanding ... I had to be in very specific shape, and there's a pandemic going on. I'm being zipped into a catsuit every day at 7am, working 12-hour days and then coming home and working out. It was intense.

LN You've been working on your feature directorial debut, Pussy Island, too, which you also wrote.

ZK I've been writing it for four years. I want to be careful about how I speak about it and what information I put out there because there are a lot of layers to the story. I was actually in London shooting Fantastic Beasts when I started to write it. I had a decent amount of time off during that film, and I was feeling a lot of frustration and anger towards men, specifically in my industry, and I felt like this wasn't a conversation that was happening at the time. Then my imagination ran away with me and I started writing a story around those feelings. Then Harvey Weinstein happened and the world changed. This story has evolved with the world evolving, which has been interesting and which is part of the reason it took so long. This conversation is happening in real time.

LN And you want it to reflect what was and is happening?

ZK Yeah, and my opinions changed and the world changed, and so the characters and their interactions have had to change. That was interesting. It was this living, breathing thing. It's been a crazy journey, writing this movie, and I'm in love with it. I'm so excited to bring it to life.

LN When you wrote it, did you imagine you'd also direct it yourself? What was the plan?

ZK Maybe not right away. I wrote the lead role for myself, assuming I'd be in it, just naturally, because I was writing it from my perspective, in a way. Then, maybe a year in, I had decided that I wanted to direct it and that I didn't want to do both. It was actually really fun, creating this

character and taking her away from me and making her something that is not a version of me. Writing something for a woman that she can sink her teeth into, as I'm constantly reading one-dimensional, boring roles. So now we have [British actor] Naomi Ackie on board. I feel very lucky to have her.

We're in prep right now. We're still figuring out when we're going to shoot – there are a lot of different factors. Schedules and locations and stuff. It's the fun part right now, where we get to see how it all falls together. It will start filming either at the end of this year or sometime next year. I'm still figuring it out.

LN Are you nervous?

ZK I am. In a really good way – nervous and also very ready. I know the story inside out. I know how to tell it. I know what I want to do. I know where I'm coming from emotionally. I'm going to learn a lot and it's going to be hard, but the challenge is good.

LN From my perspective, to see so many female directors shine in the past few years seems new. There had been odd glimpses before but I feel like there's such a great wave of women telling worthwhile stories now. And you can always tell when a woman has directed the film.

ZK Of course you can. It's been really interesting also looking for crew and seeing what's out there. I'm looking for DPs, most are white men and then white women. There are very few Black female DPs, Asian female DPs, queer DPs, queer female DPs. People are aware of that now and it's at least progress to be having these kinds of conversations. Especially as a first-time director, I want someone that's done it before. And the people who've done it before are white men. It's like being stuck between a rock and a hard place. I haven't chosen a DP yet. I don't know what it's going to look like. I'm trying to just stay open and feel it out.

LN You also just wrapped on Kimi with Steven Soderbergh.

ZK I loved working with him. It was a really fucking fun movie. It was my first time working with him. To get

that phone call and to star in one of his movies was a wild experience. He is a true genius. Watching him work, especially going into directing, was like a college education. It's so nice to meet a filmmaker who's been doing it for so long and who's still so interested and invested in finding new ways to tell stories. He wants to work. He wants to do new things. He loves filmmaking. It's amazing.

LN Have you had time for your music amid all of this?

ZK Well, the band is no more but I've been recording a solo album with Jack Antonoff for a couple of years, on and off. It's been hard with the schedule and the pandemic. Jack is a fantastic producer – he's so good at really tapping into who he's working with and not making it about him. Some producers want to make it about ... like, "I'm going to put my sound on you." It's what I experienced with my band. But for him to want to help me realise what I'm hearing in my head has been a really wonderful experience and very therapeutic. I wrote it over a long stretch of time, subconsciously just capturing this range of emotions, which has been interesting to look back on and see what I was writing about them, then and now and in between. It's personal. It's about love and loss. I got married. I got divorced. Separations, break-ups are sad but are beautiful things too. It's about the bittersweetness, that beginning and that end. It's so complex, that space, when you're in between heartbroken and mourning the loss of something and excited for what's ahead of you.

LN Do you feel happy? Your twenties are crazy, I feel. I was holding on for dear life.

ZK I was too. Now I'm holding on to my thirties and I'm like, "Can I just stay here, though? This is nice." It's great making better decisions, knowing what works for you, knowing what feels good to you, knowing what real fun is, not just the idea of fun. We're in a sweet spot. We need to enjoy it and not pretend to be adults that don't do fun things any more. It should be, "I'm in my thirties. Let's do more things."

"It's *so complex*, that space, when you're in between heartbroken and mourning the loss of something and *excited* for what's ahead of you"

Travis Scott

Photography
JOSHUA WOODS

Styling
ELLIE GRACE CUMMING

All clothing and accessories from the DIOR menswear Spring/Summer 2022
collection. Travis is wearing a knitted wool jumper with Cactus Jack
intarsia and embroidery, flared silk and wool satin trousers with Cactus
Jack embroidery (throughout) and jasper and gold-plated brass Cactus
Jack signet ring by DIOR. White and yellow gold Cactus Jack necklace
with diamonds, cultured pearls, emeralds and lacquer by DIOR JOAILLERIE.
And his own jewellery

Wool coat with satin lapels and soutache embroidery, cotton jersey
boat-neck T-shirt with Cactus Jack print, gold-finish brass Cactus
Jack brooch, white crystal Cactus Jack belt and mesh and nubuck
leather trainers by DIOR. Trousers as before. And his own earrings

This page and following spread: Oblique silk and wool satin blazer with Cactus
Jack embroidery by DIOR. White and yellow gold Cactus Jack necklace with
diamonds, cultured pearls, emeralds and lacquer (throughout) by DIOR JOAILLERIE.
And his own earrings. Opposite: Cactus Jack jacquard cashmere sleeveless jumper
by DIOR. Trousers and necklace as before. And his own watch and jewellery

Lighting: Romain Hirtz and Hugues Poulanges. Styling assistants: Isabella Kavanagh and Ewa Kluczenko. Production: Artistry Paris. Executive producer: Laura Forrest at Artistry Paris

Travis Scott is difficult to pin down – literally, for an interview or a photographic shoot, but also ideologically. He eschews and evades easy categorisation. Sure, he's a musician – he has one of the highest profiles of a new generation of rap artists. Yet to see Scott as just that is to miss the point: whether creating a McDonald's meal – he is the first celebrity to have one named after him since Michael Jordan in 1992 – performing a virtual concert on gaming platform Fortnite, or remaking himself as a modern media mogul, Scott embodies creativity in the 21st century. While somehow juggling an aura of mystery with a stratospheric level of fame, he matches a hazy, autotune-inflected musical output that defines the sound of modern hip-hop with a creative auteurship that goes beyond hit singles. Scott's creative collective Cactus Jack encompasses a record label, a publishing arm and an array of merchandise with graphics devised by him. Perhaps inevitably his manifold talents attracted the attention of the equally multi-hyphenate creative Kim Jones at Dior – he thought they should collaborate.

Words EMMA HOPE ALLWOOD

Jones, of course, has brought the work of visual artists into the Dior universe on numerous occasions since stepping into his role as artistic director of menswear in 2018: the pneumatic robots of Hajime Sorayama; the playful, cross-eyed characters created by Kaws; and art-influenced clothing in partnership with artists Raymond Pettibon, Daniel Arsham and Peter Doig. But this latest collaboration exhaustively explores the elastic definition of the term 'artist' today. "I have always collaborated with artists. This time I said to myself, why not a musician?" Jones says. "Creating is a collective effort and, let's be honest, a creative director is surrounded by a whole team of creatives. You can't accomplish your ambitions for a house like this if you're doing it alone. It's not about talent or celebrity, but if someone produces something I find cool, I want to interact with him."

Scott was born Jacques Bermon Webster II in Houston, Texas, in 1991: he renamed himself after a favourite uncle, Travis, and the American rapper Kid Cudi, whose real first name is Scott. Thus rechristened, he achieved global success as a recording artist: after dropping out of university to pursue music, his first commercial EP, Upper Echelon, was released in 2013 – since then, he has been nominated for eight Grammy awards. His 2018 album Astroworld has gone triple platinum in the US and, after the release of his last single – fittingly titled Franchise – in September last year, he became the first artist to have three songs debut at No 1 in less than a year on the Billboard Hot 100. Spotify currently ranks him as the 24th most popular artist in the world, ahead of Lady Gaga, Taylor Swift and the Beatles.

He and Jones first met six years ago, when the latter was head of menswear at Louis Vuitton, clashing modern luxury with streetwear in a manner that's now commonplace – not least at Dior. The label's much hyped Air Jordan collaboration was previewed on Scott's feet at the house's menswear show in Miami in December 2019. The next step was for them to collaborate for Spring/Summer 2022, on the first Dior catwalk collection created with a musician or a record label, dual-branded as Cactus Jack Dior.

The collaboration, however, isn't about two brands coming together – rather, it's about the relationship between Jones and Scott, an intimate connection. The two have been in contact since that first meeting, talking, texting and ultimately gestating this possibly inevitable hook-up. "Kim is a friend of mine. I probably wouldn't be doing this if he wasn't involved," Scott says. "He is such an inspiration. I was a fan even when I was in college, so it's crazy to be working with him. Going to the atelier and watching things being sewn and made by hand, it was insane."

This wasn't just a case of Scott slapping his name on a label and calling it a day. It never is with any of his collaborations: Scott and Cactus Jack have also worked with Nike, Bape and PlayStation, and his McDonald's hook-up wasn't just a meal – incidentally, it consisted of a quarter pounder with cheese, bacon and lettuce, fries with barbecue sauce and a Sprite – but a full line of merchandise. "This is the first time that a luxury house is collaborating with a musician and involving him in all the creation process," says Jones in an implicit acknowledgment of the fact that while rappers like Scott are often on the moodboard or seated in the front row, they're rarely found in the atelier or joining a designer for a bow at the end of the runway. Their creative process began with Scott visiting Dior's archives. "Travis knew exactly what he wanted," says Jones. "He understands

what young people want, knows how to appeal to them. He also knows what the brand is about. We wanted it to be Dior with Travis's element on top."

On his 2016 track High Fashion, Scott raps a list of designer names: Maison Margiela, Louboutin, Givenchy. But he isn't keen to label either himself or his sound. He has bristled at a music industry keen to pigeonhole the latter as hip-hop: "I would just describe it as different pieces of my brain," he has said. The same approach applies to his personal appearance – the two go hand in hand, blending sports and formalwear, street and couture. That is what influenced Jones for this Cactus Jack Dior show: Scott's own style, filtered through his eye and the workmanship of Dior, a conversation in cloth.

Scott's home state of Texas served as an inspiration – it was, coincidentally, the first place in America that Christian Dior himself visited, in 1947, a bit of Dior folklore that connected now to then. As such, the set of the show offered a visual mash-up of Dior's childhood rose garden in Normandy with an imaginary rendering of the Lone Star State – all fluorescent fibreglass cacti, larger-than-life bleached bison skulls and desert sand (no matter that Scott actually grew up in the lush Houston suburb of Missouri City). The colour of the clothes came from there too. "The pink is the sky over Houston, the green is the cactus, the brown is the soil," shares Jones. "We tried to connect worlds and take where I'm from and the identity of Houston, Texas, and spread it across the collection," Scott adds.

Of course, Scott provided the soundtrack for the Cactus Jack Dior catwalk in June – the Paris menswear show debuted two new songs by Scott, one titled Escape Plan, the second Lost Forever, featuring rapper Westside Gunn. He also included a song originally leaked in 2019, In My Head, featuring Swae Lee and CyHi the Prynce, with a different beat and additional ad libs. All three are set for release on the forthcoming Utopia LP, his fourth album to date. As we go to print, it's scheduled to drop sometime later in 2021 – but precise details are hazy. Scott values his mystique.

What does the music sound like? Ambient, unexpected, kind of earwormy, lo-fi yet high-tech. It's a bundle of contradictions, which is – as Scott says – connected to the clothes. His personal style has been described as grunge – which it is, with beaten-up jeans and flannel button-downs and even Nirvana T-shirts making appearances. Then he'll tote a crocodile Hermès Haut à courroies bag below an Ozzfest T-shirt. "I think high end and evening couture have always been in the metaverse of things I'm into," says Scott, who cites the tailoring as his favourite part of the Dior collection. And there was a philanthropic element too: a series of shirts hand-painted by American artist George Condo will be sold to raise money for a new foundation Scott is establishing, which will support students with scholarships in collaboration with New York fashion institution Parsons.

"I have been thinking about young people a lot recently. With the pandemic, it's a very difficult time for them," says Jones. "Studying, going to university, following their dreams, it's all a lot more difficult today with Covid-19. And yet Dior is doing incredibly well in spite of this crisis. We need to use our power and the means at our disposal to support the kind of initiatives in which we believe."

As Scott puts it, "I'm just a kid from Texas." Maybe this collection will end up helping the next kid from Texas too.

Balenciaga
Couture

Photography
OLA RINDAL

Styling
MARIE CHAIX

This page: Adama is wearing a padded satin faille stole and opera coat with BB embroidery and moulded polyurethane sunglasses by BALENCIAGA COUTURE. Opposite: Lisa is wearing an oversized knitted vicuña wool turtleneck, tailored fresco wool trousers, antique brass earrings with Swarovski crystal rhinestones, fitted jersey gloves and glazed leather boots by BALENCIAGA COUTURE. Domed flocked velvet hat by PHILIP TREACY

"Fear." The designer Demna Gvasalia is talking about the emotions, namely his own, triggered by the daunting task of presenting his first couture collection. It's May 2021 – the show is in July. "This is a little bit like a therapy session," he'll later add, laughing. His feelings are heightened because this couture collection is not just for himself, but for the august, austere house of Balenciaga, where couture – arguably – was raised from applied to pure art at the hands of its founder, Cristóbal Balenciaga, a legend in his own lifetime, deified since. He retired in 1968 and died in 1972. Couture bearing the label Balenciaga has never been designed by anyone other than him – until now. "This is the house where couture for me is kind of like innate, the essence," Gvasalia says. "I felt it was my obligation." But still, there's fear. "Fear of not being enough. Fear of having to fill these very big shoes, left by 'the master of us all'." He isn't laughing. "It's not just a legacy – it's Cristóbal Balenciaga's legacy."

Portrait by BFRND

Words ALEXANDER FURY

Gvasalia has every right to be afraid, given that the history and prestige of the house of Balenciaga is, possibly, unparalleled in modern fashion. Others come close, granted. Christian Dior ensured his name's immortality by resuscitating Paris haute couture after the strictures of the second world war, by saving women from nature and creating a fashion moment with his 1947 debut that outmoded all before it. Gabrielle Chanel emancipated women not once but twice, first in the 20th century's teenage years, and then again after her comeback in 1954, inventing a uniform of modernity, eschewing fickle fashion in favour of eternal style. Yves Saint Laurent, Dior's dauphin, rebelled in the 1960s and then refined, dedicating himself to the perfection of his craft. They are all couture greats, names whose work changed fashion. Yet the sombre Spaniard Cristóbal Balenciaga is feted as the greatest of all. Even those contemporaries – and others – openly acknowledged it. It was Dior who first called him "the master of us all", comparing the couture to an orchestra composed and conducted by Balenciaga. "Balenciaga alone is a couturier," said Chanel – who rarely praised anyone except herself. "The others are draughtsmen or copyists." Madeleine Vionnet called him "un vrai"; Balenciaga's friend and devoted disciple Hubert de Givenchy declared he was the greatest single influence on his career.

Almost half a century after his death, Balenciaga is still revered as the most significant figure of 20th-century haute couture, a defining architect of fashion as we experience it today. Balenciaga founded his couture house in San Sebastián, Spain, in 1917 – it was named Eisa, a diminutive of his mother's surname Eizaguirre – expanded to Madrid and Barcelona, and in 1937 opened as Balenciaga in Paris, at 10 avenue George V. When that address – and the other branches – closed in 1968, the New York Times ran the news under the headline "Nothing Left to Achieve, Balenciaga Calls It a Day". Nothing left to achieve because, in the 51 years in between, Balenciaga had reinvented how people dressed. His clothes were paradoxically formal and fluid, could appear heavy and architectural yet were magically weightless, "like a sea swell", wrote Pauline de Rothschild, who, like pretty much every other woman of note, wore Balenciaga.

"One never knew what one was going to see at a Balenciaga opening," wrote Diana Vreeland, breathlessly, in her 1984 memoirs. "One fainted. It was possible to blow up and die." Balenciaga's most passionate client was Mona von Bismarck, who featured in Cole Porter lyrics and Vogue photo spreads, and who ordered everything, including cinnamon-coloured gardening clothes, from the couture house. She was immortalised by Cecil Beaton in Balenciaga's trapeze-line draped-back satin evening dresses, shot from behind to show the collar elegantly dipping at the nape. When the house closed she retired to her room for three days, to mourn.

In May, when Gvasalia and I meet at the Balenciaga archives, held in a vast warehouse on the outskirts of northern Paris, he has already been preparing for his couture debut for 18 months. Balenciaga had originally planned to present the line in July 2020 but was stymied by the Covid-19 pandemic and lockdowns that achieved what two world wars and the Nazi occupation could never do in halting the Paris haute couture shows for a year. With hindsight, however, Gvasalia says he's been thinking about couture for six years – since he first began designing for the house in 2015. Surprising, because you wouldn't immediately connect Gvasalia's designs to couture, for many reasons. They are ready-to-wear obviously, their slick surfaces and sharp silhouettes revelling in an industrial quality inherent to their manufacture, while aesthetically and ideologically they sit as far away from the fluffy extravagance that characterises most modern haute couture, focused as it is on event dressing. When Cristóbal Balenciaga closed the fashion house in 1968 he reportedly told a distraught client, "Why do you want me to go on? There is no one left to dress." Ready-to-wear, he recognised, was the future, but he had no interest in it.

People store priceless fine art in the out-of-town repository where Balenciaga keeps its archive, a space segmented into aircraft-hangar-sized spaces crammed with stuff whose collective worth is equivalent to the GDP of entire nations. The Balenciaga archive houses some unusual things alongside clothes – the remnants of Cristóbal Balenciaga's personal library and art collection, the furniture from his homes piled on shelves, even an elevator padded in cordovan leather that once ferried clients in his couture house. It has examples of ready-to-wear clothes by Cristóbal Balenciaga's successors – lesser-knowns such as Josephus Thimister, who designed Balenciaga from 1992 to 1997, and the famous 21st-century trio of Nicolas Ghesquière, Alexander Wang and Gvasalia. There are also pieces actually made by Cristóbal's own hands – holy stuff. Each collection, Balenciaga purportedly sewed one black dress entirely – he learnt the craft directly from his mother, a seamstress, and was venerated for his faultless technical ability alongside his creativity. Balenciaga would frequently make clothes for himself to wear, including such oddly un-Balenciaga garments as a ski anorak, sewn together on the eve of his departure for holiday. One 1960s collection featured a coat with sleeves that were based on Balenciaga's own raincoat – Women's Wear Daily, which often snubbed its nose at Balenciaga's hauteur and the reverence with which he was held in the fashion industry, dubbed it a "Balenciagaberry". Balenciaga wouldn't sketch, rather he worked directly on the fabric of toiles, manipulating material in three dimensions until they achieved the effects he craved – a methodology echoed in Gvasalia's own, where he chops up existing garments to shift forms on the body.

Anoraks, raincoats, brand mash-ups, high and low – there's a whole bunch of unanticipated parallels you can find there between Gvasalia and Balenciaga. The most enduring connection between the two, however, is their quest for modernity – although the meaning of modernity in 1960s Parisian high society and circa 2021 is, of course, fundamentally different. Back then, it revolved around haute couture – today, women wear tracksuits rather than tweed suits, sportswear for everyday that can perhaps be traced back to Balenciaga's revolutionary semi-fitted suits of 1951, which traced an eased line that foreshadowed not just the silhouette of the 1960s, but a whole modern idea of comfort in dress. "Parkas, denim jackets, five-pocket jeans," says Gvasalia. He's talking not about ready-to-wear here, but his couture. He's talking about how he can make couture feel modern, for him.

"When I started, there were a lot of Cristóbal dress references because that is the base," Gvasalia says. "I need to bring that elegance into this time. But I also want clients who don't walk through a palazzo in Venice, in the *robe manteau* of Mona von Bismarck." He laughs. "It's somebody who, I don't know, travels in haute couture. Because there are people who do that – I don't know them, but I hope to know them." Gvasalia has always been superb at unpicking his thought processes: he makes for an incredibly engaging interview. Here, next to Cristóbal Balenciaga's old furniture, he is giving an ad hoc synopsis of his new take on couture. "It's a trench coat. It's a tailored suit. I will even have a couture T-shirt. I need to extend it. For couture to be modern, it has to be a wardrobe." He pauses. "We cannot get locked into the ballroom."

When you enter the Balenciaga archive, you are given a small oxygen monitor: the airflow is controlled and the climate, generally, is maintained at -7.8C (18F), a temperature so low fire cannot ignite. Off to the side is a rail of new (old) acquisitions from auction houses: a sculpted sheath dress in searing yellow duchesse satin from 1962, a black cashmere evening coat from 1951. In the back, there are several racks from which recent Balenciaga collections hang. Gvasalia won't look at those, he tells me. He is wearing a long black coat, like the inverse of the traditional white couture worker's smock, his hair closely cropped. He's looking at an elaborately embellished bodice, contained in a grey cardboard archive box – the type known, in the trade, as "coffins", because dead clothes sleep inside them. The bodice, swollen with tissue padding as if still inhabited by a living body, is pale silvery blue silk jacquard, a base for embroideries of strewn flowers in glass beads with crystal droplets. It's a little raggedy, threads plucked and hanging loose, as if it's been bashed about, with uncharacteristic disrespect, for half a century or so. Only it hasn't: the piece is new, the top of an evening dress from his forthcoming couture collection. "This we have been working on, I think, for two months," Gvasalia says. Its decoration is executed by the young French embroidery atelier Jean-Pierre Ollier and painstakingly sewn to seem, for want of a better term, a bit fucked up. Other pieces from the collection are too, like a sack-back evening coat in a poison green silk taffeta that is permanently crumpled, as though it slid off its hanger to the bottom of a wardrobe long ago and was left to moulder.

"I like the idea that couture is an effort to come as close as possible to perfection," Gvasalia says, incongruously, staring down at the plucked surface. "I think Cristóbal's idea of couture was that. He was a perfectionist."

Understatement of the century: Balenciaga was an absolute obsessive, "a haunted man" according to his parish priest and confessor Father Robert Pieplu, "haunted by a great plan, a vision of the world". That vision accepted nothing short of perfection. Sleeves were a fixation, his couture house resounding with anguished cries of "*la manga*" as Balenciaga ripped his garments apart with his own hands, remaking again and again. He would not permit anyone else to pin his designs in his presence and, when he was asked to design the uniforms for Air France in 1968, he wanted to fit each of the 6,000 outfits himself. Conversely, Gvasalia has never been interested in achieving perfection. "Perfection doesn't really exist. I don't really believe in that," he says. "I feel I always look for beauty in places that are not conventionally understood as that." Gvasalia's clothes, first for the label Vetements (which he co-founded in 2014 and left in 2019) and latterly for Balenciaga, have made a feature of their unusual fabric treatments and odd proportions – inbuilt creasing, bleaching, puckering and mismatched prints, coats tugged across the body and deliberately misbuttoned, shoulders cut to slide forwards, to almost round the back.

Back in 2016, when I spoke with Gvasalia for a profile for this magazine around his first ready-to-wear show, he recounted a story of Cristóbal Balenciaga draping fabric on a client, "of how this woman was transformed. How he changed the posture, the attitude," Gvasalia said. "For me, that was the most important part. That was, for me, the source of inspiration. How do we do that today? How do we transform the attitude?" Gvasalia, though, is more likely to create a hunch than hide it: a Schiaparelli-pink satin faille coat in this couture collection looks a bit like it has a sofa cushion stuffed between the shoulder blades, an extension of a collar line Gvasalia drew from the stand-away collars of Balenciaga's 1960s suits and translated into his clothes right from the start. His Oxford stripe shirts and denim jackets dip delicately at the nape, a nod to Mona von Bismarck.

Attitude is all-important to Gvasalia. Attitude can mean both a physical posture – a gesture, a stance – and a mindset. It can also denote truculent behaviour. All three are evident in his approach. If today Gvasalia is in a reverential mood, it hasn't always been the case. He has affixed Balenciaga's name to tracksuits and trainers, to T-shirts with reconfigurations of the election merchandise of 2016 Democratic presidential nominee Bernie Sanders. Cristóbal Balenciaga was, by contrast, avowedly apolitical: he fled the Spanish Civil War in 1937, yet the final dress he created was a wedding dress for General Franco's granddaughter Carmen Martínez-Bordiú in 1972. When Balenciaga decided to close his couture house, it was in the midst of sociopolitical upheaval – news breaking of the May 1968 Paris student protests, the world transforming before his eyes. However, Gvasalia reacts to those streets, translating the attitude of its founder into unexpected clothes, including hooded sweatshirts, leather jackets and jeans. Born and brought up poor, Balenciaga was a snob: he declared his house must dress only thoroughbreds and quoted Salvador Dalí – another Spaniard – when he stated, "A distinguished lady always has a disagreeable air." So you may think he wouldn't

"Perfection *doesn't really* exist.
I don't really believe in that"

like sweatshirts labelled with his name – even if they're cut with a cocoon back or to mimic the hip-thrust stance he instructed his models to adopt. Yet many of Balenciaga's garments also have humble origins: his semi-fitted suits were based on the smocks worn by sailors in Getaria, the coastal village in Basque country where he was born. His father was one of them.

Gvasalia's father repaired cars; his mother was a housewife. While Balenciaga was apolitical, Gvasalia wasn't permitted that luxury. He was born in Georgia, though his family was displaced via a process of ethnic cleansing by Abkhaz separatists that ultimately expelled a quarter of a million Georgians from their homes between 1992 and 1993. He and his family relocated first to Ukraine and, with the Iron Curtain having fallen, Gvasalia's father shifted, unexpectedly, to a lucrative business of importing hitherto restricted goods into Russia – mineral water, caviar. Fashion wasn't such a great leap for Gvasalia, although he first got a degree in economics before going against his parents' wishes and studying how to design clothes. He then began to work with other brands in Paris – namely Maison Martin Margiela and Louis Vuitton – before starting Vetements. It's a far cry from the apocryphal origin story of a precocious Balenciaga, remarking as an 11-year-old on the elegance of the Marquesa de Casa Torres as she passed in a tailleur by the turn-of-the-century couture house Drecoll. Sometimes he's 13, sometimes she's wearing Worth. In all the stories, she allowed him to copy it, which he did with prodigious skill, and a star was born.

As Gvasalia and I speak, surrounded by remnants of the maison's past on the outskirts of Paris, preparations are underway to disinter the literal house of Balenciaga on avenue George V. The man himself didn't live there, of course – although his directrice of couture, an icy woman referred to only as Mademoiselle Renée and a fervent acolyte, had an apartment on the top floor. Cristóbal Balenciaga's own home was around the corner on avenue Marceau, at number 28, but his life was in 10 avenue George V. There's a charge to the building – an imprint remains of the events it bore witness to. Balenciaga sat there, brooding and melancholy, devising silhouettes, inventing fabrics, shifting fashion. His clothes were sewn there, in stark ateliers that his former assistant André Courrèges described in religious terms: "Pure white, unornamented and intensely silent. People whispered and walked on tiptoe, and even the clients talked in hushed voices." Those clients saw Balenciaga's clothes in fashion shows from which the press was habitually excluded, in oddly fanciful white salons with stucco scrolls, Louie-hooey curve-backed couches and urn-shaped lamps on plaster pedestals. In complete silence, a *cabine* of models of unconventional beauty – less flatteringly dubbed "monsters" by the press – paraded clothes that, in their masterful cut, transformed not only the direction of fashion, but also the ways in which people saw themselves. Sleeves sliced at three-quarter length elongated arms; collars shrugged away from the neck extended the profile – silhouettes breathed easy, bodies were free.

For the past 30 years or so, those stately salons where Balenciaga showed clothes that redefined fashion, had been stripped back to brick. Most recently, they were stacked with boxes of Balenciaga's bestselling Triple S trainers – a symbol if ever there was one of the couture house's recalibration to the demands of the 21st-century luxury market. "Blasphemous," is the word used by Gvasalia. Now the boxes are gone, replaced by a breathtakingly precise facsimile of the original interior – stucco, sofas, urns and all – less reproduction than resurrection, executed by a Berlin architectural practice named Sub and based on plentiful archival footage and photographs. But it isn't exactly right: the walls are grimy, white darkened to a dingy grey, the silken curtains tidemarked. Like those creased silk dresses and plucked embroideries, its attitude is disrespect – as if the house of Balenciaga has been left to rot.

The inspiration, Gvasalia said, was the relatively recent unearthing of an apartment in the 9th arrondissement of Paris once owned by an actress named Marthe de Florian. It was closed up at the outbreak of the second world war and only opened again in 2010: water had leaked in, staining walls, curtains had faded and greyed with dust. Gvasalia wanted the same in George V. "It has to really feel like the passage of time, which I think is the most beautiful thing," he says. Hence a 'patination' team spent the month before the show basically living from the space, "spilling Coca-Cola in the morning, smoking, dipping ash a little bit everywhere", according to Gösta Andreas Lönn Grill, one of the team's designers, to speed up the ageing process and make it seem as if 53 years had elapsed since the white carpets were last trod. "It's a time machine, somehow," says Gvasalia. Or like a tomb cracked open: the Norwegian "olfactory artist" Sissel Tolaas even created a scent by taking molecules from that leather-clad elevator, from old textiles and from the key notes of the fragrances worn by clients attending those final couture shows. "They really smell like the past," Gvasalia says.

Gvasalia's couture ateliers are based not at avenue George V but at Balenciaga's headquarters on the Left Bank, a cruciform building that formerly housed a hospital, built around an old chapel. Surgery meeting religion feels very Balenciaga – and Gvasalia and the atelier workers all operate wearing white cotton coats, the face masks necessary for such up-close and personal work in the midst of the Covid-19 pandemic giving the scene an undeniably clinical bent. Each garment is fitted on a new *cabine* of models who, like Cristóbal Balenciaga's, are unconventional: a forty-something digital-marketing strategist named Susanne Theimer from Cologne, a collector of avant-garde art called Karen Boros, the contemporary artist Eliza Douglas (who opened this couture show and also Gvasalia's first ready-to-wear show in 2016), and Kamala Harris's fashion-conscious, newsworthy stepdaughter Ella Emhoff. Other faces are hidden under the collection's many giant flying saucer hats by Philip Treacy. There are also men – Gvasalia proposing couture inspired not only by Cristóbal Balenciaga's designs but his own attire. The house collaborated with Huntsman, Balenciaga's Savile Row tailor, on suiting in crisp barathea and fresco wools, like he would have worn. One alone required three weeks of hand-stitching to perfect. "There is not a single machine stitch on it," Gvasalia says. "That, for me, is kind of the epitome of craftsmanship."

Couture on any model's body is a proposition for a client – an unreality, even if it isn't worn by a supermodel. Yet Gvasalia doesn't intend this to be a vanity project: this is couture to be bought and sold. The house has engaged a directrice, formerly of Jean Paul Gaultier and Yves Saint Laurent. She was gardening when she received the call. "I think that's the challenge of couture today," Gvasalia says. "It's far from dying out. Of course, if you see couture as something for old rich ladies and don't dust it off, then it doesn't have a future. But if you put that craft in the spotlight, it can have a relevance. Even for the younger generation – especially when everything is available, when every brand does a logo T-shirt, that's exactly when people start to value other things. I'm not talking about masses, it's a small circle of people who can appreciate this, but they are there. And it does balance the rest." By the rest, Gvasalia means the rest of Balenciaga's offering today – the ready-to-wear, the handbags, the trainers and logo T-shirts. But the couture – which has its own label and logotype, its own packaging, and shows independently from the ready-to-wear, and only once a year – stands alone. "I like the idea of it being two separate things," he says. "There is more of an aesthetic influence that I believe will be transmitted to the ready-to-wear. This sophisticated elegance. But not trying to mimic the complexity of craftsmanship that I can have in couture. Because it will never be possible, within the price range as well. This is why I don't even want to try that." He pauses. "I'd rather have couture as an inspiration."

Relaunching Balenciaga's couture operation is a tricky business. Haute couture requires phenomenal investment – prices begin in the upper five figures, and soar, due to the hours of handwork invested in every piece. It is entirely made to measure, for each individual client, so no corners can be cut. Balenciaga has not only employed a directrice but has assembled, from scratch, workrooms devoted to tailoring and *flou* – the evocative French term for light dressmaking – in the most traditional and formal manner. Every sample garment is labelled with the name of the atelier in which it is produced and the model's name it is specifically fitted to. As Cristóbal decreed, each model wears only garments specially made for them. The house has also collaborated with craft houses and fabric manufacturers who originally worked with Balenciaga to devise new weaves and techniques: the embroiderers Maison Lesage and Atelier Montex, the textile houses of Dormeuil, Jakob Schlaepfer, Taroni and Forster Rohner. "It's quite touching to go back to the craft," Gvasalia says. "It died out, in a way."

The archival references, by and large, aren't the milestones that fashion dorks would expect Gvasalia to reimagine. There's no rehash of the 1950 evening gown of two balloons of taffeta, the feather-embroidered extravaganzas of the 1960s, the extraordinary trapezoid four-sided cocktail dress of winter 1967 that made sitting impossible. There aren't even the Spanish laces, the embroidered toreador boleros, the cocoon coats, those semi-fitted little skirt suits. "I didn't use my brain so much, I used my instinct," Gvasalia says of the design process. "Every time I listen to my gut, it's always a decision that makes sense in the end."

Back in the archive, off to one side, there is a massive, blown-up publicity portrait of Cristóbal Balenciaga propped against a concrete column. It is Balenciaga in the 1950s, when he was in his sixties – no longer matinee idol handsome, as when he first opened his house in Paris, but still good-looking, albeit with deep frown lines, one hand hiding a receding chin of which he was always self-conscious. Portraits of Balenciaga are rare – he was the first couturier who refused to bow after his shows and declined interview requests until after his retirement. He also never employed a press attaché. His photographic likeness seems to stare dispassionately at a beyond-life-sized mid-century portrait by Bernard Buffet of his wife, Annabel, regal in a 1959 Balenciaga ballgown. She looks like an infanta, albeit painted in a spiky, expressionist style rather than the faultless technique of Diego Velázquez, whose stately Las Meninas constantly echoes in Balenciaga's clothing. He also admired Francisco de Zurbarán, whose work depicted not the richness of the Spanish court but the simplicity of nuns, monks and martyrs. Perhaps it was to emulate the almost sculptural draped fabrics of Zurbarán that Balenciaga challenged the Swiss textile firm Abraham to invent a new fabric, gazar, an architectural and crisp silk that held its shape like plywood. Inspired by cotton bandages, it took them three years to perfect. For a decade after its creation in 1958, Balenciaga carved shapes out with gazar, transforming women into walking bubbles, upturned pyramids or arum lilies of fabric.

An example of the latter, a sculptural wedding dress from 1967, will be revisited by Gvasalia as the finale look for his couture show. It's an unconventionally direct homage – one of those well-avoided milestones. "I couldn't not do it," Gvasalia says. "It's impossible without that. But we tried to do something else with it. We were like, 'OK, let's do it like this, or let's do it like this. Let's change the darts here.' Trying to be more clever," he rolls his eyes. "Or, I don't know, like more construction conscious than Cristóbal. And we just ended up replicating the dress. There was no way it could be better." They did change the fabric – the silk-wool mix has a worn feel, as if it had been drawn from the archives. "And we did change the hat, that particular hat, into a veil." The headpiece, originally, was known as the "coal scuttle", a helmet of fabric that resembles something out of Star Wars and has been ripped off endlessly since. "There is something quite absurd about the wedding dress in today's context," Gvasalia says. Which is strange, given that bridal gowns are often seen as contemporary couture's raison d'être – if you're going to spend six figures on a dress, it's probably for holy matrimony. After all, that last dress Cristóbal Balenciaga ever made, after his couture house closed and just months before he died, was a wedding dress.

Gvasalia taps the box holding his newly made old-looking bodice, its neckline scooping shallow across an imaginary collarbone. It will later be attached to a wide skirt, worn over men's wool trousers. "In that dress, I do reference Cristóbal's silhouette of the Infanta, where he references Velázquez paintings," Gvasalia says. "Luckily we do have this history, so we can build on that." A reference

"We tried to step into *those pictures* from the *past*"

to a reference – you find that elsewhere in the collection. Sometimes the reference is even to Gvasalia's own work at Balenciaga, his translation of Cristóbal's couture attitude into ready-to-wear bouncing right back to couture again. Take look 17, a hazmat-orange gabardine suit with the jacket shrugged off the shoulders, neck wrenched wide open – it's an open reference to his debut Balenciaga show, where he pulled the necks apart on trench coats and padded jackets to emulate the shape of grandiose opera coats. "But this orange jacket, it required so much work that could never have been done in ready-to-wear," Gvasalia says. "In my first collection for Balenciaga, when I started opening the shoulder line ... that was a very easy construction. You made a huge dart, basically, swinging the shape to the back. But when you wear it, it doesn't behave the same way. This was like an upgrade, completely crazy, pattern-making acrobatics." He smiles, shrugs. "It's couture."

Two months later, the first Balenciaga couture show since 1968 – the 50th in total, a satisfying number – takes place at 11.30am on the 7th of July. The context is historical: the recreated salons are filled with spindly gold chairs, a carnation placed on each. The air does indeed smell old. "I wanted to underline the timelessness of couture," Gvasalia said. "We tried to step into those pictures from the past." The show was staged during the first physical haute couture presentations since January 2020. That was important for Gvasalia – he waited to showcase the collection until he could do so in person – what's another few months when you've waited since 1968? "The screen makes everything so flat – and of course, you cannot see that broken embroidery, the craft," he says. "There is something quite majestic about couture being worn."

When the show began, no one really realised. It began without the thud of music common to most shows, and especially to those of Balenciaga under Gvasalia – his husband, Loïk Gomez, a French musician under the moniker BFRND, creates all the soundtracks. This collection, however, would be shown in silence, another unexpected homage to Cristóbal and to haute couture tradition. "Cristóbal loved silence," says Gvasalia. It's quite intimidating. "Here it's all about the garments." Silence, he says, makes the experience not less but even more intense. "I wanted to use microphones, to amplify. But that would be fake. With a lot of fabrics we're using, you do hear them. There are trains, a carpet that rubs. It's almost fetishistic."

The collection dances between those different interpretations of attitude, between respect and repudiation. Models wear embroidered evening gowns, sure, but also the tailoring based on Cristóbal's personal wardrobe, while Mona von Bismarck opera coats morph into the ski anoraks he sewed in his own ateliers. Male models walk in high heels – Gvasalia wanted them to change the posture and deportment of the wearers, many of whom had to be specially trained. "The gay guys were fine," Gvasalia says. The collection's striking, sometimes searing colours are even drawn from Balenciaga fabric swatches in the archive – the orange, the pink, an electric blue, sealed in cardboard boxes so untouched by time. Polka dots come from the archives too. Gvasalia's couture T-shirt is in padded silk, with a

matching stole. It's an accessory he uses a lot, a couture gesture. There are also lots of gloves, sometimes built into tops to streamline and perfect. Jewellery is based on original pieces displaced, so elaborate spherical brooches can become earrings or perhaps cocktail rings. Pauline de Rothschild once stated that the wit was on the head chez Balenciaga – Cristóbal's milliners were also his life partners, Ramón Esparza and Wladzio Jaworowski d'Attainville, so they were perhaps afforded more liberties than most. Here, the sole headpiece is a Treacy dome, like a shallow inverted fruit bowl, flocked with velvet or high-gloss lacquer. "It's like a car varnish," says Gvasalia. "I wanted to have some kind of almost futuristic touch. A bit alien."

Jeans in Balenciaga's couture salon are also alien and futuristic. Gvasalia's denims are woven in Japan, riveted and buttoned in sterling silver, lined in silk. "People think I literally just take one thing and put a brand name on it," Gvasalia says. "It's not that at all." There is, perhaps, a sense that Gvasalia – still, after six years – feels the need to prove himself worthy of the Balenciaga name. "Accepting the wedding dress – the ingenuity of how this wedding dress was made in the 1960s – was letting go of that fear of not being innovative in every look. Not transforming everything that I took for this collection as a reference from Cristóbal into something completely new," he says. "For a designer like me, that's difficult." Following Gvasalia's rumpled Astroturf-green opera coat and the fucked-up Infanta evening gown, Cristóbal Balenciaga's wedding dress swept through the salons of his house. He hadn't changed a thing.

After the show, a lull. The evening afterwards, there's a dinner in the new art foundation established by the Pinault family in the centre of Paris. Gvasalia wears the high-heeled men's shoes he had debuted barely nine hours earlier. There's a performance by Bryan Ferry – "I thought he felt quite couture," Gvasalia said, laughing. The next day, he travelled back to Zurich with his husband.

"For me, it was the beginning of a new era." Gvasalia sounds a bit fuzzy on the phone from Switzerland. But he's pleased. "I'm not talking about Balenciaga, but about myself as a designer. It was a moment I have been looking forward to and been quite afraid of."

Is he still afraid? "I feel at peace," Gvasalia says. "I never really knew that feeling within the context of my work, to feel at peace. I always felt quite agitated, nervous, before the show, anxious. I had this anxiety before the show yesterday – I forgot how it feels, actually. It's been over a year since I had to do a show in real life. It felt again like the first time – something physical, in your stomach, almost. I couldn't understand if I liked it or not, and just before the show I realised I love it. It's the tension – fashion is about a tension, and then you release. I felt like I released something that has been incubating in me for a long time. Not only one year, I think much longer. That release brought me to this feeling of peacefulness."

Gvasalia breathes out. "It's not really about that collection so much as my personal relationship with fashion. Through couture, I found peace with it."

This page: Lisa is wearing a swing-back gabardine jacket and skirt, stretch mesh pantashoes and jersey gloves by BALENCIAGA COUTURE. Domed flocked velvet hat by PHILIP TREACY. Opposite: Azenor is wearing a tulle minidress with sequin embellishment, moulded polyurethane sunglasses, embossed leather iPhone clutch, tights and glazed leather pumps by BALENCIAGA COUTURE

This page: Lisa is wearing a padded satin stole and T-shirt, Japanese denim jeans, moulded polyurethane sunglasses, antique brass earrings and double-finger ring with Swarovski crystal rhinestones, jersey opera gloves and glazed leather boots by BALENCIAGA COUTURE. Opposite: Sori is wearing a satin faille coat dress, antique brass earrings with Swarovski crystal rhinestones and jersey gloves by BALENCIAGA COUTURE

This page and opposite: Marius is wearing a waisted barathea wool suit with trompe l'oeil shirt cuffs and onyx buttons, stainless steel glasses and glazed leather boots by BALENCIAGA COUTURE

This page and opposite: Adama is wearing a belted Japanese cotton trench coat, knitted vicuña wool turtleneck, washed Japanese denim jeans, moulded polyurethane sunglasses, embossed leather tote and glazed leather boots by BALENCIAGA COUTURE

This page and opposite: Boris is wearing a swing-back Japanese denim jacket and jeans, moulded polyurethane sunglasses and glazed leather boots by BALENCIAGA COUTURE

This page: Binta is wearing a silk wool wedding dress with train and technical knit veil by BALENCIAGA COUTURE. Opposite: Sori is wearing a polka-dot swing-back silk shirt with bow corset, trousers and glazed leather boots by BALENCIAGA COUTURE. Her own earring

This page: Gritli is wearing a silk taffeta opera coat, jersey top, antique brass earrings with Swarovski crystal rhinestones and jersey gloves by BALENCIAGA COUTURE. Opposite: Marie Agnès is wearing a domed flocked velvet hat by PHILIP TREACY

Hair: Akemi Kishida at Blend Management using ORIBE. Make-up: Anthony Preel at Artlist. Models: Binta Diacko at Fever, Marie Agnès Diène at The Claw, Adama Konate at Girl Mgmt, Azenor Le Dily at Supreme, Gritti and Sori at Keva Legault, Marius and Boris at Tomorrow Is Another Day and Lisa Williamson at The Face. Casting: Julia Lange Casting. Casting associate: Mathilde Curel. Photographic assistant: Léa Guintrand. Styling assistants: Emmanuelle Ramos and Matthieu Bertorello. Hair assistant: Yulia Pantiukhina. Make-up assistant: Azusa Kumakura. Production: TheLink Mgmt. On-set producer: Gwenaelle Wieners

Miu Miu

Photography JAMIE HAWKESWORTH
Styling KATIE SHILLINGFORD

Anita is wearing a wool crepe coat with contrasting collar
and suede boots by MIU MIU, Autumn/Winter 2011

If Prada is the elder statesman in the empire Miuccia Prada presides over with her husband, Patrizio Bertelli, Miu Miu is its intuitive, impulsive counterpart. Titled after the affectionate moniker by which the designer has been known by her closest friends and family since she was a child, Miu Miu has the sensibility of sibling rebellion. Each bears an echo of the other: Miu Miu's intellect is light-hearted compared to Prada's heavyweight approach; Prada questions luxury, whereas Miu Miu toys with its trappings. While also profoundly radical, Prada is more serious, the public face of Miuccia Prada and indeed the family dynasty – carrying the name of her mother, Luisa, who ran the company once her own father, Prada's founder Mario Prada, stepped down. Miu Miu, which launched in 1993, is conversely just Miuccia Prada's. It is a place where she can express herself freely. Prada is now co-creatively directed by Miuccia Prada and Raf Simons. Miu Miu is personal.

Words SUSANNAH FRANKEL

"The show in the mountains was personal – exactly that," Miuccia Prada says. Entitled Brave Hearts, it was filmed in March 2021, with Europe in the throes of the third wave of the pandemic. With references to both Tyrolean and Highland dress, Miu Miu's Autumn/Winter collection also draws on the dress codes adopted by its designer as a young woman. Those were unconventional. "I had so much fun in the mountains, skiing in a skirt," she remembers. "I skied in a bikini too. I did it back then. It was perfectly normal. And the mountains are my favourite place in the world. I am in love with the mountains. I enjoy them at any moment, under every circumstance. I don't know why."

Prada's clothing designs have always been drawn from her personal experience, personal history, personal tastes. She dressed in Saint Laurent as a rebellious, left-leaning student in the 1970s; later in the 1980s, butting against the direction of contemporary fashion, she bought her clothes from children's tailors and from suppliers of uniforms for nurses and chambermaids, before deciding to design her own. Miu Miu is of course no exception: it began life as a small collection of minimal, vintage-inspired pieces, the sort of thing she might dream of wearing. If the sobriety of Prada reflected the life of a committed feminist and businesswoman – albeit a creative one, with impeccably refined taste – Miu Miu spoke of the side of Miuccia Prada that grew up wanting to wear pink when her mother dressed her in navy, that secretly hitched up her skirt as she left her house to go out, and that skied in a bikini.

Miuccia Prada likes bravery – she is herself brave. And it is a quality she admires in others. "Bravery is something women always need," she commented at the time the collection was shown. "This talks about the fantasies of women, their imaginations and dreams of different places, different ideas. Following your dreams is courageous – that takes bravery and strength." Still, for Miuccia Prada, while women's fantasies are often the starting point of a conversation, fashion is always seen in the context of it being in the first instance a service to men (at Prada) but to women at both Prada and at Miu Miu still more so.

And so, at the Italian ski resort of Cortina d'Ampezzo, against a backdrop of the Dolomite Alps, models walked through the snow in boots – from ankle to thigh-high – and chubby coats in teddy bear fur, bombers, jumpsuits and miniskirts in Miu Miu's signature matelassé leather and boudoir satins in a sugary colour palette that seemed as sweet as it was incongruous, as apparently delicate as the look is ultimately fierce. Juxtaposing clothing designed to protect its wearer from the elements with more quintessentially feminine pieces – those aforementioned fantasies, evocative of an empowered sense of seduction – oversized satin padded jackets were layered over lingerie-inspired slip dresses in featherlight silks or lacy sweaters and skirts embroidered with twinkling sequins. Striped, pop bright and pastel crochet nursery knits framed faces and made for cosy cardigans, arm warmers, socks and tights. And yes,

there was indeed a bikini of sorts: a bralet and skirt – the dimensions of the latter, an over-anxious mother might not unreasonably argue, are more reminiscent of a belt. One can only imagine what Miuccia Prada's own parents had to say on the matter of their daughter skiing in her swimwear all those years ago now. Not that she would have let that stop her.

Idiosyncratically, sport has always been a passion for Miuccia Prada, long before the fashion world caught up. She was among the first designers to put sportswear on the runway: for Prada's final Spring/Summer show of the millennium she introduced Prada Sport, inspired by Bertelli's love of sailing and Prada's announcement of its involvement in the America's Cup in 1997. The red and white logo mirrored that of the lettering on the Prada Challenge boat, and the label, reintroduced in 2018, is now called Linea Rossa. Designer sportswear proved a rapidly expanding commodity across the board and Prada, with its luxe-industrial heritage, was well placed to capitalise on that. Clean shapes and technologically advanced fabrics with equally pragmatic shoes and bags were shown alongside the main collection, which was very much about both fashion and luxury in a more traditional sense: full, pleated canvas skirts and coats with broad, pleated ribbon edges, crumpled chiffon dresses, skirts and knickerbockers in tea-stained shades and richly coloured crocodile skirts and jackets all made an appearance, sometimes embellished with saucer-sized mirror embroideries. The wilful contrariness of the Prada handwriting – the space somewhere between the real and the unreal, the functional and the fashionable, the earthly and the otherworldly – was already well established.

Miuccia Prada needs no introduction, but here are the basics of her upbringing and career, the elements that formed her and still frame her current status and state of mind. Born in 1949, she grew up in Milan and left that city's Statale University with a doctorate in political science in 1970. A committed activist, she was a member of the Unione Donne Italiane, dedicated to establishing equal rights for women. She studied mime at the Piccolo Teatro before joining the family business in the mid-70s. She met Bertelli in 1978 and they married in 1987, a year before she began designing her own clothes. For her wedding, Miuccia Prada wore a dress made by the Ferrari sisters, designers of clothes for the children of Milan's elite, scaled up to her size. With Bertelli, she launched the famous Prada nylon backpack in 1984, debuted Prada women's ready-to-wear in 1988 and Miu Miu five years later. Today, Prada is a multi-billion-dollar public company. It was floated on the Hong Kong stock exchange in 2011, yet remains under their control both creatively and financially.

To help differentiate Miu Miu from Prada, principally shown in its hometown, the label staged catwalk shows in each of the major fashion capitals until landing, lastingly, in Paris in 2006. There Miu Miu was first presented at 34 avenue Foch, a hotel particulier in a chic residential arrondissement.

From the start, Miu Miu exuded the spirit of the renegade debutante, all puffed sleeves, empire lines, pie-crust collars and slightly off party dresses. The clothes perhaps owe a debt to the Ferrari sisters too, and to Cirri in Florence, which Miuccia Prada once said made the best sailor dresses around. They often play with childlike elements, taking liberties with scale by blowing up or shrinking details. When they are more adult – in the Autumn/Winter 2011 collection of broad 1940s shoulders and mid-calf skirts, for example – models somehow still resemble young girls dressed in looks far too old for them. There are mismatched graphic prints – of swallows in flight or kittens at play – and unlikely fabric combinations: paillettes on sludge-coloured wools. Elsewhere, 50s Americana meets 80s Anglophilia or 70s psychedelia, varsity jackets are worn over big knickers (Miuccia Prada calls them panties), leather is oversized, silver and inlaid with everything from art deco florals to stars, and French terry towelling bathrobes double up as summer coats.

Such diversity of fabrication, silhouette and thematic makes the fact that Miu Miu is so immediately identifiable and distinct from its sister, Prada, more remarkable still. Across these pages the overview of Miu Miu is Miuccia Prada's own, having delved into her archives to select pieces that best show her vision of her label. The edit reflects both past and present tense: the pieces are chosen from the label's back catalogue but with the designer's current mood and viewpoint in mind. They are the styles she feels are relevant for now. Miu Miu is always reactive: the shows are put together in a matter of weeks, sometimes even days. It is spontaneous, immediate, instinctive.

When we speak at the end of May, Miuccia Prada is alone. She is as elegant and conscious of the importance of good manners and humour as always, and a quietly contemplative mood prevails, one that acknowledges that we are living in a world that remains frightening in its uncertainty. While the designer's circumstances – as she herself is the first to admit – are privileged, there is a modesty to the conversation, if not quite so much to the surroundings. An opulent olive-green velvet covers the walls of the room she is working from and that same fabric, in brown, a plump daybed. Pieces from the personal collection of modern art Prada and Bertelli have been building for a quarter of a century hang behind her – a fluffy white Pietro Manzoni Achrome like a lost cloud, a John Baldessari pop portrait of Bruce Lee, the eyes cut out.

Since the first lockdown in March 2020, she has been based here, away from the crowds and mainly focused on her job. As perceptive and aware of the world as she always has been, she is grateful for the time that has afforded her – time to work, time to watch and to read, time to think. Many column inches have been dedicated to her wardrobe in the past and that too has moved with the times. Today she is wearing an oversized white cotton T-shirt that it's somehow life-affirming to imagine her rolling out of bed in – and a pair of vintage diamond earrings that reach almost to her shoulders. Some things shouldn't change.

Then as now, Miuccia Prada is the ultimate brave heart: a woman for whom courage and risk-taking are second nature – the driving force.

Susannah Frankel
Can we talk first about the Miu Miu show in the mountains?

Miuccia Prada
I'm not sure I would do it again now but at that point you didn't need many people, which was a good thing, and also there was so much snow. I said it's now or never. Then everybody got excited. It was a long discussion because of the difficulties of there being no physical show. That is much more complex for me but also more interesting. You have to turn your ideas into a bigger picture. If you call directors, good movie directors, they are not, I think, very good at doing fashion, and fashion people, of course, they don't know how to make movies. So we had to improvise, to reinvent our jobs. It all came out of this idea of bravery. The mountains, the walking in the snow, the symbol of being brave. Back then I was fixated on women being brave.

SF You're always brave.

MP I try to be. I wanted to be. We

decided to go, we dealt with whatever happened. We had very bad weather but also very good weather.

SF In one way the collection was mountain appropriate – the big trousers, the big boots, the Tyrolean references, the Highland references – but in another way it was about a skirt covered in jewels. That's very you. The conservative and radical, the appropriate and the inappropriate, often in one look.

MP That is what I always aim for and it comes instinctively.

SF It's about you.

MP Yes, it's me.

SF You were one of the first people to actually combine high fashion and sport in the 90s with Prada Sport.

MP I remember back then I never wanted to dress myself in sporty things. I didn't like them. Then I was always into inappropriate things.

And I asked myself why when you do sport, or ski, do you have to become another person? I want to keep my love of fashion, my ideas. I don't want to transform myself into someone else, into a sporty man or a sporty woman, wearing what everyone else is wearing. That was the origin of it.

SF And today you still combine two apparently contrasting worlds. The idea of the couture gesture – the gloves are big woolly gloves but they're still long gloves, the hats, the jewellery – with something much more obviously functional.

MP That's something that I really like. I like that when you do sport you retain your spirit. So if you run, why shouldn't you wear a pair of earrings? Be covered in jewels, running along?

SF You always work with extremes.

MP I like very different things. There were men's things in that collection and then there were feminine things. Probably I like the duality in myself.

I can be very feminine, or very masculine, or both at the same time. In general, in a modest environment I like to put on the richest pieces. I like opposites together. Why? I don't know. For instance, in the Fondazione, when we did the house in gold, it was not my idea, it was Rem's idea, but I thought it was genius because it represents what I like to the maximum. What do you do in gold? The poorest, most industrial, most old-fashioned home. It's also about assessing the value of something by putting it with its opposite, making inexpensive things look or feel very rich and vice versa. I don't want to say it's a political approach because the word carries so much weight but, yes, the point of view is to find the opposite between two extremes, always, and to try to improvise. I don't question myself about that. It comes so naturally.

SF Perhaps that's the recognition that women are not simple or straightforward.

MP Yes, for sure. It's not enough to be feminine. Put simply, by mixing things you show the complexity of life, the complexity all around us. To be just one thing is boring.

SF Do you think bravery is particularly important now?

MP I think bravery is very important in general. Otherwise, why do you live? You have to try to make things, to do things.

SF In the past we talked about the idea that, in the 2000s especially, you in particular seemed to be taking bigger risks than smaller, independent labels, bigger risks than the avant-garde.

MP If you are small – niche – you can be avant-garde. It is very different in a bourgeois context. I struggle sometimes. And my husband tells me, you can't pretend to be left-wing, because the other ones are all rich, or bourgeois. It is true that with Prada and Miu Miu I want to make the impossible happen. We are a luxury group

with concepts that are not only about luxury. In fact, I don't like the word luxury but I have always appreciated beauty and sophisticated things. So it really is a constant effort.

SF A constant fight.

MP Yes, that too.

SF Miu Miu especially seems to be about female rites of passage – about a girl becoming a woman, a girl on the cusp of womanhood. Of course, that's not actually about age at all but about spirit, and about the slight fragility – but also the exceptional beauty – of that time in a woman's life, the time when you're a girl working out what being a woman means. That is something that continues, that comes up again and again at all ages.

MP That's right. That's great. It's true that Miu Miu is also about that fragility, the fact that you don't know who you are, who you want to be. You want to be beautiful, you want to be sexy – but you also want to be nasty, intelligent and political.

SF However brave you are – however brave Miu Miu is – we are all vulnerable.

MP I never think about that but, yes, actually Miu Miu is probably a lot about that.

SF People always say Miu Miu is younger but it's not about being young physically. It's about …

MP The mentality.

SF It is also the embodiment of the fact that you can be 40, 50, 60, 70, but you can still flirt.

MP I strongly believe in that. Apart from I don't go out in miniskirts, which if you have the courage to and you want to, then why not, but apart from that, when I dress I'm not dressing like an old woman. When you become old, it's not easy to have fun with how you dress. When you are older, dressing is even more about bravery.

SF One of the things that has changed since you started designing clothes is that you really can wear what you like.

MP True. Good taste, bad taste … It's very subtle.

SF This issue of the magazine is about hindsight, the idea of looking at the past to inform the future. That sentiment feels intense at the moment because the present is relatively quiet. Our present is lacking in outside experience, so people are looking back in a romantic way, though not necessarily a purely nostalgic way – it feels like something bigger than that.

MP That has something to do with looking for meaning. I hear a lot of people saying now that they don't want to go to stupid parties any more, that what they value is friendship, love. That, of course, is romantic. We are searching for something more complete, more true, not superficial.

SF You have always said you love superficial things.

MP Maybe because I would like to be that person but really I'm not. Now people are thinking more about the past, about things that count, about the heart, not about superficial things. The word romantic makes sense.

SF You have Prada and Miu Miu. Miu Miu is approaching its 30th anniversary, Prada is more than a century old. You shoulder a huge legacy. How do you feel now about that responsibility?

MP I don't think about legacy. I know I should but it's not what motivates me. Also because of our age, people say to me you should enjoy what you have done, celebrate your achievement. Listen, I'm not like that. I'm always thinking about what I can do next. I don't think of myself as someone who is ambitious but somebody told me recently, "You are a monster of ambition." In truth, I am very ambitious.

SF Historically, Miu Miu comes at the end of the ready-to-wear season.

It's reactive to what has come before it at the shows and is done quickly, in weeks rather than months. This situation must throw that slightly. The seasons are difficult to follow now.

MP   That's why in the end I am still showing in seasons. It took so much time for the fashion world to get itself together, to facilitate the jobs of journalists and buyers and so on. So now I find myself in a place where I can do whatever I want, whenever I want. But I don't know if that's right. In the first place, you lose the sense of a season and with that, a little bit, the sense of fashion. I understand that it's exciting to be free but instinctively I decided to stick with the calendar. Otherwise it's going to be such a mess.

SF   Fashion is a community – you move from one place to another as a group. The pandemic has left a vacuum.

MP   Yes, but going back to normal shows is maybe like going backwards. Before, you did your job, your clothes, your show, then it was finished. This is the beginning of a whole different chapter and it's ten times the work. But I'm afraid that now just to go back to physical shows won't feel so exciting. Maybe you should do both. But both is double the money and more work again. We are discussing this all the time. In the end, somebody said, "People like being together. Who cares about the clothes? They just like having fun, like at a concert, in a football stadium." It's more the idea of being with people. Everybody always complains. But now that it is not possible people miss it.

SF   Now you work with Raf at Prada, how has your work with Miu Miu changed?

MP   It has changed. I decided that at Prada I wanted to work with someone else to create a new idea, to have more inspiration and to share, that's a priority. The priority is for Raf and me to do something together. I'm very happy with that. So Miu Miu is now the

place where I am completely myself. When I realise that, then I want to do even more, to really concentrate, to inject more passion, more of what I like. The show in the mountains was exactly that. It was very personal. Because of the location and the implications. For sure, Miu Miu is the only place where I am alone.

SF   Is there more of a sense of your renegade spirit in Miu Miu?

MP   Absolutely. It's what I like in life. I have not always been able to be enough like that perhaps. I was when I was young, with my political ideas and activities, I kind of did it. Probably not enough. But that's what I like.

SF   I think your son said to you that, as someone in a position of power, you're obliged to speak out and say things that go beyond fashion. Do you believe that?

MP   That's a big question. I always hated it in the past. I never wanted to answer any questions that weren't specifically related to what I do, related to art or fashion. I didn't want to talk about politics or any of the things that I care about most. That is partly out of a sense of decency, about being a rich fashion designer. Having said that, because of the influence we have, we probably should speak out more. I should probably speak out more. But that goes against my spirit and my thinking completely. I'm thinking about it, about how to try to speak to people more.

SF   People often talk about a certain woman they design for. Is there a Miu Miu woman?

MP   You know that's something I don't like. I design what I think is right. It's theoretical. I never had a woman in mind, I don't have an icon in mind. I do like a renegade. Usually, every brand has its target. I don't. But I always said I do what I feel is right and if I am in contact with reality, if I know people through reading, through

movies, through meeting them, then it will work. The more I am in contact with reality the more what I do makes sense. If it works it means I was connected and my thoughts were realistic. I'm trying to do something that is relevant, to translate that into clothes, because that is my job and something that I am able to do. You know that I am fanatical about the life of people, that is the reason I love vintage. I love thinking about who the woman was who wore something, about what their life was like. People's lives. I like thinking about that a lot.

SF   You recently put exactly that idea into practice with Upcycled by Miu Miu, that idea of finding vintage clothes and letting them tell their own story all while putting your mark on it.

MP   When I did my first show for Prada, I was very much criticised for appropriation. It was the 80s, the art world did it the whole time, but in fashion it caused a scandal – a dress that was totally 60s, totally 70s. But I loved it because I like history, I like stories of periods, stories of women. I think, OK, modernity, the future, but all our ideas come from what we saw, what we heard, what we read. We are our past. How can we pretend it doesn't exist? Now, with Upcycled, it's conscious and we want to build on it, but in the first instance it came from a place of naivety, from a love of vintage and the fact that vintage pieces entertain the people who wear them. It is a piece of clothing but it expresses a whole life – how was it worn, what was it worn for, what did its original owner do while they were wearing it?

SF   In fact, that's what we love about clothes generally.

MP   Yes, because clothes are instruments for living, basically. To conquer or not to conquer, to do whatever you want. I always think dresses have to be useful.

SF   As a young woman you were active in the second wave of feminism.

"People are thinking more about the past,
about *things that count*,
about the heart, not about superficial things"

Do you think things are better now for women than they were then?

MP There's a long way to go. That is one of my biggest questions – how long does it take? Sometimes it seems like we're going backwards rather than forwards. Sometimes when you see movies about the suffragettes, you see how they really struggled. For sure in our countries, for people who are richer, more educated, things are better, but that's easy for us to say. There are still things happening to women all over the world that are terrible – unbelievable.

SF The upheaval of the past 18 months has meant we have all been forced to acknowledge a shift in our perspectives and change the way we look at things and how we prioritise.

MP I think so. Six months after the pandemic started, my son told me that if it finished now things would go back to how they were before but that if it lasted longer things would change. I am very much changed. I'm changed in general but mainly in thinking that anything I used to do in a certain way I should now do differently. I have an instinctive desire for change, for not repeating things we did before.

SF And when you're designing, thinking about bravery and about fighting, you're also dreaming.

MP I always say that I don't like dreaming. If I dream about something I want to make it happen.

SF For someone who sometimes thinks they are not ambitious that's quite an ambitious idea.

MP Now my ambition at the Fondazione is doing science. We are preparing a show for the next biennale with the most important scientists in the world. It's about the human brain. I always want to do shows that are about religion, feminism, science, big subjects that are floating in our heads but that many of us don't really understand. And they said they wanted to do it only if the Fondazione Prada in Venice becomes a permanent place for exploring ideas about neuroscience. So, yes, that's also ambitious.

SF The idea of the same woman who grew up skiing in a skirt now doing that is inspiring – uplifting. Can we talk about Miu Miu as a community of women who shop but who also exchange and share ideas about culture, about things they are excited by and that they love? You have Women's Tales, dedicated to supporting female talent in film, Miu Miu Musings, conversations between women about issues that are culturally and socially pertinent, Miu Miu Club …

MP We do and that's very important to me. I love film and know that, even now, it is not so easy for women to break through, so if we can help we should. I also believe in giving women a voice, in projecting a feminine point of view. I have this idea that, during the day, our shops are shops, about shopping for fashion. Then, during the night they are about a community.

SF Have you missed your teams during this period? Have you felt restricted?

MP For the past 18 months, I have worked on Zoom. I don't know if I miss my teams physically because I am discussing with them all the time. Sometimes when I am at work, there are so many distractions, so many empty moments, so many boring moments. Now at home maybe I've found the excuse to do other things. And that is fantastic. I want to be careful not to lose that privilege. Also, I can do so many more appointments. Before, you had to go to the office, to a bar. A ten-minute discussion might take two hours. This is easier, simpler. Also, I am lazy. I like staying home very much.

SF So there is an element of relief?

MP I am happy here. This pandemic has changed my way of thinking on so many levels. I've had more time to consider things. We were so afraid, there were so many difficulties – all the shops were closed and everything was a disaster. We were forced to react, to find new ways of doing things, new ways of taking care of clients. When we were closed there was a real sense of solidarity between human beings. Perhaps we had arrived at a point that was repetitive, generally decadent. When the world changes it signifies the rebirth of something, there is a new energy.

SF Do you have a sense of it being wonderful to spend your life making beautiful things?

MP For sure. And now I have much more time to do my job and to do it well. Before I was distracted. Even though I have barely any social life there were still too many distractions. And the idea that I could maybe stay in one place, for just one day, and think about clothes – that was such a joy.

SF You have been one of very few designers who have actually changed our aesthetic, changed the way people – women and men also – dress. At the beginning, you had to fight to be understood, people described your work as ugly, and certainly it played with received notions of taste. Now though, with Prada and Miu Miu, there is an understanding, and a love of the things you have done and still do. Do you feel proud of that?

MP Of that, yes, I am proud. I think that if I have achieved anything it is that. But it wasn't revolutionary. It was subtle. Early on the avant-garde thought I was not avant-garde enough, the classicists thought I was very disturbing. And I loved that. It is the in between that interests me. In that sense, little by little, probably because I didn't come from the fashion world, I changed things. It was only in fashion that there was this obsession with beautification in a conventional sense. In art, in the movies, in books, those ideals were questioned. And I too thought that was so old-fashioned, so conservative. Now it's normal to question those values. I think I have contributed to that.

This page: Anita is wearing a wool crepe coat with contrasting
collar by MIU MIU, Autumn/Winter 2011

This page: Mira is wearing a natte fringed top and skirt with embroidery by MIU MIU, Spring/Summer 2014. Opposite: Lucy is wearing a vichy-printed mohair coat with ruffles, technical fabric polo shirt, vichy-printed cotton poplin shirt, acrylic headband with crystals and feather and crystal necklace (in her hand) by MIU MIU, Spring/Summer 2016

This page: Garfield is wearing a cable knit wool jumper with oversized collar, denim shirt, checked wool trousers and brocade belt by MIU MIU, Autumn/Winter 2016. Leather boots with chain detail by MIU MIU, Autumn/Winter 2021. Opposite: Mira is wearing a cotton poplin dress by MIU MIU, Spring/Summer 1997

This page: Anita is wearing a gabardine dress by MIU MIU, Spring/Summer 1998. Opposite:
Mira is wearing an art nouveau floral-printed georgette dress by MIU MIU, Autumn/Winter
2001. Stylist's own tights. And suede heels by MIU MIU, Spring/Summer 2005

This page: Valeria is wearing a felt coat (over her arm), paisley crepe de chine dress and straw hat by
MIU MIU, Autumn/Winter 2000. Leather wedges by MIU MIU, Spring/Summer 2002. Opposite: Anita is wearing
a tulle dress with crystal embroidery and technical fabric sleeves by MIU MIU, Autumn/Winter 2020

This page: Anita is wearing a printed cotton poplin shirt dress, acrylic headband and knitted nylon belt by MIU MIU, Spring/Summer 2005. Opposite: Corinne is wearing a leather minidress, technical fabric shorts and ballerina flats with paillettes and crystal embroidery by MIU MIU, Autumn/Winter 2018

This page: Ludovica is wearing a printed silk jacquard minidress by MIU MIU,
Autumn/Winter 2006. Opposite: Elena is wearing a star-printed taffeta dress,
jersey T-shirt and silk jersey gloves by MIU MIU, Spring/Summer 2006

This page: Yu Shan is wearing a striped gazar minidress and collar by MIU MIU, Spring/Summer 2008.
Opposite: Garfield is wearing a volute-printed mohair suit, camellia-printed gazar shirt, embroidered
jacquard collar and tie and leather belt by MIU MIU, Autumn/Winter 2012

Yu Shan is wearing a loden dress with stud and crystal
embroidery, satin skirt and faux-fur boots by MIU MIU,
Autumn/Winter 2021

This page: Valeria is wearing a leather and shearling gilet, viscose zip-up top and loden trousers by MIU MIU, Autumn/Winter 2021. Opposite: Mohair dress and cashmere sleeves by MIU MIU, Autumn/Winter 2021

This page: Anita is wearing a polka-dot felted wool coat by MIU MIU, Autumn/Winter 1997. Opposite: Myrsky is wearing a lily-printed mohair suit, camellia-printed gazar shirt, embroidered jacquard collar and tie and leather belt by MIU MIU, Autumn/Winter 2012. Leather brogues by MIU MIU, Autumn/Winter 2003

This page: Mira is wearing a nylon bra and skirt, knitted mohair top, crocheted wool scarf
and stockings and faux-fur boots by MIU MIU, Autumn/Winter 2021. Opposite: Yu Shan is wearing
a quilted technical fabric jacket and Lurex top by MIU MIU, Autumn/Winter 2014

Opposite page: Anita is wearing a satin and crocheted dress
and faux-fur boots by MIU MIU, Autumn/Winter 2021

Hair: Paolo Soffiatti at Blend Management. Make-up: Luciano Chiarello at Julian Watson Agency. Models: Corinne at Street People Casting, Elena Burgin and Yu Shan Chen at Persona, Mira Nora Nagy at Why Not, Valeria Pavesi at Fabbrica and Anita Salinsky at Rebel Management. Streetcast models: Myrsky Kerko, Lucy Marega, Garfield Pagani and Ludovica Richiello. Casting director: Julia Lange at Artistry. Casting associate: Olivia Langner. Additional casting of Anita Salinsky by Florinda Martucciello\Sara Casana and Mara Veneziano. Photographic assistant: Cecilia Byrne. Styling assistants: George Pistachio and Fabiana Guigli. Production: Nicola Catterall and Sophie Hambling at Farago Projects. Local production: Alessandra Gabbetta, Eleonora Giammello and Alberto Angeloni at Hotel Production. Black and white printing: Peter at The Image. Retouching: Simon Thistle

Gucci Aria

Photography   Styling
WILLY VANDERPERRE   OLIVIER RIZZO

Lulu is wearing a monogrammed wool cotton cape by GUCCI

Lulu is wearing a leather harness and monogrammed polyester pantashoes by GUCCI

This page: Damian wearing a leather harness and monogrammed wool cotton Bermuda shorts with leather trim by GUCCI. Opposite: Monogrammed wool cotton coat with logo and leather trim, leather harness, monogrammed wool cotton Bermuda shorts and riding boots with leather trim by GUCCI

This page: Lulu is wearing a leather bustier and monogrammed wool cotton Bermuda shorts with leather trim by GUCCI. Opposite: Monogrammed wool cotton jacket with logo and leather trim, leather bustier and monogrammed wool cotton Bermuda shorts with leather trim by GUCCI

Diani is wearing a leather choker harness and wool jodhpurs by GUCCI.

Lulu is wearing a leather harness and polyester
Flora skirt with logo by GUCCI

This page: Daan is wearing a cotton velvet tuxedo and leather choker harness by GUCCI. Opposite: Wool evening suit with feathered sleeves and leather choker harness by GUCCI

Lulu is wearing a silk satin and lamé silk evening gown, leather harness and feathered sleeves by GUCCI

Hair: Anthony Turner at Streeters. Make-up: Lynsey Alexander at Streeters. Models: Daan Duez at Rebel Management and Lulu Tenney at Ford Models. Casting: Michelle Lee Casting. Manicure: Lotje Vleugels. Digital tech: Henri Coutant. Lighting: Romain Dubus. Photographic assistant: Samir Dari. Styling assistants: Niccolo Torelli, Louise Pollet and Jasmien Van Loo. Hair assistant: Harriet Beidleman. Make-up assistant: Raffaele Romagnoli. Production: assistant to Willy Vanderperre: Lieze Rubbrecht. Production: Mindbox. Producer: Isabelle Verreyke. On-set producer: Lise Luyckx. Production manager: Roel Van Tittelboom. Production/assistants: Charlotte Dupont and Marteen Rose. Post-production: Triplelutz Paris

"It's like pornography." Alessandro Michele uses typically atypical terminology to describe his latest Gucci collection. In an ongoing challenge to traditional seasonal nomenclature, he has called it Aria, the operatic term denoting a self-contained piece for a solo voice. Which is ironic, given that Michele's Gucci is boldly plural – especially today, drawing in myriad creative voices, aesthetic histories and ideological constructs, many parts to make the whole. This time, Michele went even further, describing his approach of openly appropriating other styles, symbols and signifiers as "hacking". To draw us back to his pornographic play on perception, he means the results seem slightly illicit, the gains maybe ill-gotten. "It's illegal, but maybe we can start to change this word a little bit," he says. "You can hack if you have permission."

Words ALEXANDER FURY

Michele, who turns 49 this autumn, has helmed Gucci for six and a half years now, a restless period of ceaseless reinvention of the century-old Italian leather goods house. Not only Gucci's clothes but its entire aesthetic universe has been transformed – hacked, not in the sense of the act of illegally infiltrating a computer system, but of violently or sharply cutting. Michele has hacked at Gucci's heritage, its history, its meaning, to reshape it into something new. I'm reminded of a turn of phrase by the German philosopher Walter Benjamin – whose work Michele admires and quotes often. Benjamin used the German word *Tigersprung* – 'tiger's leap' – to describe fashion's leap into the past to create an ever-changing present. Michele embroiders lots of tigers on things. Maybe they mean more than you would imagine at first glance.

"Gucci is a brand that started from the creativity of a family," says Michele. He's talking from his home in Rome, a few weeks after presenting his Gucci collection, via Zoom but without video. The focus instead is on his melodious, strong-accented voice, softly crooning. Michele is mesmerising in person, dressed like some kind of bejewelled fashion shaman with his long, flowing hair. But as with any great leader, his voice is enough to pull you into his world, his cult. Now he's talking about the cult of Gucci – the history of the brand, but also of the family. "They just did something unbelievable because they were not couturiers. They were just people of the *bottega*" – the Italian word for 'shop', not the Kering brand that shares that name – "that started to work in leather goods. They really used a lot of creativity to start this unbelievable trip. In Gucci there is a space for everybody. There was a space for Tom, who invented, again, the image of the brand – you know the story."

"Tom" means Tom Ford, of course, who in 1994 was appointed creative director of Gucci – a name then more commonly seen in tabloid headlines than fashion pages, emerging from a morass of familial power struggles and murder plots worthy of pulp-fiction novels and, now, a blockbuster movie – and ignited its rise to the pinnacle of the industry. What Ford did was to rebrand Gucci, as swiftly and adroitly as Michele has done, giving it a slinky, subversive sexiness that pervaded everything from evening dresses to advertising campaigns to exotic ephemera – such as a kinky leather Gucci whip – intended to provoke reactions. Michele's vision for Gucci is softer, sure – it's tough to picture Ford quoting Benjamin – and infinitely more multifaceted, as befits the vastly expanded sphere of luxury today. But it's just as powerful.

And for this Gucci collection, Michele embraced every part of the house's identity – his opening look was one hell of a tiger's leap, exhuming a keynote outfit from Tom Ford's Autumn/Winter 1996 Gucci collection, a velvet suit in a shade of scarlet that the New York Times critic Amy Spindler compared to Mick Jagger's bruised lips, slithering over a baby-blue shirt. It was sort of Scarface. More tigers. I remember it, from when I was a kid, the advertising campaign showing Georgina Grenville languishing on a sofa, staring up at a male model, Ludovico Benazzo. They were both dressed in that suit, her hand stroking a velvety thigh.

Whenever fashion quotes from its past it's never quite the same. Michele hacked at that look, shifting the proportions, overlaying the subtly sexual open shirt with an overtly fetishistic leather harness. Ironically, that has its roots in an even older Gucci – Michele tugged it from the brand's origins, the leather equestrian goods offered alongside luggage in a tiny Florentine shop established by Guccio Gucci in 1921. He learnt his trade at Valigeria Franzi, purveyor of luggage and leathers to the Italian aristocracy, but had also spent time at the Savoy in London, hauling expensive luggage. Literal first-hand experience. Guccio started off importing goods to his store, but given the excellence of Tuscan craftspeople, he began to have artisans make pieces for him locally. But he – and those leather workers – probably never imagined their harnesses and whips would be shifted from horse to human.

Then again, Michele likes to confound expectations. So, although rumours of a collaboration – or whatever you want to call it – between Gucci and its stablemate Balenciaga swirled before Michele unveiled his Aria show in April, the sheer audacity of Michele's approach was still breathtaking. This wasn't a polite example of co-branding, an anodyne sweatshirt plastered with a couple of emblems. Michele filched the patterns of Demna Gvasalia's tugged-across asymmetric coats, his curve-bottomed Hourglass handbag, stretch trouser-boot hybrids and the waist-nipped, plump-hipped suits he showed in his first Balenciaga show in 2016 – it was at that event that the two designers first met one another – and slapped a Gucci label in them, sometimes over them. He printed Balenciaga's logo atop Gucci's monogram canvas, smothering one suit with crystals spelling out both labels' names in a delirious co-branding confusion. The Gucci Jackie bag, a fiercely protected house classic first introduced in 1961 – it was given the rather less evocative serial number G1244 until last year, when it was officially renamed after its most high-profile fan, Jacqueline Kennedy Onassis – now comes stamped with a print stating, falsely, 'BALENCIAGA'. It looks like a fake.

The language of the counterfeit is something Michele is fascinated by. I should have asked him if, really, he's always hacking Gucci because he isn't a Gucci – he's perpetually working under someone else's name. But he was already talking, slowly, methodically, about his ideas. "There is a big philosophical conversation around the copy," Michele says. "And the idea of combining the language of two brands, it's also a dream of a fashionista." He breaks into laughter. "I mean, it's like history if you can combine Leonardo with Raphael, not because I feel myself like Leonardo! Maybe Demna is Raphael ... " He's laughing again. "But it's like a dream. It could be really bad, it could be a beautiful experiment. The beautiful thing is that it's forbidden, and when you say that something is forbidden, I think that it starts to be interesting, in terms of creativity."

Michele pauses, thinks. "Fashion is about life. Fashion is the closest thing to life – because every day, from the first day of our life, we put something on our body. So it's such a crazy thing to apply boundaries or limits. Because life isn't about limits."

Vivienne Westwood

Photography CASPER SEJERSEN
Styling ELLIE GRACE CUMMING

Before she began her career in fashion, half a century ago now, Vivienne Westwood trained as a primary school teacher. It's a mindset that has informed her work from the outset – occasionally, she still describes herself as a teacher, and has always created clothes that reflect that – to communicate a theory, to educate. Great teachers inspire: through her unparalleled creativity Westwood has tutored entire generations. For more than a decade her focus has been to draw attention to the plight of the planet through her clothes, of course, and also powerful graphics that trace back to her work in the 1970s. Her latest is a pack of playing cards that lays out a strategy to save the world. Across these pages, pieces by Westwood and her former pupil Andreas Kronthaler – today her husband and the creative director of her top-line collection – are joined by a new group of designers whose garments echo her working methods and draw infinite inspiration from her.

"We are looking through the lens of *a changing world.* If the human race does not turn the telescope around we face mass extinction. Climate change will reach tipping point. I've been trying to *save the world* from climate change since the foundation of Climate Revolution 15 years ago, and now I'm up to Card 37 – back and front – *I'm nearly there.* I've got my message across. *We're already working on it! Follow me*"

– Vivienne Westwood

Inheritance

A new generation of
fashion designers on how
Vivienne Westwood inspires

JUNTAE KIM

"For me, her clothes liberate the body. When I first designed menswear, I used to come up against the limitations of what men's clothes should be. But Vivienne has helped destroy these stereotypes, the idea that certain clothes are only for certain genders and classes. That means freedom."

MARVIN DESROC

"I love Vivienne's resilience. I can't think of one time that she's bent to the rules of the industry – even the word 'industry' can't be associated with her. When we talk about Vivienne, we talk about art, emotion, design – that's what I've always loved about her. She's an artist, yet has been able to last in this business without ever compromising who she is. Meanwhile Andreas's energy and spirit are out of this world. It's so refreshing to see – I love unconventional men."

CHARLES JEFFREY

"There's no denying that Vivienne and Andreas have paved the way for me and my work. I feel like I'm from the same planet as them and have my own little island on it. Matty, too. It's like we are sending smoke signals to each other and sending ships across the sea, with good tidings."

MATTY BOVAN

"Growing up I saw the world a bit differently, and I believe Vivienne did too. She doesn't believe in conformity, and she and Andreas like to push the idea of what is acceptable. That is a great, great thing to do and why their work speaks to so many people worldwide. Vivienne has taught me to truly believe in myself and to gain knowledge of how and where things are made. To question."

CECILY OPHELIA

"Vivienne is the first fashion designer I remember remembering. When I was 16, I found the phone number for the Vivienne Westwood office and rang up, asking if I could come to the studio for a meeting about an internship. I went the next day. Attending fittings with Andreas taught me so much – he is unpredictable yet meticulous, a very good combination. And Vivienne has helped me to recognise the importance of craftsmanship and sustainability. Valuing the process of time serves both as a therapy and a protest against the voracious cycle of the fashion treadmill."

JULIAN CERRO

"My favourite show is Spring/Summer 1994, Café Society. Kate Moss, topless, licking a Magnum ice cream, wearing the shortest skirt ever, with 18th-century make-up. What more could you want?"

HASEEB HASSAN

"Growing up in Pakistan, I wasn't really aware of fashion, let alone the idea I could choose it as a career. Vivienne and Andreas have helped me open up and explore ideas while also being unapologetic about my background. For me, studying fashion is going against the grain – Vivienne and Andreas's work taught me to be myself and to believe in what you do if you feel passionately about it."

STEVEN STOKEY-DALEY

"Vivienne Westwood represents the characterful unpacking and subversion of the British wardrobe – the art of dressing, of reappropriating content within garments, of reinterpreting that into fashion."

A SAI TA

"What's so special about Vivienne is her spirit, her attitude and the fact that she didn't come from a traditional fashion-school education – you can see that she plays by her own rules. Vivienne taught me to do me, to speak my mind, to be brave and fearless. Education doesn't only have to come from school – if anything, you must unlearn what education systems have taught and search wider."

MICHAELA STARK

"It is, I'm sure, glaringly obvious how much Vivienne has influenced my practice as a designer. She paved the way for people like me – with courageous moves like opening a store with 'SEX' written out the front in giant pink letters. She helped open the door for provocative female designers."

FLINT J MCDONALD

"It's the appreciation of the past for me, how she translates that to the now. I've always been into history and historical garments – the construction and cut of those clothes is so interesting to dissect and play with. Westwood triumphs at that. Playing with British heritage as she and Andreas do is a real turn-on for me. And their appreciation of quality – I'm a sucker for a luscious fabric."

EMMA CHOPOVA & LAURA LOWENA

"Westwood was a designer we always looked up to as kids. The combination of preferences, punk and historical dress has had a very strong impact on us and has shaped us so much as designers. The DIY attitude inspired us to get into fashion – to just try making stuff without the fear of everything [having to be] perfect."

Interviews TED STANSFIELD

This page: Charley is wearing a printed silk blouse and knitted wool balaclava with bunny
ears by GARETH WRIGHTON. Latex bra and opera gloves by ATSUKO KUDO. And yellow gold and
crystal T-bar chain necklace by ANDREAS KRONTHALER FOR VIVIENNE WESTWOOD. Opposite:
Michaela is wearing a printed cotton corset and underwear with pearl ties by MICHAELA STARK

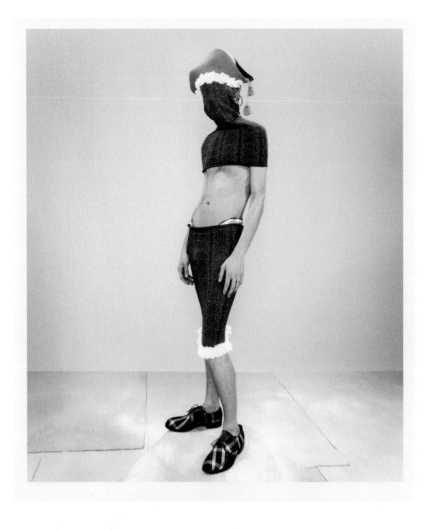

This page, from top: Tom is wearing an intarsia knitted wool top and skirt and crocheted cotton thong by ALINA ISPAS. Felted wool pirate hat with gold tassels by VIVIENNE WESTWOOD WORLDS END. His own jewellery (throughout). And tartan recycled polyester brogues by VIVIENNE WESTWOOD. Nicola is wearing a muslin Destroy top and leather Rocking Horse ballerina shoes by VIVIENNE WESTWOOD WORLDS END. Pleated patchwork wool tartan skirt and embellished wool beret by CHOPOVA LOWENA. Yellow gold and resin earrings by ANDREAS KRONTHALER FOR VIVIENNE WESTWOOD. And printed nylon tights by LAUREN PERRIN. Opposite, from left: Charley is wearing an argyle wool sweater vest and oversized pleat-front cotton shirt by SS DALEY. Devoré and cotton trousers by FLINT J MCDONALD. Wool hat with floral appliqué by PAULA MIHOVILOVIC. And knee-high oak nut wood boots by ANDREAS KRONTHALER FOR VIVIENNE WESTWOOD. Tom is wearing a cotton jacquard bodice, crinoline top with pussy bow collar, checked cotton stole (underneath) and metal ring with spoon charms (in his hand) by FLINT J MCDONALD. Argyle merino wool leggings by ANDREAS KRONTHALER FOR VIVIENNE WESTWOOD. Jewellery as before. And leather Rocking Horse boots by VIVIENNE WESTWOOD WORLDS END. Taira is wearing a cotton jacquard corset top and trousers and cotton catsuit with leg of mutton sleeves by FLINT J MCDONALD. Wool beret by VIVIENNE WESTWOOD. Paper and brass drop earrings by ANDREAS KRONTHALER FOR VIVIENNE WESTWOOD. Cotton socks by BURLINGTON. And leather Rocking Horse ballerina shoes by VIVIENNE WESTWOOD WORLDS END

This page, from left: Charley is wearing a cut-out cotton top and lace-up skirt by HASEEB HASSAN.
Wool beret by VIVIENNE WESTWOOD. Latex opera gloves by ELISSA POPPY. Hand-illustrated tights by
LAUREN PERRIN. And leather Rocking Horse ballerina shoes by VIVIENNE WESTWOOD WORLDS END. Nicola is
wearing a knitted wool top and skirt and charm belt by MATTY BOVAN. Crystal necklace (as a headpiece)
from PEBBLE LONDON. And leather Rocking Horse boots by VIVIENNE WESTWOOD WORLDS END. Opposite: Kyra
is wearing a hand-beaded wool jacket by CECILY OPHELIA. Her own jewellery (throughout)

This page: Sakeema is wearing a printed cotton jersey T-shirt by VIVIENNE WESTWOOD WORLDS END. Knitted Lurex skirt by ALINA ISPAS. Yellow gold and resin earrings and yellow gold and crystal T-bar chain necklace by ANDREAS KRONTHALER FOR VIVIENNE WESTWOOD. And her own jewellery. Opposite, from left: B is wearing a striped silk jacquard corset dress with leg of mutton sleeves and patent leather boots by ANDREAS KRONTHALER FOR VIVIENNE WESTWOOD. Latex leggings by ATSUKO KUDO. Taira is wearing a cotton jacquard and PVC shirt dress, argyle merino wool cardigan, brass and paper beaded choker and knee-high oak nut wood boots by ANDREAS KRONTHALER FOR VIVIENNE WESTWOOD. Nicola is wearing a draped PVC latex dress by ANDREAS KRONTHALER FOR VIVIENNE WESTWOOD X ATSUKO KUDO. Coated cotton bustier and yellow gold and resin earrings by ANDREAS KRONTHALER FOR VIVIENNE WESTWOOD. Latex opera gloves by ATSUKO KUDO. And crystal-embellished leather boots by ANDREAS KRONTHALER FOR VIVIENNE WESTWOOD X GINA

This page, from left: Nicola is wearing a cotton jacket with printed corset panel and cotton bondage trousers by JUNTAE KIM. Printed wool beret and leather Rocking Horse boots by VIVIENNE WESTWOOD WORLDS END. Tom is wearing an embroidered cotton denim jacket and trousers by JUNTAE KIM. Printed wool beret and tartan recycled polyester brogues by VIVIENNE WESTWOOD. And jewellery as before. Opposite: Kyra is wearing a double-breasted strapless wool dress and distressed knitted wool jumper by ASAI. Felted wool pirate hat with gold tassels by VIVIENNE WESTWOOD WORLDS END. Brass and paper beaded choker by ANDREAS KRONTHALER FOR VIVIENNE WESTWOOD. Jewellery as before. And leather belt by MATTY BOVAN

This page: Charley is wearing a moulded rubber bust cast by SINÉAD O'DWYER. Gold-toned brass necklace by CHOPOVA LOWENA. Opposite, from top: B is wearing a printed cotton top with feather trim and crocheted cotton jumpsuit with fringe detail by JULIAN CERRO. Felted wool pirate hat with gold tassels by VIVIENNE WESTWOOD WORLDS END. And knee-high oak nut wood boots by ANDREAS KRONTHALER FOR VIVIENNE WESTWOOD. Sakeema is wearing a crocheted stretch cotton top and tights by MARVIN DESROC. Jewellery as before. And leather Rocking Horse boots by VIVIENNE WESTWOOD WORLDS END

Opening spread: Taira is wearing a bouclé corset by DILARA FINDIKOGLU. Striped cotton poplin shirt by HODAKOVA. Argyle merino wool leg warmers by ANDREAS KRONTHALER FOR VIVIENNE WESTWOOD. And leather Rocking Horse ballerina shoes by VIVIENNE WESTWOOD WORLDS END. B is wearing a printed latex top by KATIE SHANNON. Printed cotton trousers by MOLLY TURNER. Brass and paper beaded choker by ANDREAS KRONTHALER FOR VIVIENNE WESTWOOD. Latex opera gloves by ATSUKO KUDO. And tartan recycled polyester brogues by VIVIENNE WESTWOOD. Sakeema is wearing a printed cotton jersey T-shirt by VIVIENNE WESTWOOD WORLDS END. Knitted Lurex skirt by ALINA ISPAS. Yellow gold and resin earrings, yellow gold and crystal T-bar chain necklace and knee-high oak nut wood boots by ANDREAS KRONTHALER FOR VIVIENNE WESTWOOD. And jewellery as before. Tom is wearing a striped cotton shirt and cotton skirt by KATYA ZELENTSOVA. Crocheted Lurex skirt with feather trim (worn as a headpiece) by ALINA ISPAS. Cotton socks by BURLINGTON. Tartan wool brogues by VIVIENNE WESTWOOD. And jewellery as before. Charley is wearing a ruched nylon and silk bodysuit with attached TABITHA RINGWOOD shoes by SINÉAD O'DWYER. Brass and paper beaded choker by ANDREAS KRONTHALER FOR VIVIENNE WESTWOOD. And crystal necklace from PEBBLE LONDON. Previous spread, left page: Taira is wearing a ruched velvet top, asymmetric cotton top and skirt by CHIE KAYA. Right page, from left: Taira is wearing a corduroy blazer with floral appliqué by SS DALEY. Wool corset by ASAI. Latex leggings by ATSUKO KUDO. And yellow gold and resin earrings, brass and paper beaded choker and knee-high oak nut wood boots by ANDREAS KRONTHALER FOR VIVIENNE WESTWOOD. Sakeema is wearing a ruched cotton dress by JULIAN CERRO. Wool and cotton underwear by ALINA ISPAS. Argyle merino wool leggings by ANDREAS KRONTHALER FOR VIVIENNE WESTWOOD. Gold-toned brass necklace by CHOPOVA LOWENA. Jewellery as before. And leather Rocking Horse boots by VIVIENNE WESTWOOD WORLDS END. Charley is wearing a printed silk blouse and knitted wool balaclava with bunny ears by GARETH WRIGHTON. Latex bra and opera gloves by ATSUKO KUDO. Deconstructed wool trousers by ASAI. Yellow gold and crystal T-bar necklace by ANDREAS KRONTHALER FOR VIVIENNE WESTWOOD. Cotton socks by BURLINGTON. And leather Rocking Horse ballerina shoes by VIVIENNE WESTWOOD WORLDS END. Kyra is wearing a double-breasted strapless wool dress and distressed knitted wool jumper by ASAI. Merino wool leggings by ANDREAS KRONTHALER FOR VIVIENNE WESTWOOD. Felted wool pirate hat with gold tassels and leather bondage boots by VIVIENNE WESTWOOD WORLDS END. Brass and paper beaded choker by ANDREAS KRONTHALER FOR VIVIENNE WESTWOOD. Jewellery as before. And leather belt by MATTY BOVAN. Tom is wearing a houndstooth wool overcoat by STEFAN COOKE. Ribbed cashmere wool vest, PVC and wool cuffed trousers and yellow gold and crystal T-bar necklace by ANDREAS KRONTHALER FOR VIVIENNE WESTWOOD. Knitted wool headband with bunny ears by GARETH WRIGHTON. Jewellery as before. Cotton socks by BURLINGTON. And tartan recycled polyester brogues by VIVIENNE WESTWOOD

Hair: Eugene Souleiman at Streeters. Hair for portraits of Vivienne Westwood and Andreas Kronthaler, and Michaela Stark: Kei Terada at Julian Watson Agency using OUAI. Make-up: Janeen Witherspoon at MA and Talent. Models: B at Idal, Charley Dean Sayers at Premier Model Management, Nicola Dinan at Xdirectn, Tom Goddard at Contact, Kyra Kaur and Taira at Storm Management and Sakeema Peng Crook at Crumb. Casting: Nicola Kast at Webber. Casting assistant: Julia Gilmour. Set design: Amy Strickland at Webber. Digital tech: Nic Bezzina. Digital tech for portraits: Sam Hearn. Photographic assistants: Matt Moran, Bradley Polkinghorne, Sean Morrow and Jack Storer. Styling assistants: Isabella Kavanagh, Ioana Ivan and Cari Lima. Hair assistants: Claire Moore, Massimo Di Stefano and Carlo Avena. Hair assistant for portraits: Takumi Horiwaki. Make-up assistant: Elizabeth Owen Perry. Set-design assistants: Harry Stayt and Molly Marot. Set-design assistant for portraits: Lizzy Gilbert. Production: Artistry. Producers: Jess Rogers and Sian Moodliar. Production assistant: Arthur Millier Radnall. Post-production: Frederik Heide at She Post Production

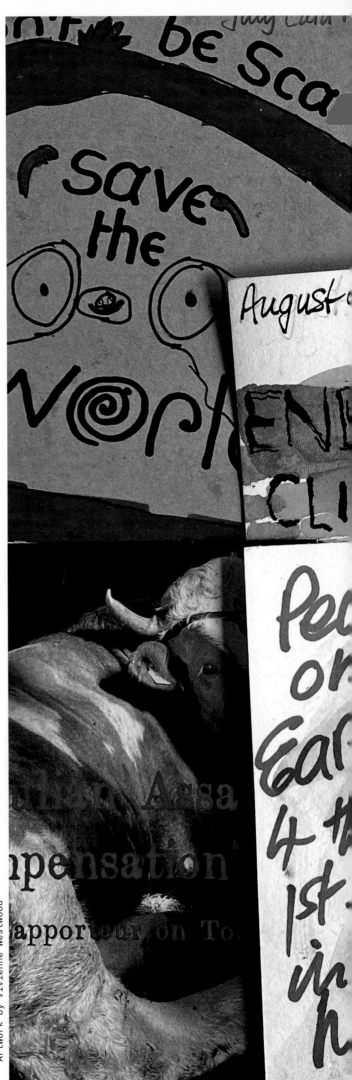

Artwork by Vivienne Westwood

In Search of Lost Time

Photography JACKIE NICKERSON
Styling KATIE SHILLINGFORD

Louise is wearing an oversized plastic jacket and polyurethane dress by NOIR KEI NINOMIYA

Louise is wearing a leather opera bubble dress by JW ANDERSON. Latex stockings by ELISSA POPPY. And upcycled deadstock trainers by MATTHEW NEEDHAM X HELEN KIRKUM

Quilted habotai cannage peacoat and ribbed cashmere jumper by DIOR. Crocheted plastic mask custom-made by JANINA PEDAN

Louise is wearing an oversized technical cotton coat with contrast stripes by GUCCI. T-shirt yarn knitted balaclava custom-made by ELEANOR BUTLER-JONES

Zinnia is wearing a ribbed cashmere and feather top and technical stretch wool and feather trousers by BOTTEGA VENETA. Latex gloves by ELISSA POPPY. And nylon and suede trainers by EYTYS

Zinnia is wearing a viscose jumper and snood by KENZO

Louise is wearing nylon tracksuit coats (as a coat and a skirt) and fleece sweatpants by BALENCIAGA. Latex gloves by ELISSA POPPY

Louise is wearing a superfine wool jacquard bodysuit and gloves by PRADA.
Oversized acetate sunglasses by TOM FORD. And nylon boots by RAF SIMONS

Quilted cotton coat by LOEWE

Louise is wearing a quilted nylon jumpsuit and shearling mittens by MIU MIU. Crocheted plastic mask custom-made by JANINA PEDAN

Cotton jacket, midi skirt and trousers, wool turtleneck, cotton hood and velvet platform Mary Janes by MARC JACOBS

Louise is wearing a laminated jersey body by SAINT LAURENT BY ANTHONY VACCARELLO. Crocheted balloon mask custom-made by ELEANOR BUTLER-JONES

Nylon duvet jacket by RICK OWENS. Plastic
head-dress custom made by JANINA PEDAN

Zinnia is wearing a flag intarsia stretch jersey and velvet turtleneck body by BURBERRY. Ribbed cotton and mosquito net mask (worn as a balaclava) by DAVID WEKSLER

Louise is wearing a printed velvet dress by LOUIS VUITTON X FORNASETTI. Cotton sweatpants by UNDERCOVER X EVANGELION C(KHARA). And leather boots by LOUIS VUITTON

Louise is wearing quilted canvas salopettes by CHANEL.
Hooded recycled polyester ribbon top by NANUSHKA

Zinnia is wearing a cut-out ribbed cotton jumpsuit and cropped padded leather jacket by GIVENCHY. Latex gloves by ELISSA POPPY

This page: Zinnia is wearing an oversized nylon tabard with faux-fur lining by MARNI. Lacquered nylon trousers by MONCLER GRENOBLE. Opposite: Technical linen coat by KENZO. Braided mask custom-made by JANINA PEDAN. Latex gloves by ELISSA POPPY. And Knot drop earrings in yellow gold with diamonds by TIFFANY & CO

Hair: Soichi Inagaki at Art Partner. Make-up: Anne Sophie Costa at Streeters using MAC. Hair colourist for Louise Robert: Tasha Spencer at Bleach London. Models: Louise Robert at Viva London and Zinnia Kumar at The Society Management. Casting: Noah Shelley at Streeters. Digital tech: Christopher Blythe at Lightmill. Photographic assistant: Pierre Lequeux. Styling assistant: George Pistachio

Time
Regained

Photography WILLIAM WATERWORTH
Styling REUBEN ESSER

This page: Warren is wearing a single-breasted wool coat, rollneck, tailored trousers with satin stripe and embroidered beret by DIOR. Opposite: Arthur is wearing a double-breasted wool suit and cotton poplin shirt by GUCCI. Silk pocket square from COSTUME STUDIO. And his own cotton scarf, rings and leather boots (throughout).

This page: Warren is wearing a single-breasted wool overcoat, tailored wool trousers and leather Derby shoes by DUNHILL. Cotton poplin shirt and silk tie from COSTUME STUDIO. Opposite: Warren and Arthur are wearing pleated wool shirt dresses with leather details by BURBERRY

LOEWE. Tailored wool trousers from COSTUME STUDIO. Opposite: Single-breasted technical fabric coat and wide-leg trousers by PRADA. Leather boots from COSTUME STUDIO

Grooming: Olivia Coumaile using Boy de Chanel and Le Lift Fluide by CHANEL. Models: Warren Hendy and Arthur Poujois. Casting: Nachum Shonn. Videographer: Joel Kerr. Photographic assistant: Orlando Osinowo. Styling assistant: Lauren Rucha. Printing: Eastend Printers Ltd. Post-production: Alessandro Raimondo

Ada, or Ardor: A Family Chronicle

Photography
OLIVER HADLEE PEARCH

Styling
ROBBIE SPENCER

Steinberg is wearing a long-sleeved viscose
bra top by JACQUEMUS. Striped PVC shirt
by CLÉMENT PICOT. And silk and vegan leather
skirt with lace trim by Y/PROJECT

This page: Quinn is wearing a double-breasted corduroy coat by PRADA. Silk skirt by Y/PROJECT. Twisted silk slip dress by GENEVIEVE DEVINE. Wool jumper and wool cashmere tights (throughout) by MIU MIU. And embroidered cotton poplin shorts by PALOMO SPAIN. Opposite: Steinberg is wearing a wool blazer with chiffon details and cotton and silk skirt by DRIES VAN NOTEN. Satin camisole with metal studs by MIU MIU. Long-sleeved cotton top by Y/PROJECT. Taffeta dress with oversized collar by MSGM. And tights as before

This page: Steinberg is wearing a long-sleeved viscose bra top by JACQUEMUS. Striped PVC shirt by CLÉMENT PICOT. Silk and vegan leather skirt with lace trim by Y/PROJECT. And cropped trousers as before. Opposite: Cropped wool jumper by MIU MIU. Crinoline dentelle dress with wire by JISOO BAIK. Cotton top (underneath) by Y/PROJECT. And tights and Mary Janes as before

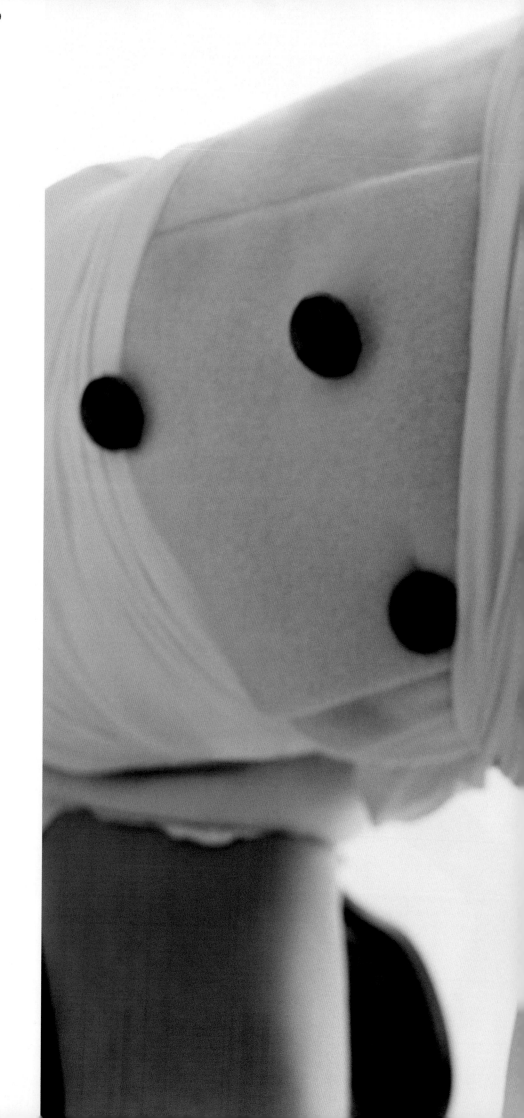

Quinn is wearing a draped Lycra body
by MAXIMILIAN. Double-breasted wool coat by
ISABEL MARANT. Taffeta blouse with oversized
collar (throughout) by MSGM. And leather
boots by JIL SANDER BY LUCIE AND LUKE MEIER

This page: Steinberg is wearing a geometric cotton puff top by MARCO RIBEIRO. Silk satin cropped top with sequin embroidery and detachable cotton collar by GUCCI. Tulle skirt (throughout) by NOIR KEI NINOMIYA. And trousers as before. Opposite: Faux-fur and Lurex coat by BALENCIAGA. Long-sleeved viscose bra top by JACQUEMUS. Layered padded silk dress by KENZO. And tulle skirt by MOLLY GODDARD

This page: Steinberg is wearing a New Zealand wool jersey top and skirt (knit in collaboration with PAUL AARØN) by CHIE KAYA. Stylist's own socks. Tights as before. And satin platform Mary Janes by MARC JACOBS. Opposite: Quinn is wearing an oversized printed nylon down jacket by KENZO. Laced polyester padded coat by OTTOLINGER. Off-the-shoulder satin dress by FENDI. Hooded leather gilet by GIVENCHY. Skirt, trousers and Mary Janes as before. Mohair bonnet by MIU MIU. And stylist's own socks

Quinn is wearing a microfibre nylon and cotton
jersey jacket with portable inflatable fans by
FEYFEY YUFEI LIU. Blouse as before. And mohair
bonnet by MIU MIU

This page: Steinberg is wearing a smocked cloqué organza dress, leather harness belt with crystal embellishment and lace-up leather brogues with tracker soles by SIMONE ROCHA. Skirt as before. And stylist's own nylon tights. Opposite: Quinn is wearing an acrylic, cotton, cupro and polyester coat dress by JUNYA WATANABE. Blouse and skirt as before. T hoop earrings in 18-carat yellow gold by TIFFANY & CO. And over-the-knee leather platform boots by PRADA.

Hair: Yann Turchi at Bryant Artists. Make-up: Masae Ito at Blend Management using GLOSSIER. Models: Quinn Mora at Premier Model Management and Steinberg at Ford Models. Casting: Noah Shelley at Streeters. Photographic assistants: Ben Coppola, Mathieu Boutang and Bella Sporle. Styling assistants: Met Kilinc, Sabine Groza, Yann Steiner and Louna Guerreiro. Hair assistant: Magdalena Loza. Make-up assistant: Louise Rouger. Production: Art Partner. Special thanks to Hammer Lab and Aly Studio

Music
for
Chameleons

Make-up PETER PHILIPS for DIOR BEAUTY
Photography THUE NØRGAARD
Styling RAE BOXER

Alyssa is wearing Rouge Dior Universal lip balm in 000 Diornatural Satin Finish by DIOR. Vintage leather jacket and polyester jersey from LES MAUVAIS GARÇONS. And silver chain necklace by TANT D'AVENIR

This page: Milk is wearing Diorshow On-Stage Liner in 091 Matte Black and knit shearling jacket by DIOR. Opposite: Diorshow Pump 'N' Volume HD Mascara in 090 Black and Rouge Dior lipstick in 999 Matte by DIOR. Cotton T-shirt from SUPER VINTAGE. And silver chain with vintage metal pendant by TANT D'AVENIR

This page: Elisa is wearing Dior Addict Lip Glow lip balm in 000 Universal Clear by DIOR. Stylist's own vintage hoodie. Opposite: Elio is wearing Diorshow 24H Stylo waterproof eyeliner in 091 Matte Black by DIOR. Cotton T-shirt by PALACE. Vintage plaid cotton shirt from OH LUMIÈRE. And silver chain with pendant by TANT D'AVENIR.

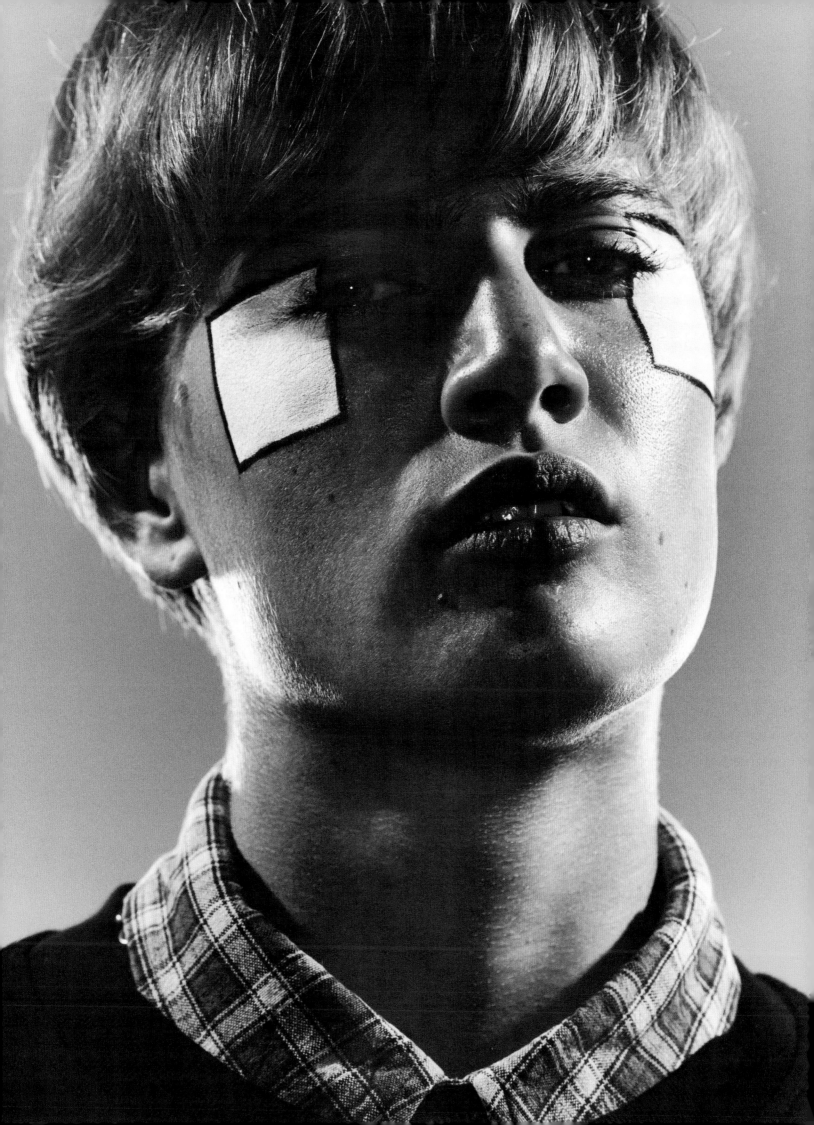

Silver chain necklace by TANT D'AVENIR. Opposite: Lucas is wearing Dior Hydra Life Matte Dew Hydration Sorbet Drop Emulsion by DIOR. Silver earring from PASSAGE. Make-up: Peter Philips, Creative & Image Director for Dior Make-up. Hair: Christian Eberhard at MA and Talent. Models: Victoria Fawole at The Claw, Lucas M at Tomorrow Is Another Day, Elisa Nijman at Poparazzi, Alyssa Sardine at BM Model Management, Elio S at Mikas and Mila van Eeten at Viva. Casting: Daniel von der Graf. Manicure: Hanae Goumri at The Wall Group. Digital tech: Juliette Eberg Kral. Photographic assistants: Stan Rey-grange and Alexis Parrenin. Styling assistants: Marianne Chateauneuf and Morane Guérineau de Lamerie Michalet. Hair assistants: Christophe Pestel and Gabrielle Pondybias. Make-up assistants: Elodie Barra, Jindian Yang and Julie Camus. Manicure assistant: Chloé Desmarchelier. Production: Simon Malivindi. Ashleigh Hayward and Bigaël Da Silva at One Thirty-Eight Productions. Production assistants: Arthur Debriffe and Anaëlle De Oliveira. Post-production: Studio RM.

# #

1017 ALYX 9SM
alyxstudio.com
4 Moncler Hyke
moncler.com

A

Acne Studios
acnestudios.com
Adidas
adidas.co.uk
Alexander McQueen
alexandermcqueen.com
Alighieri
alighieri.co.uk
Alina Ispas
instagram/alinaispas
Ambush
ambushdesign.com
Andreas Kronthaler
for Vivienne Westwood
viviennewestwood.com
Asai
asaitakeaway.com
Atlein
atlein.com
Atsuko Kudo
atsukokudo.com

B

Balenciaga Couture
couture.balenciaga.com
Berluti
berluti.com
Bianca Saunders
biancasaunders.com
Blumarine
blumarine.com
Bottega Veneta
bottegaveneta.com
Burberry
burberry.com
Burlington
burlington.de

C

Cartier
cartier.com
Cave Things
cavethings.com
Cecily Ophelia
cecilyophelia.com
Chanel
chanel.com
Charles Jeffrey
Loverboy
loverboy.net
Charvet
charvet.com
Chato Lufsen
chatolufsen.shop
Chie Kaya
instagram.com/kayachieee
Chopova Lowena
chopovalowena.com
Cinabre
cinabre-paris.com
Clément Picot
instagram.com/clementpicot__
Comme des Garçons
Homme Plus
doverstreetmarket.com
Commission
commission.nyc
Cormio
cormio.com
Costume Studio
costumestudio.co.uk
Courrèges
courreges.com

D

David Weksler
davidweksler.com
De Pino
instagram.com/_de_pino
Dilara Findikoglu
dilarafindikoglu.com
Dior
dior.com
Dries Van Noten
driesvannoten.com
Dsquared2
dsquared2.com
Dunhill
dunhill.com

E

ERL
erl.store
Eleanor Butler-Jones
eleanorbutlerjones.com
Elissa Poppy
elissapoppy.com
Ellery
ellery.com
Ermenegildo Zegna XXX
zegna.com
Ernest W Baker
ernest-w-baker.com
Eyland Jewellery
eylandjewellery.com
Eytys
eytys.com

F

Falke
falke.com
Fantabody
fantabody.com
Fendi
fendi.com
Feyfey Yufei Liu
feyfeyworldwide.com
Fila
fila.co.uk
Flint J McDonald
instagram.com/flintjmcdonald
Fornasetti
fornasetti.com

G

Gareth Wrighton
instagram.com/gareth_wrighton
Genevieve Devine
instagram.com/genevieve_
florence_devine
Gina
gina.com
Givenchy
givenchy.com
GmbH
gmbhgmbh.eu
Gucci
gucci.com
Guess Activewear
guess.com
Guess Jeans
guess.com

H

Hanes
hanes.com
Haseeb Hassan
instagram.com/h.hassan__
Helen Kirkum
helenkirkum.com
Hermès
hermes.com
Hi-Tec
hi-tec.com

Hodakova
hodakova.com
Hunza G
hunzag.com

I

Isabel Marant
isabelmarant.com

J

JW Anderson
jwanderson.com
Jacquemus
jacquemus.com
Jil Sander by Lucie
and Luke Meier
jilsander.com
Jisoo Baik
instagram.com/jisoo_baik_
John Lobb
johnlobb.com
Julian Cerro
instagram.com/julianarchangel
Juntae Kim
instagram.com/juuntaekim
Junya Watanabe
doverstreetmarket.com
Juun J
juunj.com

K

Katie Shannon
instagram.com/wasserbebei1
Katya Zelentsova
katyazelentsova.com
Katz Dancewear
katz-dancewear.co.uk
Kenzo
kenzo.com
Kiko Kostadinov
kikokostadinov.com

L

Lacoste
lacoste.com
Lauren Perrin
laurenperrin.com
Lemaire
lemaire.fr
Les Girls Les Boys
lesgirlslesboys.com
Les Mauvais Garçons
instagram.com/
lesmauvaisgarconscostumes
Levi's
levi.com
Loewe
loewe.com
Loro Piana
loropiana.com
Louis Vuitton
louisvuitton.com
Lucile Guilmard
instagram.com/lucile_guilmard
Ludovic de Saint Sernin
ludovicdesaintsernin.com

M

Manolo Blahnik
manoloblahnik.com
Marc Jacobs
marcjacobs.com
Marco Ribeiro
marcoribeiro.fr
Margaret Howell
margarethowell.co.uk
Marni
marni.com
Marsèll
marsell.it
Martine Rose
martine-rose.com

Marvin Desroc
instagram/marvindesroc
Matthew Needham
matthew-needham.com
Matty Bovan
mattybovan.com
Maximilian
brownsfashion.com
Michaela Stark
michaelastark.co
Missoni
missoni.com
Miu Miu
miumiu.com
Molly Goddard
mollygoddard.com
Molly Turner
instagram.com/mollyjlturner
Moncler Grenoble
moncler.com
Moose Knuckles
mooseknucklescanada.com
MSGM
msgm.it

N

Nanushka
nanushka.com
Noir Kei Ninomiya
doverstreetmarket.com

O

Off-White
c/o Virgil Abloh
off---white.com
Oh Lumière
instagram.com/ohlumiere
Oswalde
instagram.com/oswalde.shop
Ottolinger
ottolinger.com

P

Palace
palaceskateboards.com
Palomo Spain
palomospain.com
Pantherella
pantherella.com
Passage
passageparis.com
Paul Aarøn
instagram.com/
paulaaronknitwear
Paul Smith
paulsmith.com
Paula Mihovilovic
instagram.com/courage_hail
Pebble London
pebblelondon.com
Peter Do
peterdo.net
Petit Bateau
petit-bateau.co.uk
Phipps
phipps.international
Prada
prada.com

R

Raf Simons
rafsimons.com
Raggedy Threads
raggedythreads.com
Rick Owens
rickowens.eu
RIMOWA
rimowa.com

S

SS Daley
matchesfashion.com
Saint Laurent by
Anthony Vaccarello
ysl.com
Salvatore Ferragamo
ferragamo.com
Simone Rocha
simonerocha.com
Sinéad O'Dwyer
sineadodwyer.com
Slim Barrett
slimbarrett.com
Spanx
spanx.com
Speedo
speedo.com
Sportmax
sportmax.com
Stefan Cooke
stefancooke.co.uk
Stella McCartney
stellamccartney.com
Super Vintage
instagram.com/
supervintageparis
Supriya Lele
supriyalele.com

T

Tabitha Ringwood
tabitharingwood.com
Tant d'Avenir
tantdavenir.com
Tela
tela9.com
Telfar
telfar.net
The Attico
theattico.com
The Contemporary
Wardrobe Collection
contemporarywardrobe.com
Tiffany & Co
tiffany.com
Tom Ford
tomford.co.uk
Trasparenze
calzetrasparenze.com

U

UK Tights
uktights.com
Undercover
undercoverism.com

V

Valentino
valentino.com
Vaquera
vaquera.nyc
Versace
versace.com
Vic Matié
vicmatie.com
Vivienne Westwood
viviennewestwood.com

W

We11done
we11-done.com
Wolford
wolfordshop.co.uk
Woolrich
woolrich.com

Y

Y/Project
yproject.fr

Legacy

Legacy is a big word for an artist. Part inheritance and part archive.
Especially for a performance artist. How can I possibly convey
the mindset, the values, the process behind good performance art?
Performance art is experiential. It is in the 'here' and the 'now'.
You have to be present. You need to be present.

   How do we reanimate the documented but un-documentable?
How do we share something that existed – but is no more?
How do you archive emotions?

   Perhaps we cannot. At least not in the classic sense.

   What we cannot do on paper, film or any known modality, or any
that will be invented in the future, we can do through other people.
Artists and participants. Through their hearts, minds and memory.

   Performance is participatory. There is no performance without
people.

   This is the reason I founded MAI (Marina Abramović Institute).
To provide a platform for other artists to share their work.
And for participants an opportunity to be part of that sharing.

   To communicate and disseminate the artistic values, the mindset
and the process of true performance art.

   MAI explores, supports and presents performance in every way and
every form possible and creates public and participatory experiences.

   MAI strives to be in difficult places at times of fragility.
We have been in the outskirts of São Paulo in Brazil, in Ukraine
during the invasion of Crimea, in Athens during the financial crisis
and in Istanbul during the most polarised elections of the past 30
years. We want to capture art where it is most important at the moment
it is conceived.

   Perpetual movement is at the heart of our practice. We are nomads
of ephemerality.

   MAI is committed to inclusive artistic practices. We strive for
an art made of transparency, vulnerability and truth.

   Being an artist is a constant search for process. And we have
opened our process to prepare artists for performance to everybody.
That said, even the distinction might be obsolete or even redundant.

   – Marina Abramović

Guest-edited by
MARINA ABRAMOVIĆ

Atlas de Ulla, Spain, 2002. Courtesy Marina Abramović Archive

The Cleaning the House workshop was developed by Marina Abramović over more than four decades of teaching. Its title refers to Abramović's metaphor of the body as our only 'house'.

Hosted by MAI, and held all over the world, the workshop challenges the body's physical and mental limits, forcing it to respond to and reconnect with its environment. This training is a method towards achieving heightened consciousness and a deepened understanding of oneself.

During the workshop, participants are asked to refrain from eating and speaking, to bring body and mind to a quiet, calm state. They are led through a series of long-durational exercises to improve individual focus, stamina and concentration. The workshop offers the opportunity to be in nature, away from distractions, and to participate in a carefully timed set of exercises and activities to improve both our determination and our ability to generate new ideas.

This type of preparation provides the proper process and setting for a complete internal reset, essential not only for performers as they approach their work, but also for other practitioners and professionals across all disciplines.

Cleaning the House

"The workshop challenges the body's physical and mental limits, forcing it to respond to and reconnect with its environment"

Maria Stamenković Herranz studied at the Vaganova Ballet School in Novi Sad, in the former Yugoslavia, and later graduated from the Rambert School of Ballet and Contemporary Dance in London and Maggie Flanigan Studio in New York. An interdisciplinary performance artist, Herranz strives to illuminate the hidden structures we create to feel safe, but that in turn also limit us. Her work continually seeks to lay those structures bare, "to desolate them and forge a path of return", she says, "beyond nation states and borders, back to the truest sense of home – the body itself". In her 24-day blindfolded performance This Mortal House, the artist constructed a labyrinth inside Istanbul's Sakıp Sabancı Museum. For eight hours a day, six days a week, she built the structure brick by brick from the inside out, using the mythological blueprint of the labyrinth that the craftsman Daedalus built in Knossos, Crete – designed to imprison the Minotaur, the maze was so elaborate that Daedalus himself had difficulty escaping it. In the following piece Herranz describes the revelatory experience of performing This Mortal House last year in Istanbul.

This page, opposite and following spread: Maria Stamenković Herranz, This Mortal House, 2020, Akis/Flux, MAI at Sakıp Sabancı Museum, Istanbul, Turkey. Photograph by Korhan Karaoysal stamenkovicherranz.com, @mariasherranz

Maria Stamenković Herranz

This Mortal House

Akış/Flux, Sakıp Sabancı Museum, Istanbul
11 February – 8 March 2020

The performing artist legacy for me
feels like,
the recipe of a good bowl of
    minestrone
that's been passed on.
In the pot of minestrone,
there is a variety of ingredients
that coexist together.
The minestrone can be a shared
    experience
and an individual one.
The minestrone is passed on through
    generations.
It's an experience
that is specifically prepared
so we
eat it
share it
digest it
and have the moment
to let it disappear.
But we have a recipe,
written on a piece of paper,
that is passed on from generation to
    generation.
Without this piece of paper
we wouldn't be able to sometimes
    taste some of the best dishes
that give us not only an ultimate
    experience of some sort
but as well enable us to have
conversations of history,
speak of cultural heritages
and have an understanding
and awareness of the time passing,
without mentioning
the invaluable necessity
of transformation
that is a basic human need.
Having come from the theatre
dance
to performance art,
in each form
I question how,
as a performing artist,
moving through these various forms,
I can pass the legacy of the
    performing work.
I discovered there are two key
    ingredients:
presence
and
creating a trace.
Being present creates impact.
Impact creates echo.
Echo creates a trace.
And if you create a good cauldron for
    the trace to sit in
then you have a recipe
that can be passed on
and you create a legacy.
Leaving traces

is inevitable as human beings
and I strongly believe
that our stories
our heritage
our individual experiences
impact our shared experiences,
and thus allow for the performing
    artist
to be part of an important aspect
through the practice of ephemeral
    art,
and be a valuable asset
to the development of our society.
Given the times we live in,
shared experiences
have taken on

new dimensions.
Today
there is something
in moving forward,
a heightened sensibility,
a vital necessity,
that one
not only acts
on behalf
of oneself,
but on behalf
of others
and for those
that come
after us.
Years ago,
in 2004,
when I met Marina Abramović,
I was instantly awed
by her sincere desire
to know about my work.
She was genuinely curious
about how my mix of
the west and east
harmonised with one another.

Since I grew up
with a Spanish mother
and a Serbian father,
I recognised
that the similarities
with those of my father
in fact
were quite uncanny.
My father was born the same year
    as Marina Abramović.
They grew up in the same system,
have the same humour.
When I saw Marina's work for the
    first time
my blood moved,
it was like being home.

I recognised the energy,
I recognised how my culture
    channels pain,
depth
and humour.
But above all
I recognised
the resilience,
the wild warrior strength,
with which our culture had to survive
from century to century.
When I was invited to collaborate
    with Marina
as a performer,
and later commissioned as a
    performance artist by MAI,
I felt like destiny was doing its thing.
We work and perceive energy very
    similarly.
We tend to put our gazes in kindred
    directions.
We are moved by a deep longing to
    connect;
to be transformed in unison,
but so as to fight

to keep our own fires afloat,
even when the winds are against us.
I feel that we both strongly believe
how positively the performing
arts
can change individuals at a deep
and cellular level.
We both set up protocols
for those shifts to occur.
From the moment I saw her work

came to a standstill.
My focus
and the dedication of my performing
career
came to an end.
A birth
to a new beginning.
Somehow
unconsciously
I felt it before I began.

All I understood
was
I had to let my body
be the vessel
and
lead me through
the darkness.
After years of classical training
I've travelled a long road
of letting go.
This allowed
for the work
to come to fruition
right in front of
my blindness.
The audience
saw
before I could.
Somehow
I understand now,
I turned the mirror inwardly
and let the visitors
reflect their own image.
When I think of it now,
I feel such purity
lending such trust
to people.
Somehow
it's the connection
I still long for today.
I had such a deep desire
to disappear
as a performance artist.

I knew instantly it was inevitable
that I was going to be part of her
legacy.
For we both speak the same
language.
In 2020
I was asked
to create a new long-durational
performance
for the
Sakıp Sabancı Museum in Istanbul.
I was
at a very particular moment
in my life.
With This Mortal House,
I feel I reached a shift in my work.
With this performance piece
the many years of life's experiences
I gathered

I was electrified
leading up to the start.
The protocol I created
came from a deeper
place than I could explain in words.
As Dostoevsky points out in the book
The Adolescent:
"There is immeasurably more left
inside
than what comes out in words."
It felt like falling off a cliff
right from the start.
Having no idea
how I'd pull the concept through
was in fact
the beginning of the transformation.
To allow the unknown
to lead me
was the path I had taken.

I had
this burning desire
for the protocol
to grow into its own animal,
be its own entity,
and let people
look at themselves
through me
and not at me.
I remember
somehow
it gave me such an
enormous feeling of freedom.
Even now
I know it's the
hardest piece
I have ever made.
I still carry
the physical traces
in my eyes
to this date.
At times I am afraid
there is something wrong with them.
But it teaches me too
that the body decays
by nature
and that acceptance
is part of the process.
This has been
a transformational experience,
both as a human
and as an artist,
an inevitable threshold I had to
cross.
In the past few days,
I began perceiving
a form of static energy.

"I had to let my body be the vessel and lead me through the darkness"

I saw my hands
while blind.
I discovered a key.
Now looking back
cocooning seemed to have played
a big part in this process.
Sometimes I wish
to go back
to this place
for I seemed to be more happy then
than now
for some reason.
Perhaps resetting
in full swing
allowed me to cross the bridge.
Although I was alone
I never felt lonely.
The visitors of Istanbul
lent me such kindness.
Their smells,
their whispers,
their kind footsteps,
their energy of genuine respect.
I fell in love with this city,
I felt
nostalgic
every second
after I left.
Throughout
I carved words
into the bricks.
My last
before
I destroyed it:
Don't
Look
Back.

Carlos Martiel, Monumento I, 2020, El Museo del Barrio, New York, USA. Photograph by Walter Wlodarczyk carlosmartiel.net, @martielcarlos

"Through performance I've modified my body and mindset, just like a sculptor transforms a piece of marble or wood"

Performance artist Carlos Martiel uses his body to address the lived experience of the Black male body. Born in Cuba, where he graduated from the San Alejandro National Academy of Fine Arts, he now splits his time between New York and Havana. Here, he chose to have the following interview, first published in Hypermedia magazine, translated into English. His interviewer is the Cuban-American artist, writer and curator Coco Fusco, who has also used her body to confront racial representation and colonial legacies. Together, the artists talk about the origins of Martiel's family, his interest in blood as an expressive material, and his sculptural focus in performance.

Carlos Martiel

Carlos Martiel has created some of the most striking performances ever made by a Cuban artist. Over the past 15 years, he has transformed his body into a symbol of subjection, survival and collective resistance, with memorable renditions of the stories and experiences of those who have been marginalised and displaced.

I became acquainted with Martiel's work through my dear friend and colleague [Cuban artist] Sandra Ceballos. Its sheer, raw imagery impressed me: his bleeding arms extended, his head under a soldier's boot, his eyelids covered in excrement. It looked as if he were slashing himself, scarring and submitting his flesh to distress without a second thought.

Back when I was writing a book on performance art and its links to Cuba's political arena, I knew I had to include a discussion about Prodigal Son, the performance in which Martiel pierces his own chest with his father's revolutionary medals in an unforgettable commentary on the price paid by those who volunteered for the Cuban Revolution.

Since his departure from Cuba in 2012, Martiel has extended his historical references to address his experiences in Latin America, Europe and the United States. He has reappropriated the masochistic tendencies of body art in the 1970s and repurposed those gestures as political allegories of the social condition of Black bodies throughout the African diaspora, evoking stories of slavery, subjugation and de-territorialisation.

Coco Fusco
Your ancestors were Jamaicans and Haitians who arrived in Cuba as farm workers. How does your background influence your artistic practice?

Carlos Martiel
I come from the offspring of Jamaican and Haitian immigrants who settled in Banes, in the province of Holguín, in the mid-1920s, to try to get by. As a kid, my grandmother used to tell me, at bedtime, the experiences of her early childhood and all the hardships and upheavals that her parents had to go through in order to raise nine children, before they could move to Havana. I really enjoyed collecting all those memories from her. Despite the challenges present in her stories, she always shared them with a sense of pride.

In time, as I matured, my Haitian and Jamaican roots became a fundamental pillar in my life, so much so that I applied for Jamaican citizenship four years ago.

Evidently, being an artist, and doing work focusing on the body, identity and immigration, I have come to make different works relating to who I am, because art is a process of individual affirmation, as well as of ancestral acknowledgment. In recent years I've made pieces like Legado [2015], Basamento [2016] and Muerte al olvido [2019], all of which explore my search for an identity, the recovering of my family history and the memory of all the bodies that are a part of me.

CF How did you come to leave Cuba and find a base in another country to develop your artistic work?

CM I made the decision to leave Cuba when beginning my second year at ISA [Instituto Superior de las Artes, Havana]. At the time I wanted to make the most of my possibilities in life, I wanted to travel through Latin America, and I yearned for a world that the Cuban context kept dismissing for me, due to its restrictive reality. I felt repressed in my own country. Deep down, I knew I was an artist. The main element of my work was my body and experience, so I didn't overthink what could happen to my work outside Cuba, because I felt that I was my own work material.

CF Your trajectory could be divided into stages – your years in Cuba, your departure and time in Ecuador, and your migration to the United States. What were the most important experiences you had in each one of these stages?

CM The most relevant part of the first phase of my work in Cuba was the discovery of my body as a tool of work, which led me to the use of blood. When I began studying at the academy I made a series of drawings with different media – coal, beeswax,

Carlos Martiel. Fundamento (Basis), 2020. New York. USA. Photograph by Jorge Sanchez

iron oxide diluted in vinegar and my own blood. Of all the materials I used, blood was the most constant one and the one that became, little by little, a prominent feature in my drawings.

For the blood drawings, I had to go to clinics and ask the nurses on duty if they could do it for me as a favour. Which in time became a hindrance, because they only drew very little blood or refused to do it altogether, since some of them questioned the use I intended for it. The time came when I wanted to make a specific type of work and couldn't, because I was lacking the material that I was conceptually interested in using. Still, given the issues that I was drawn to, that frustration made me understand that the way to keep working was my body, and that's how I decided to begin to do performances and make myself the object and subject of my own practice.

Quito and Buenos Aires were a trial for me. If something is to be said about that period in my work, it is my capacity for resilience when exploring the unknown, remaining faithful to the path I had drawn with my body.

When I arrived in Ecuador I had already made some works, but my departure from Cuba took me out of my comfort zone. I was completely destabilised when I faced the challenge of knowing what to do in order to keep existing as an artist without diluting myself. During that time I realised that the most important thing in my work was context, and that confronting what I didn't know could provide a lot of material for it.

That is when Cuba became a thing of the past for me and I began to make a series of pieces in which my experience as a migrant became the centre of my creative focus. Coming to the United States was another moment of destabilisation in my work, but I came to terms with it because I had already experienced life in other countries.

What I can say about the past few years of work is that I now feel the extent of the responsibility it has acquired when meeting the demands of a specific context, and the commitment that I feel to my voice as a Caribbean immigrant, a Black person and a homosexual.

CF   You have said that if you weren't a performance artist, you would be a sculptor. What does performance offer you as a medium? Why focus your energy on it in particular?

CM   I see the performance artist as a sort of *behique*, a pagan saint – and I don't mean those that stand on altars – a scapegoat, an intellectual terrorist. When art is born out of the need to express the inner conflicts of human beings, it's able to connect with whomever, regardless of your birthplace, your skin colour or your gender. The ritualisation of the body through art creates empathy.

In my experience, performance has been the medium to manifest my needs and rights, as well as those of others – the universe of the oppressed is all too large. Working with and from my body has been a process of individual empowerment.

The path of the body has not been easy for me, because as an artist one feels the world in a different way. A creator lives tormented by meaning and sometimes this overflows – you don't know what to do with everything you know you have and must express in some way. Coming to the conclusion of making performance art and working with my body was a cumulative process, which emerged from my non-conformance with different types of realities that I came across. I was a teenager with many questions regarding what it means to be Black in Cuba. I was ashamed of my sexual orientation and felt suffocated by the social and political circumstances of my country and my inability to change them. Performance was my salvation, my act of self-liberation and resistance, and it still is to this day.

CF   Your main medium is your body as an object. You don't use your voice, and in most of your pieces you barely move. You invite us to behold your body being manipulated in various ways – perforated, sewn up, bloody, buried, restrained. Can you elaborate on the bodily metaphors that are predominant in your work?

CM   That's why I said once that had I not become a performance artist, I would have been a sculptor. Through performance I've modified my body and mindset, just like a sculptor transforms a piece of marble or wood.

My work is born out of an individual dimension, often auto-biographical, that acquires a social dimension during the creative process. It's a permanent exercise of corporeal sincerity.

In performance, one can say a lot with no words or gestures, because the body's possibilities are endless and bodies don't require speech to understand each other. The bodily metaphors I make and use to produce sense and share knowledge are just the way in which my mind processes my reality and that of other bodies which I feel deeply connected and attached to.

CF   How do you approach your vision and experience of Blackness in Cuba, and how different is it from what you went through abroad?

CM   From birth to death, being a Black body is and will be a permanent struggle, not out of choice, but because racism is the foundation of most contemporary societies and violence against Black bodies is a global phenomenon.

After leaving Cuba I had the opportunity to live in three countries – Ecuador, Argentina and the United States. Despite having to, more often than not, confront racist people to extents I would never have imagined before, the racist experiences I suffered in Cuba had the most impact on me, maybe because they happened while I was growing up and getting an education.

I remember that there was a moment in my teens when I wouldn't walk out on my own around Old Havana or El Vedado, because I used to get stopped by policemen at every corner. As a child, I also recall that most of the jokes made by my friends aimed to ridicule and humiliate Black characters. I remember that the word "negro" was used against me as an insult countless times, as if being Black were a criminal offence or something to be ashamed of. "*Negro y maricón, lo último*" – a popular saying in Cuba that could translate as, "Black and a faggot, that's rock bottom."

I look back at all of this now, because I've had to revalue my body, embrace the jewel of my Blackness and come to understand that there isn't a single problem with my being Black. But in my childhood and teenage years I didn't have the tools I have now to defend myself.

Living in the United States and experiencing first-hand the harsh reality of racial inequality, an immeasurable anger builds up in you. I'm not telling you anything you don't know or haven't experienced yourself. Racism has destroyed too many lives here, both literally and figuratively. Racism here is a daily experience because people allow themselves to be racist without thinking for a second about what is wrong in their behaviour.

If I have learnt anything in the United States, it's that my rights and my life are worthy, and that any effort I might make to fight racism will fall short. There is no such thing as second-class lives, therefore we can't keep accepting our bodies vulnerabilised, fragilised or assassinated.

Translated by Adrian de Banville

Brazilian artist Paula Garcia explores ideas of resistance in her work, building her creative process through rupture, denial and uncertainty. In the following essay she discusses Noise Body, a performance during which she is locked into a suit of magnetised armour and covered in heavy metal objects, before a group of collaborators throw handfuls of large nails at her. The jagged sound of metal colliding with her armour ricochets around the gallery space until Garcia can no longer stand under the weight of material.

In her subsequent work, Crumbling Body, the artist again harnessed magnetic forces, which act for her as an analogy of the invisible forces – social, political, psychological – that control us, as well as a way of exploring both the limits and the strengths of the human body. Garcia also works as an independent curator and a project curator at Marina Abramović Institute.

"The result was an image of the system and of the body fettered, buried ... At the same time, I emerged much stronger"

Paula Garcia

Paula Garcia, Crumbling Body, 2015. Photograph by Erika Mayumi. paulagarcia.net, @paula_garcia

Noise Body

In performance art, the confrontation is direct, especially between you and your limits, and that is what I wanted to work with. I gradually realised with this practice how the work modifies me, even more so because most of the experiences consist of placing my body in situations of discomfort or contradiction. When I wear the armour in Noise Body, there is no way of knowing what will happen. I had not managed to wear it for the duration of any of the rehearsals before I performed for six hours for the first time in 2014, for the exhibition The Artist Is an Explorer, co-curated by Marina Abramović at the Beyeler Foundation in Switzerland. The suit of armour had to be locked with a key and I felt claustrophobic in all preparatory attempts. But during the performance, I managed.

The experiences of the Noise Body series really modified me. Crumbling Body, the work I did during the exhibition Terra Comunal, in 2015 in São Paulo, was extremely challenging. The action of gathering scrap metal with magnets confronts the sensations of heaviness and lightness. The walls and ceiling were impregnated with magnetic force; as the parts and debris spread, a kind of inverted burial space happens. For two months, six days a week, eight hours a day, I worked in this room throwing iron waste, up to 30 kilograms, at the magnetised walls and ceiling. After filling the walls and ceiling, the pieces were removed and placed in the centre of the room and thrown on the walls and ceiling again.

" ... in a society where the non-white, female, queer and trans body is constantly at risk, there is something eerily protective about seeing Garcia's body covered with layers of metal" – Rui Chaves, Making It Heard: A History of Brazilian Sound Art

I am aware that if I had not attended Marina's Cleaning the House workshop shortly before the beginning of the exhibition, I might not have been able to experience things as I did during Terra Comunal with such commitment. Every day I used elements and practices we exercised in the workshop. For me, the mental confrontation is much more challenging than the physical confrontation. More than throwing metal parts against the wall, I am throwing energy.

On the first day of the performance, I used a lot of force and I hurt myself. I was excited with all the energy. The following day, Marina called to tell me she wanted me alive. This talk of hers, as an artist and friend, was so important. She spoke about my presence in the space, saying that even if I slept there three days in a row, it would still be intense. Over the following days, I started incorporating the silences and pauses as part of the process. I now realise that I lived through a period in that box in which there was a profound truth, with no deception. There was fury, obsession, fatigue, and there was an exchange of potent energy – "Everything that you, as

an artist, transmitted in that space, people received back," Marina said. Those teachings will undoubtedly be part of my legacy in the future.

"A tension sets in between a body that is brittle and malleable, and metal, which is firm and rigid. And the sound arising from it comes from a mechanical, material connection between these metallic objects as they fall to the ground. Thus, the aural dimension in her works does not depend on the audibility of sounds. Sound hovers over the performances and imposes itself as a powerful presence" – Lilian Campesato, Making It Heard: A History of Brazilian Sound Art

The concept of Noise Body represents a body that is defined by a sum of three factors: precariousness, uncertainty and risk. The magnets are elements of my work that serve to discuss the concept of forces. Not only of the invisible subjective kind, but also of the more evident social forces that work to consolidate a system of power that ends up shaping things like bodies, feelings, subjectivities and truths. In these performances I try to showcase bodies in disassembly, crumbling. Ultimately, what I propose in my actions is a performative use of my body as a platform where different forms of conflict are carved out. At the end of the performance, when I would attract the iron pieces to my body, the result was an image of the system and of the body fettered, buried, like a body with no organs. At the same time, I emerged much stronger.

"We'll defend ourselves with truths ancestral strengths changing moons"

Regina José Galindo, El dolor en un pañuelo, Guatemala, 1999. Photograph by Marvin Olivares reginajosegalindo.com, @galindoreginajose

Born and raised in Guatemala, Regina José Galindo has been writing poetry since she was a teenager, and later used many of her texts as the foundations of her early performances. With the country's context as a starting point – in particular the bloody history of Guatemala's 36-year civil war – she explores the ethical implications of social violence and injustices related to gender and racial discrimination. Galindo uses her body to transform her outrage into powerful public acts, such as the performance ¿Quién puede borrar las huellas? (2003), in which she walked barefoot through the streets of Guatemala City, repeatedly dipping her feet in a bowl of human blood to protest the presidential candidacy of former military dictator Efraín Ríos Montt. Here she chooses a small selection of her poems for Document. As carefully constructed as her performances, they are works that question whose voices and stories get to be heard and how to speak of violence.

Regina José Galindo

we will defend

We'll defend ourselves
with our fists
our nails
our teeth
our vocal cords
our vaginas
our uteruses
our ovaries.

We'll defend ourselves with truths
ancestral strengths
changing moons.

We'll defend ourselves with poems
weavings
drawings
voice.

We'll defend ourselves, each
and every one of us
because together we're one
and without even one of us
we won't be all of us.

We'll defend ourselves, all of us
before we all fall
and not a single one of us
remains.

Vamos a defendernos entre todas
y cada una
porque todas somos una
y sin una
no somos todas.

Vamos a defendernos entre todas
antes de que todas caigan
y de nosotras
no quede ninguna.

Regina José Galindo, La Intención, La Focara, Italy, 2015.
Photograph by Ana María Lamastra

Regina José Galindo. ¿Quién puede borrar las huellas? Guatemala, 2003. Photograph by José Osorio

For every cornfield you
        burn
we'll plant a hundred seeds

For every foetus you kill
we'll raise a hundred
        children

For every woman you rape
we'll come a hundred times

For every man you torture
we'll embrace a hundred
        joys

For every death you deny
we'll weave a hundred
        truths

For every gun you grip
we'll make a hundred
        drawings

For every bullet lost
a hundred poems

For every bullet found
a hundred songs.

They follow me as I walk
and no one silences me.

They stop me in my tracks
and no one silences me.

They're my shadow
and no one silences me.

They kick at my dignity
and no one silences me.

They tear my name to shreds
and no one silences me.

They make up lies
and no one silences me.

They put me in jail
and no one silences me.

They accuse me of everything
and no one silences me.

They explode me with shouts
and no one silences me.

They insult my blood
and no one silences me.

They throw me in a pit
and no one silences me.

They steal my light
and no one silences me.

They shatter my teeth
and no one silences me.

They pull out my molars
and no one silences me.

They gag my mouth
and no one silences me.

They cut out my tongue
and no one silences me.

They burn my face
and no one silences me.

They tie my hands
and no one silences me.

They slice at my feet
and no one silences me.

They dig out my eyes
and no one silences me.

They yank out my fingernails
and no one silences me.

They brand my skin
and no one silences me.

They spread my legs
and no one silences me.

They come inside me
and no one silences me.

Blood seeps from my veins
and no one silences me.

The punches hurt
and no one silences me.

They crush my intestines
and no one silences me.

They stab me through the heart
and no one silences me.

I go dry with thirst
and no one silences me.

My dreams kill me
and no one silences me.

They kill me with hunger
and no one silences me.

They kill my life
and no one silences me.

They try to erase me
and no one silences me.

The voice
– my voice –
comes from somewhere else
from deeper within.

They
haven't understood it.

The Berlin-based artist Yiannis Pappas was born on the island of Patmos, Greece, famous for being the site where the Bible's apocalyptic Book of Revelation was written, and where a Unesco-listed monastery has stood since 1088. It's a connection with religion and nature, the sacred and holy, that has surfaced in his work – his master's thesis was based around five weeks he spent in a monastery on Mount Athos in 2013; his piece Holy Vestments (2009) took the form of a robe made of golden ping-pong balls that was inspired by a Byzantine emperor. Working with video, photography, performance and installation, Pappas creates work that is underscored by a critical interest in space – as sites of physical and symbolic enactment – exploring how different places are sustained collectively and individually throughout history. Here the artist discusses Telephus, a 175-hour performance that took place at the Bangkok Art Biennale, in which he methodically wrapped parts of his body in plaster, eventually building a mountain of casts into a monumental sculpture.

"In long-durational performance, the audience is also the body of evidence: it is part of the legacy while a collective participatory memory is created"

This page, opposite and following spread: Yiannis Pappas, Telephus, 2018, Bangkok Art Biennale: Beyond Bliss, for the live exhibition A Possible Island? curated by Marina Abramović Institute at Bangkok Art and Culture Centre. Photograph by BACC/Jukkrith yiannispappas.com @pappas.yiannis

Yiannis Pappas

Telephus

A Possible Island?
Bangkok Art Biennale, Bangkok Art
and Culture Centre
18 October – 11 November 2018

The body can be used as a powerful tool. I use it to conceive sociopolitical genealogies and statements; it is the medium through which I visualise 'body politics' as it has been established in today's society. Through my practice I observe how state institutions enforce abstract power interests over the individual by way of accessing our biologies. My works are site-specific performances that seek to leave traces of temporality throughout mythological or historical events.

In the case of a performance artist, the human need for legacy could be considered the implicit knowledge that is transferred from body to body and operated beside any form of tangible material boundedness. Ultimately, the shared experience of the performance act is all that remains.

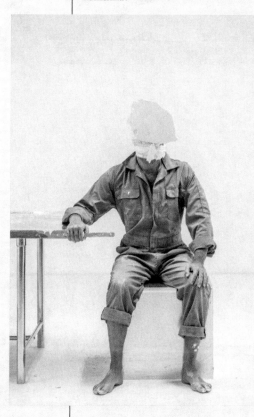

For the 175-hour performance I presented at the first Bangkok Art Biennale for A Possible Island?, the live exhibition curated by MAI, I was continuously and repeatedly wrapping different parts of my body with plaster. I ended up with a huge pile of cast parts that had been removed from my body and formed a sculpture in its own right. The act of wrapping my body parts with plaster alluded to the Greek myth of Telephus. The words Ο τρώσας και ιάσεται, an ancient Greek proverb meaning "Only he who inflicts the wound can cure it," refers to a prophecy that was given by the oracle of Apollo to Telephus about the way he should heal his wounds caused by Achilles. After the completion of the performance, the cast sculpture was donated to the Bangkok Art and Culture Centre.

A second reference of this performative work alluded to a statement made by Georgios Papadopoulos, the leader of the junta that ruled Greece from 1967 to 1974. In a statement, Papadopoulos described Greek society as a "patient" and assumed for himself the role of medical doctor. As a doctor with knowledge and authority, he would save the patient's life by restraining them on a surgical bed under anaesthesia to perform the operation. This, he suggested, was the only way to not "endanger" the life of the patient during the operation.

This statement became known as "Greece in the cast".

The medical practice of anaesthesia and the immobilisation of the patient through the cast were here presented as a necessity for Greek society to recover from its illness. Despite not knowing the Greek context, much of the audience in Thailand received the coded message, translated through the performative act and the medical references. Many people identified their own sociopolitical experiences and struggles in those of Greece.

Through these two references that informed the work – the myth of Telephus and the allusions to military regimes – I see two forms of legacy. In the first case, a material memory of the performance was donated and archived in the museum. The second case concerns an immaterial legacy, a genealogical political solidarity that was shared between me and the audience in Thailand. The paradoxical act of casting my body, of seeking to 'fix' it, to 'civilise' it, offers a critique on the ways personal asphyxia can be transformed into a collective one.

The pandemic showcases human imperfection brilliantly, as well as our inability to embrace our existential position in the one and only environment where we all belong: nature.

One of the oldest and strongest emotions of mankind is fear. Covid-19 gives us a chance to confront the concept of memento mori (remembrance of death). At the same time, it makes us think about our individual legacies. The idea of temporality through my performative body work is what I wish to remain of me. When a long-durational performance is over, my state of mind focuses on understanding through the sharing of immaterial temporal indications that affect human life, such as the shared experience with the audience in Thailand.

In long-duration performance, the audience is also the body of evidence: it is a part of the legacy while a collective participatory memory is created. Beside the traditional forms of documenting such a performance (videos, photographs and traces/objects of the action) there is the collective experience between the performer and the public – which might become a polyphonic tribute or a shared testimony to the actuality of the work.

Estileras, Calçado de Monstro, S/S 2020. Enantios Dromos and Brendy Xavier are wearing Calçado de Monstro De Rolezinho and Velociraptor by Brendy. Photograph by Pe Ferreira estileras.com.br, @estileras

Boni Gattai and Brendy Xavier are Brazil-based performance, transdisciplinary and multimedia artists working under the name Estileras. Their practice subverts traditional fashion structures, questioning the exclusivity and secrecy that permeate the market. They are interested in experimental actions, in the relationship between improvisation and material creation, and in collectivity as a tool for changing and powering an artistic network. Their performances are often supported by live videos, photographs and soundtracks, and involve creating anarchic, wearable art out of recycled garments. Here they describe Monster Shoes, a six-hour performance in which they cut, spliced and stitched discarded shoes into Frankenstein-like layered, mutated platforms, posting the creation of each new 'monster' on Instagram in real time, broadcast live through Marina Abramović Institute.

Estileras

Calçados de Monstro
(Monster Shoes)

The improvisation involved in creating an outfit for a party was the start of Estileras – the point where self-expression meets reality. The impulse of translating the excitement and anticipation of a night out revealed a pattern of deconstruction of clothing, a glimpse of a practice where the aesthetics are defined by defiance.

By finding new ways to wear old clothes, playing with already-made stitches and using our limited mastery of sewing (safety pins everywhere), fashion conventions can be twisted. We found that performance was the perfect space for sharing our process while also embracing the risk of reality, letting errors into our not-so-final works.

For Calçados de Monstro (Monster Shoes) we created a live web series of the same name where the premise was to set a time frame during which we would create things for our feet with what little we had available. It was an open performance where the results would be a surprise not only for the viewers but also for ourselves. And through livestreaming we were able to incorporate video as a part of the performance – rather than just recording an act, the act was only possible because there was a camera with us. The camera called on us to perform for it, to open our movements and ideas to the world. It was a nod to experimenting with reality as a medium. Maybe by letting art be part of life we can deglamorise fashion and access its processes.

This feeling of letting time and space limit the action to produce something that pulses with improvisation and experimentation is present in everything we do. And with it, the necessity of bringing our friends with us, bonding connections through collective bodies of work. It is obvious that almost every form of art we consume – movies, music, shows, and so on – is inherently a collective text. So why do we often spotlight only a few nodes in the network when the potential of a project is defined by the commitment of those involved? Especially with fashion, the designer is always paramount, while the rest of the team have to be satisfied with written credits at the end. From this clog in the machine, we went looking for alternatives and ways to make every part of the engine recognised as being essential. This led to Estilera Fudidamente Inserta (2019–2020, at Casa de Criadores in São Paulo), a three-part project, in collaboration with art collectives Inserto and FudidaSilk, where there was no backstage, no face unseen, no name unheard nor any link unattached. For a whole day we opened every detail to the public, followed by a runway show where the models and staff walked together down the stage.

What we have now could not have existed without the effort of those before us, and all that will be from now on will also have a mark of our presence. Connections are endless and have no boundaries, they tie the past, the present and what is coming to be with everything that is externalised and created. A ramble of nodes. If we could touch these lines that put us in contact with the world, tie them together, we might unveil a glimpse of the invisible.

From the collage of materials and the assembly of people we've created objects closer to the uncertain and difficult aspects of life. Their online history aims to shine a light on all the other lines.

"If we could touch these lines that put us in contact with the world, tie them together, we might unveil a glimpse of the invisible"

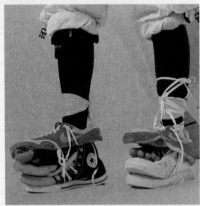

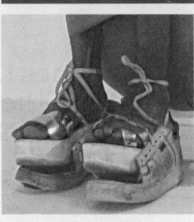

Estileras, Calçado de Monstro, S/S 2020. This page, from top: Boni is wearing Calçado de Monstro, Falaram Desleixo. Photograph by Estileras. Brendy is wearing Calçado de Monstro. Tudo de Uma Vez. Photograph by Estileras. Ray Castelo is wearing Calçado de Monstro, 100% Jesus by Ray Castelo. Photograph by Estileras. Slim Soledad is wearing Calçado de Monstro. Photograph by Brendy. Opposite: Calçado de Monstro S/S 2020. Igi Ayedun is wearing Calçado de Monstro, Meu Primeiro Saltinho by Boni. Photograph by Pe Ferreira

Turkish artist Halil Atasever grounds his practice in reflections of the human condition. Using familiar objects such as fabrics, prayer rugs or clothes, he seeks to establish a clear visual language that reveals multiple layers of meaning during his performances. Here he describes his work Slaughterhouse, a confrontation with white-collar identity and its promise to provide protection and prosperity while increasingly tying employees down. Cross-legged on the floor of a cavernous gallery space in Istanbul, Atasever quietly unpicked the seams of dozens of white shirts, laying each piece of fabric on the floor until they created a vast, imprisoning mosaic. The meditative performance was part of Akış/Flux, a collaboration between Sakıp Sabancı Museum, Akbank Sanat and Marina Abramović Institute.

This page and following spread: Halil Atasever. Slaughterhouse, 2020. Akış/Flux MAI at Sakıp Sabancı Museum Istanbul Turkey. Photograph by Canberk Ulusan. halilatasever.wordpress.com. @ataseverhalil

Halil Atasever

Slaughterhouse

Akış/Flux, Sakıp Sabancı Museum
Istanbul
17 November – 13 December 2020

Slaughterhouse was a 22-day long performance: the main act was to unstitch 52 men's white shirts with a seam ripper six hours a day in front of a dark blue wall.

It was a fascinating opportunity to perform a long-durational piece curated by MAI in Sakıp Sabancı Museum. And a tiring experience as a whole. Waiting for the driver to give me a lift to the museum, watching the streets sliding by, passing the Bosphorus Bridge and finally reaching the museum in the middle of the pandemic. Changing clothes, going to the toilet one last time and starting to unstitch. Six hours a day, the same action, over and over again. Arriving back home at about 7pm. Eating healthily with my elderly diabetic mom and watching TV.

MasterChef Turkey is on our relatively small living-room TV. The contestants on the screen are trying to cook the best surf and turf in under 50 minutes.

During the performance, cutting the shirt threads was the gateway to my deepest pitfalls. I do not know if it was supposed to be, but every day was a new therapy session in which I constantly faced off my rooted ideas of being a man, being an artist, being a son. As if it isn't hard enough to be a human, these layers all bring additional necessities, like to-do lists, phone alarms, contracts. But how many of them really work?

With a few apples left on the side table, I'm trying to forget everything I thought while unstitching the shirts.

One of the contestants is making parfait using okra. Surprisingly.

A performance itself is basically the guardian of Dionysus. Upon thousands of years of cultural history, I find it confusing to draw the line between rational and irrational. Apollo is not Apollo any more.

It took me a while to detach myself from postmodern theories and go back to the basics. I can never

embrace the uniqueness of personal thought when the world is full of people suffering from lack of access to drinking water. Whatever identity we carve out from our organic body, however we fully decorate our perceived self, it is not worthwhile unless we feed someone who is hungry.

Dad, where are you now? They are cleaning fish on the show, and I remember as clear as daylight how you loved eating sardines.

I lost him nearly three years ago and we will never eat fish together again.

It all started with him. The son of an immigrant family whose main source of income had always been fabrics, mainly men's shirts – now his son unstitching shirts to rationalise himself.

He always wanted me to be a lawyer or a manager in a multinational company and never lost his hope to see me in suits. He saw it too. I could never let the economically uncomfortable side of being an artist hunt me down. Moreover, it has been beneficial for me to work as a white-collar worker from time to time.

The battlefield is hidden somewhere in my mind. The stories and the teachings of my dad are doing their best to attack my deviant plan to be a 'well-known' and 'established' artist. There has never been a true winner of this war and there probably never will be.

My mom asks who won the previous round. The red or the blue team?

I moved to London nearly four years ago. Established my design business and have survived quite well so far. However the crucial question that appeared and struck me every day during performance hours was what to do next when I go back to London. Oh no – please don't tell me I cheated on the purity of my performance and dived deep to probe daily problems while performing such

a sacred piece. It always comes as a package. Doesn't it?

Once a week they shoot the show in a different city in Turkey.
The teams are trying to cook the best local dishes. Another city, same contest.

Married couples, mortgage rates, travel plans, all these things I admire in some ways, and I am disturbed by knowing that they will probably never cross my ongoing path. None of the rational plans of modern life build a narrative upon touching 'another'.

Trying to walk the thin line of self-centred, self-dependent stories of ours and the commonalities of these stories with others. The others. Something we learn during our childhood. As we are detached from our mothers, our being is totally out and separate from another being. Is it? If we cannot construct the outlines of our body blending with another entity, why do we even work so relentlessly to leave something behind? The trigger points, all we can sew with our bare hands.

One of the contestants cuts her hand with a meat knife.

The world is full of rational ideas and logical explanations. Becoming more and more self-centred. The encapsulating presence of science and technology gave us cellphones, hospitals, spaces. But the buildings collapse, organic stuff rots, icebergs melt – more than ever now. Temporariness in its finest form.

I care about my irrationality. Bending the rational with irrational actions. Trying to form a new essence. Attributing new meanings to the objects. Defining new thought realms. Creating trigger points. Believing the capability of leaving a mark on the receiver's mind.

It has been a 22-day transformative journey.

And still I have not tasted surf and turf.

"Every day was a new therapy session in which I constantly faced off my rooted ideas of being a man, being an artist, being a son. As if it isn't hard enough to be a human"

Académie des Beaux-Arts, Paris, 1995.

"There is a vitality, a life force, a quickening that is translated through you into action, and there is only one of you in all time. This expression is unique, and if you block it, it will never exist through any other medium, and be lost. The world will not have it. It is not your business to determine how good it is, not how it compares with other expression. It is your business to keep it yours clearly and directly, to keep the channel open. You do not even have to believe in yourself or your work. You have to keep open and aware directly to the urges that motivate you. Keep the channel open. No artist is pleased. There is no satisfaction whatever at any time. There is only a queer, divine dissatisfaction, a blessed unrest that keeps us marching and makes us more alive than the others" – Martha Graham

Edited by HANNAH LACK

STEFAN
COOKE

Isamu Noguchi

Photography KANGHEE KIM
Words KATIE KITAMURA

The multifarious work of Isamu Noguchi has travelled the globe,
redefining the boundaries of sculpture both during his lifetime
and beyond. In celebration of his creativity and to coincide with a
new retrospective at London's Barbican, the acclaimed New York-based
novelist Katie Kitamura conjures a dozen illuminating fragments
inspired by the visionary Japanese-American artist's life and work.
Her writing is presented alongside photography capturing fresh
perspectives of the artist's works housed at the Noguchi Museum in
Queens, New York, which is dedicated to preserving his legacy.

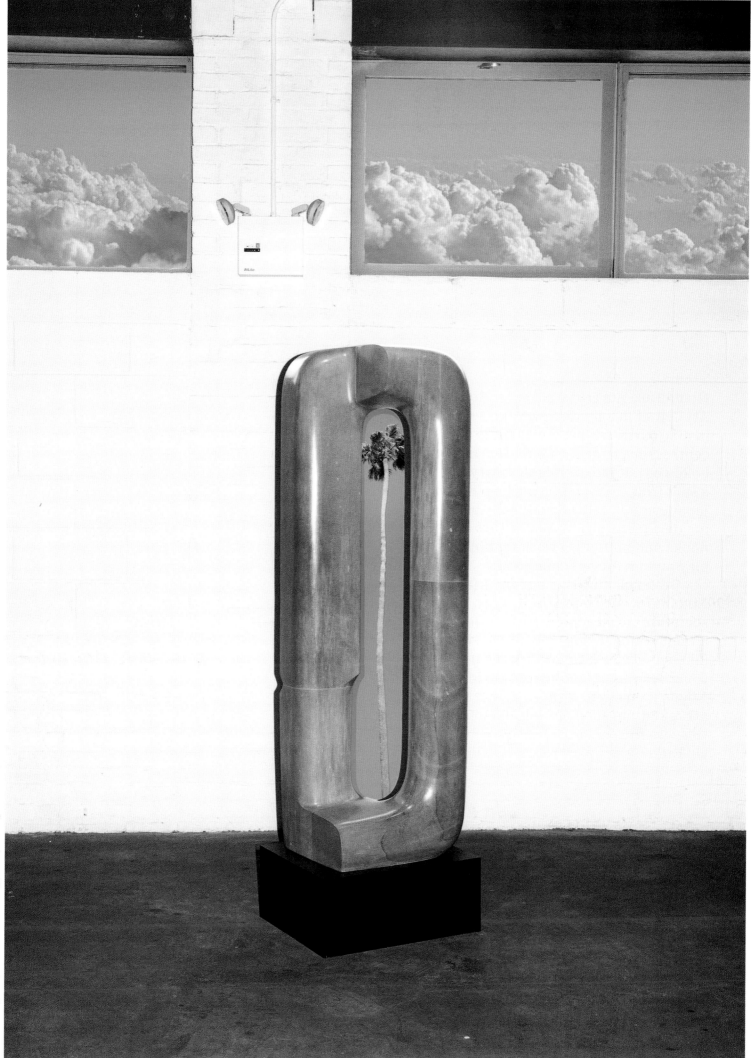

Isamu Noguchi, In Silence Walking, 1970, Bardiglio marble

1

Momo Taro sits atop a hill at the Storm King Art Center in upstate New York. A sculpture in nine parts, it is set low to the ground and centres on a large split boulder. One side is hollowed out into a sizeable cavity, evoking a split fruit. The sculpture is inspired by the Japanese folk tale about a baby boy found inside a giant peach. Momo Taro contains nooks and hollows, a work that invites the play and privacy of childhood.

Several months before his death, Noguchi went to Storm King to visit his sculpture. As he approached the hill, he saw a small child playing on it. She asked him to join her within the cavity of the peach and together they disappeared inside. When Noguchi emerged a short time later, tears streaked his face. Of all his sculptures, this was the one he described as "made for children".

Isamu Noguchi, The Whole, 1984, granite

Isamu Noguchi, Jack in the Box, 1984, hot-dipped galvanised steel

2

A scene from a childhood far from the idyll of Momo Taro. It is 1918, at the crowded port in Yokohama. The boy is 13 and known as Isamu Gilmour. His white American mother is there to see him off on the Amerika-maru, bound for Seattle. From there he will travel further inland, to a boarding school in Indiana. He is armed with a newly acquired American passport and is understandably anxious. The trip is the first of many kinds of exile.

Just as he is about to board, his Japanese father appears. The boy has not seen him in five years, and yet the father insists that he remain in Japan. The parents argue, until the boy makes his way up the gangway and boards the Amerika-maru. The first sundering of many. At times, it can seem as if both the life and the work are engaged in stitching those two parts together again, America and Japan. But that is an oversimplification.

3

He arrives in the United States in 1918 – the year of the flu pandemic and the final year of the first world war. After crossing on the Amerika-maru and a three-day train journey, he reaches Indiana. A process of assimilation ensues. A series of adjustments. He is soon entrenched in the culture of his progressive boarding school, struck by the open landscape of the Midwest. His teachers note his artistic aptitude, in particular his wood carving, a skill learnt in Japan.

Still, he is isolated. His mother is far away and communication is further hampered by the convulsions of war. In the autumn of 1918, the school suddenly closes and is converted into a military training camp. He remains there, unsupervised, surrounded by soldiers. Later, flu sweeps through the camp and he falls seriously ill.

He is eventually retrieved by a school administrator, who enrols him in a public school where he is racially bullied. Later still, he attends a high school where he goes by the name Sam Gilmour. War, abandonment, illness, bullying. However, the contacts he makes in Indiana stand him in good stead, and on the advice of a mentor there, he applies to Columbia University and is soon eastward bound.

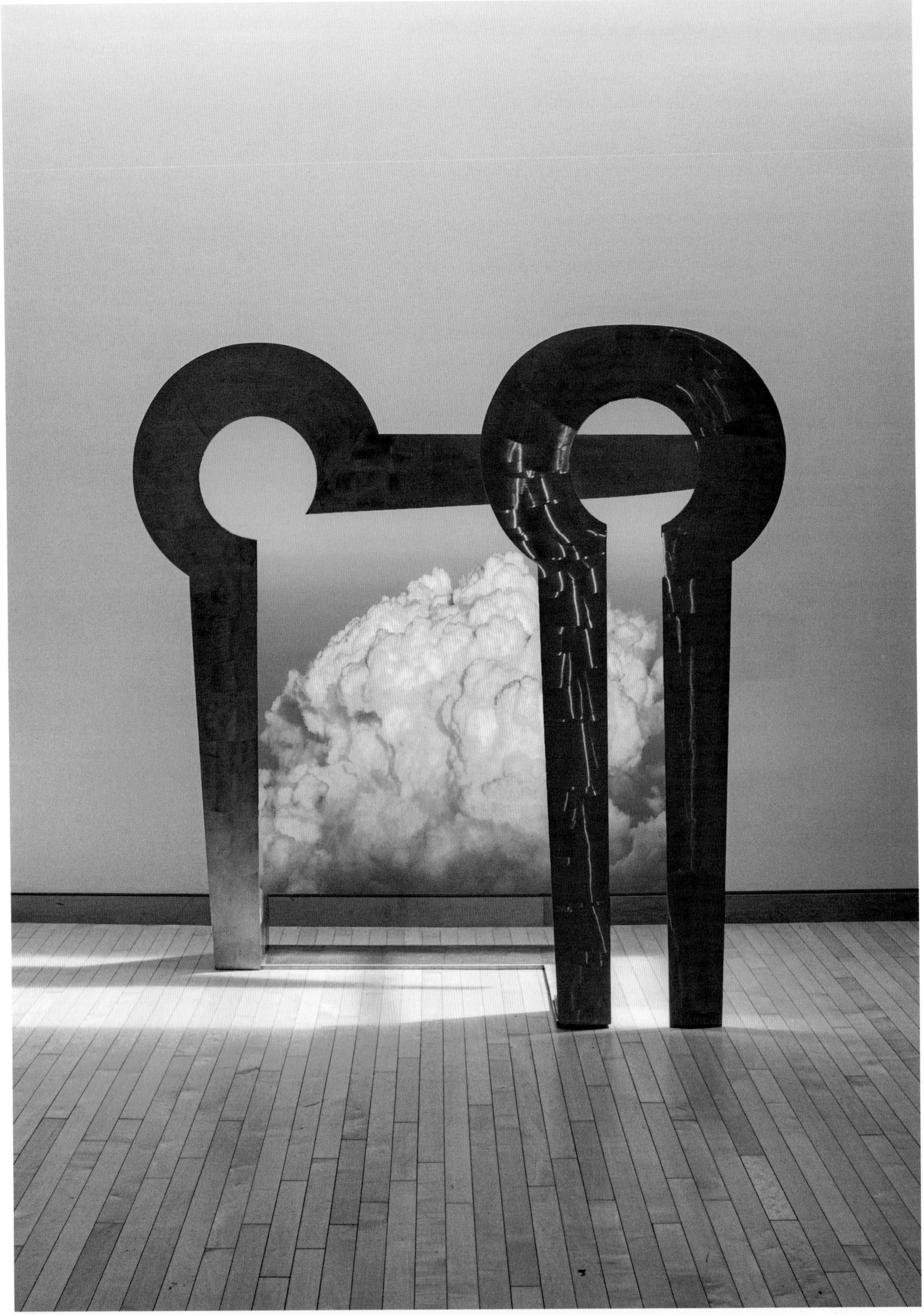

Isamu Noguchi, Sentinel, 1973, stainless steel

4

The rapidity of his ascent through New York is startling. He is 19 when he is given his first solo exhibition, and his work is exhibited in Paris and at the Grand Prix de Rome in New York. Perhaps most significantly, he takes his father's name and becomes Isamu Noguchi. No longer Sam Gilmour, or even Isamu Gilmour. The sculpture Noguchi produces during this time is perfectly executed and perfectly conventional, classical busts and nude plasters. But he is barely into his twenties when he abandons this style and travels to Paris on a Guggenheim Foundation fellowship. He quickly obtains an introduction to Constantin Brâncuși and then a position as his studio assistant. Later, Noguchi would describe the studio as "a laboratory for distilling basic shapes", and in that laboratory he begins to assemble the foundation of his aesthetic preoccupations – the simplicity of modernist forms, a deep reverence for materials.

5

An inexhaustive list of friends and collaborators: Alfred Stieglitz, Marcel Duchamp, Constantin Brâncuși, Martha Graham, Frida Kahlo, Buckminster Fuller, Merce Cunningham, Marcel Breuer, Frank Lloyd Wright, Man Ray, Ginger Rogers, George Gershwin, Arshile Gorky, Richard Neutra, Robert Motherwell, Anaïs Nin, Alexander Calder, George Balanchine, Igor Stravinsky, Akira Kurosawa, Toshiro Mifune.

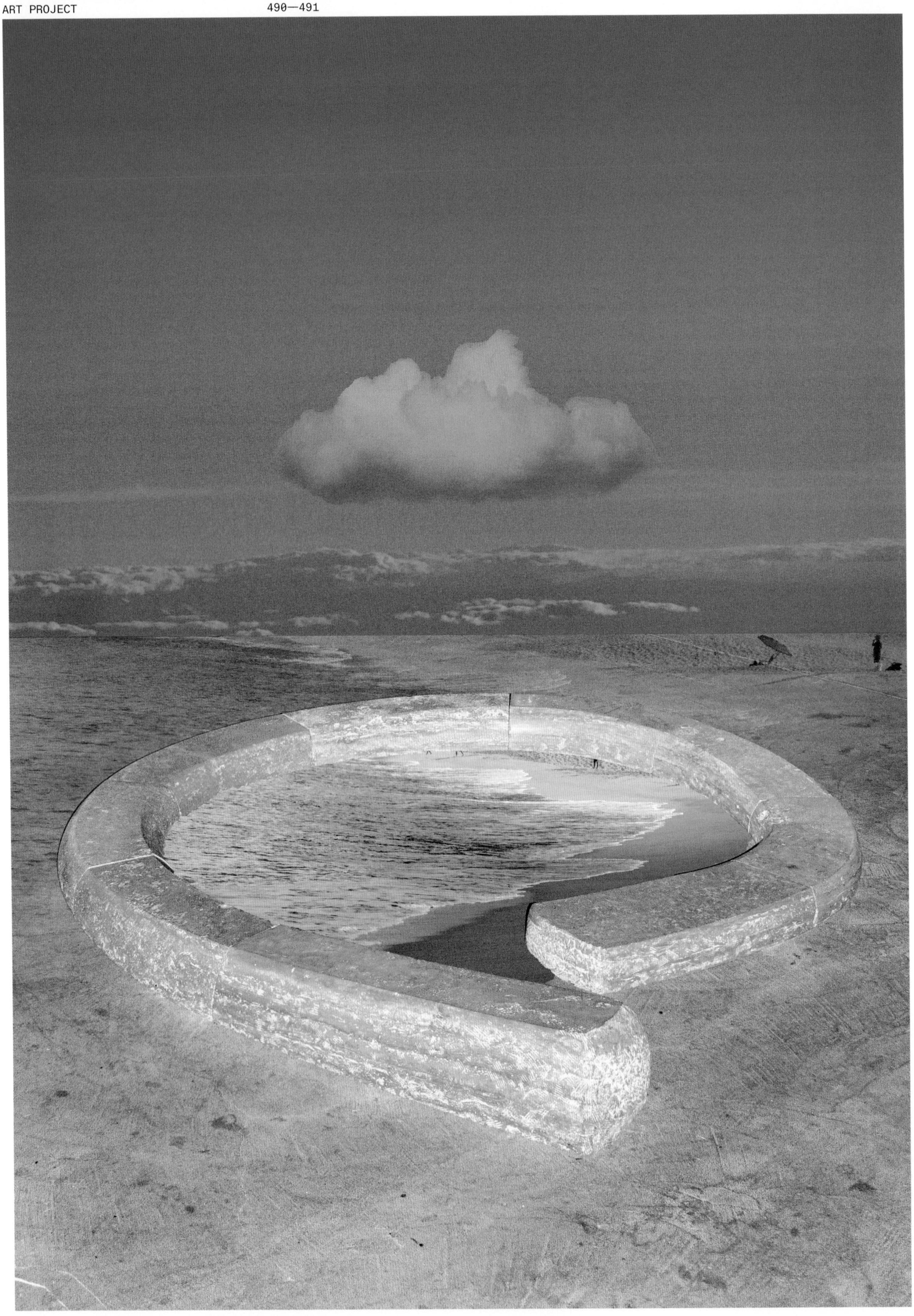

Isamu Noguchi, Magic Ring, 1970, Persian travertine

6

In 1931, Noguchi spends nearly nine months in Japan, immersing himself in its art and culture. But the trip is also marked by a series of uneasy encounters with his father. Those meetings are emotionally distressing, not least because of his father's increasingly nationalistic politics. Japan's swelling militarism bewilders and repulses Noguchi, and he leaves just as Japan invades Manchuria, returning to New York both troubled and relieved.

Just over a decade later, Roosevelt signs Executive Order 9066, and the United States begins interning Japanese citizens and immigrants. Noguchi flees the west coast, only to return and, in a gesture at once bold and deluded, enters the internment camp in Poston, Arizona. He remains there for six months. He enters with the hope of making the camp a model community with parks and playgrounds and craft programmes for the prisoners. But as the weeks pass, it becomes clear there are neither the funds nor the will to enact any of these projects.

From this dusty incarceration, Noguchi writes I Become a Nisei, a short and troubling text in which he makes a puzzling plea for assimilation, the conversion of Japanese Americans into "an eager army for democracy". Even more confounding is his delusion about internment, which he describes as an "opportunity ... it is planned to build here a community, dedicated in democracy and to the proposition that the spirit of freedom may be nurtured and grow even in confinement". There's an ugly convolution to that sentence, a tortured logic. I find myself trying to understand who Noguchi was writing for. Was it an imagined public? Was it only himself? How afraid was he, how wracked by the precariousness of his incarceration, to cling to such a naive delusion?

7

From Poston he writes a letter to Man Ray:

"Dear Man ... Here time has stopped and nothing is of any consequence, nothing of any value, neither our time or our skill. Our sphere of effective activity is cut to a minimum. Our preoccupations are the intense heat, the afternoon dust storms ...

O! For the sea!
" 	" an orange

8

In part because of his furniture and lighting, Noguchi's sculptural forms travel wide and far. The Akari light sculptures, the Noguchi coffee table, disseminate through homes around the world, in the pages of magazines and catalogues and internet browsers, in both licensed and unlicensed reproductions. Those pieces have been cannibalised by the culture and sometimes regurgitated in distorted form.

Strangest of all was the unveiling of Floor Frame in the White House Rose Garden in 2020. The ceremony was performed by the first lady married to an American president who had previously refused to condemn the internment of Japanese Americans, saying only that "war is tough" and, "I would have had to be there at the time to give you a proper answer." The first lady wore a skirt with a pattern that matched the jagged form and breaks of the sculpture; in this way, the most vulgar of administrations ushered the sublime restraint of Noguchi's sculpture into the White House.

Still, as the director of the Noguchi Museum told the New York Times, "The key for us is that this will be on display in perpetuity at the White House. Administrations come and go, but artwork remains."

Isamu Noguchi, To Bring to Life, 1979, basalt

Isamu Noguchi, Akari Light Sculpture, c1956, paper, bamboo and metal

9

The Noguchi Museum, much like Donald Judd's Chinati Foundation, was conceived by Noguchi as the ideal context for viewing his work. But unlike the cavernous spaces at Chinati, the Noguchi Museum is intimate and human-scaled. When I arrive, I am directed into the garden, populated by a handful of masked visitors. Almost immediately, I experience the fluidity of Noguchi's space – the way his sculptures, their installation, the disposition of the space all invite movement.

I circle the work, stepping forward and back and to the side. I feel how much I am embodying perspective, a specific point of view. Often when I look at a piece of art, it feels like an encounter with another mind, like contemplating some consciousness and context that is distinct from my own. But looking at Noguchi's work is a deeply internal experience that returns me to myself. The object that I am looking at no longer seems fixed or absolute, but instead vibrates with possibility.

10

When I was a teenager, my father suddenly announced that he had accepted a position at a Japanese university. He commuted between California and Kyoto for several years, living in a small, two-bedroom apartment in an anonymous high-rise building. Then, when my parents decided to return to Japan in a more permanent way, they purchased a *machiya* in the old weaving district of Kyoto. The house, unusually large by Japanese standards, had a mirrored dance studio on the ground floor and was rumoured to have belonged to a yakuza.

My parents meticulously restored the *machiya*, installing fresh tatami and *shoji* and restoring the *tori-niwa* and the *engawa*. In the end, they created a living space that was, as their neighbours noted, strenuously Japanese. But after two long decades in the United States, this was what coming home looked like. A distillation of sorts, or perhaps an incantation.

Following his marriage to singer and actor Yoshiko Yamaguchi in 1951, Noguchi moves to Kita-Kamakura, living in a traditional Japanese farmhouse that is more than 200 years old. A brief period of marital peace and creative productivity ensues, with Noguchi creating both ceramic and Akari sculpture. Eventually, though, Yamaguchi begins to find Noguchi's rigorous aesthetic restrictive. Everything "had to be in accord with the tone of the house ... he did not tolerate anything that did not match with his aesthetic". The couple separate not long afterwards.

11

In the final two decades of his life, the commissions and solo exhibitions that eluded him for years arrive in a cascade. There is a retrospective at the Whitney Museum in 1968 – his first in the United States – and a slew of large-scale commissions follows. These include the monumental Black Sun in Seattle, the fountains for the Expo 70 in Osaka, the Horace E Dodge Fountain and Philip A Hart Plaza in Detroit, the sculpture garden at the Houston Museum of Fine Arts, the sublime California Scenario garden in Costa Mesa, the Bolt of Lightning ... A Memorial to Ben Franklin in Philadelphia, the Challenger Memorial in Miami, culminating in the US Pavilion at the 1986 Venice Biennale. He is, by this point, widely considered one of the 20th century's great sculptors.

But equally there are the works that went unmade, that exist only as sketches and models and visions. Works that remain potential.

12

On the bus to school, my son sits beside me and we read our books. At a certain point, he becomes interested in my book, the recent Hayden Herrera biography of Noguchi. I show him the photographs of Noguchi as a boy and then a young man, I flip through the book and find the plaster models of Play Mountain and Contoured Playground. My son examines the soft mounds and divots, the pyramid and chutes.

My son has a tactile relationship with books, he squeezes and holds them close to his body. When there is something that he likes – a joke, a turn of phrase or an image – he folds down the corner of the page so he can revisit the precise moment that struck him or gave him pleasure. Now, as the bus rounds a corner, he leans into me. He examines the model for the unrealised Riverside Park playground, a landscape of ideal childhood, then reaches across and presses the corner of the page down, sealing the crease with his fingers.

Intimacies by Katie Kitamura, published by Jonathan Cape, is out now. Noguchi is at Barbican, London EC2, until 9 January 2022

Isamu Noguchi, The Void, 1970, Portuguese rose aurora marble

Appendix I

A BRIEF BIOGRAPHY OF ISAMU NOGUCHI
(1904-1988)

Over his six-decade career, the artist Isamu Noguchi's body of work expressed his deep humanist values and democratic belief that art should be accessible to all. He created sculptures, but also sunken gardens, costumes and props for George Balanchine, sets for Martha Graham and mass-produced goods from Bakelite baby monitors to lamps and modernist coffee tables. Born in LA in 1904, Noguchi moved to Japan with his American mother aged two, living there until he moved to school in Indiana at 13. Those formative years shaped a peripatetic artist: he would later complete an apprenticeship in Paris with Constantin Brâncuși in 1927, spend time in Mexico with Frida Kahlo, be voluntarily interned in a camp in Arizona during the second world war and go on to keep studios in both Mure, Japan, and New York. Prior to his death in 1988, Noguchi opened The Isamu Noguchi Foundation and Garden Museum in Queens, New York, in 1985 – a culmination of his commitment to art in public spaces. His profound belief in the social significance of sculpture is reflected in his public artworks, including the Unesco garden in Paris (1956–58), the History Mexico frieze in Mexico City (1936), the Expo 70 fountains in Osaka, the Playscapes playground in Atlanta (1975–76) and Sky Gate, a soaring outdoor installation in Honolulu (1976–77). Grappling with a shifting sense of identity throughout his life, Noguchi ultimately came to describe himself as a citizen of "Spaceship Earth". He bequeathed to the planet an expansive, generous legacy of works that engage with mankind in all its messy contradictions.

Appendix II

AN INDEX OF ARTWORKS REFERENCED

Momo Taro, 1977-1978
Storm King Art Center,
New Windsor, New York,
USA
Granite

Akari Light Sculptures,
1951-1988
Paper, bamboo and metal

Noguchi Coffee Table
(IN-50), 1944
Wood and glass

Floor Frame, 1962
White House Rose Garden,
Washington DC, USA
Bronze

Black Sun, 1969
Volunteer Park,
Seattle, Washington, USA
Granite

Horace E Dodge and Son
Memorial Fountain, 1981
Philip A Hart Plaza,
Detroit, Michigan, USA
Stainless steel, granite
and water

Philip A Hart Plaza,
Detroit, Michigan, USA
1971-79

Bolt of Lightning …
Memorial to Ben Franklin,
1933-84
Monument Plaza,
Philadelphia,
Pennsylvania, USA
Stainless steel

Challenger Memorial,
1985-87
Bayfront Park, Miami,
Florida, USA
Steel and paint

What Is Sculpture?
US Pavilion, Venice
Biennale, Venice,
Italy, 1986

Play Mountain
(model), 1933
Plaster

Contoured Playground
(model), 1941
Plaster

Riverside Park Playground
(model), 1963
Plaster

All artworks by Isamu
Noguchi © The Isamu
Noguchi Foundation and
Garden Museum/Artists
Rights Society

Introduction and biography by HANNAH LACK

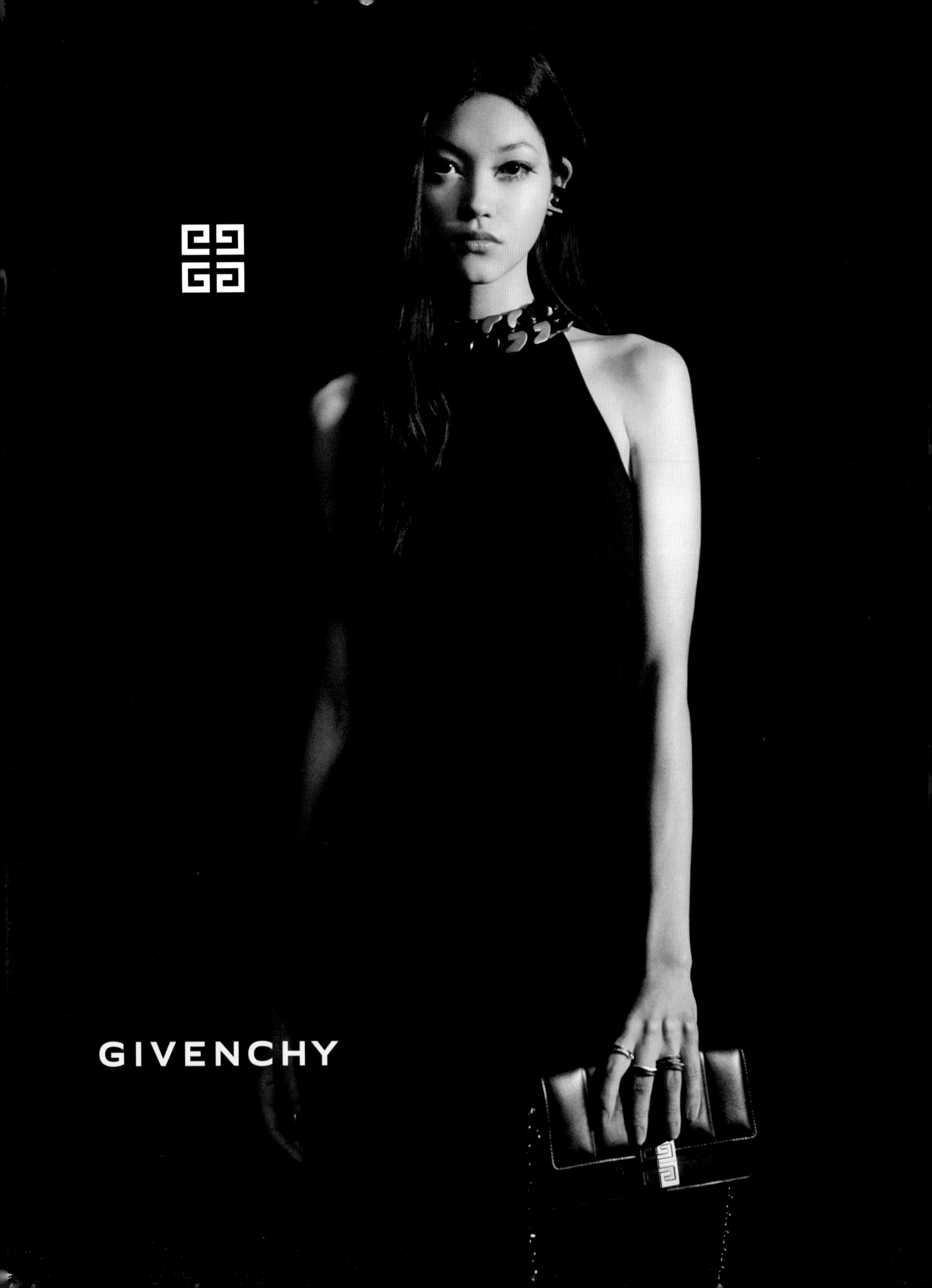
GIVENCHY

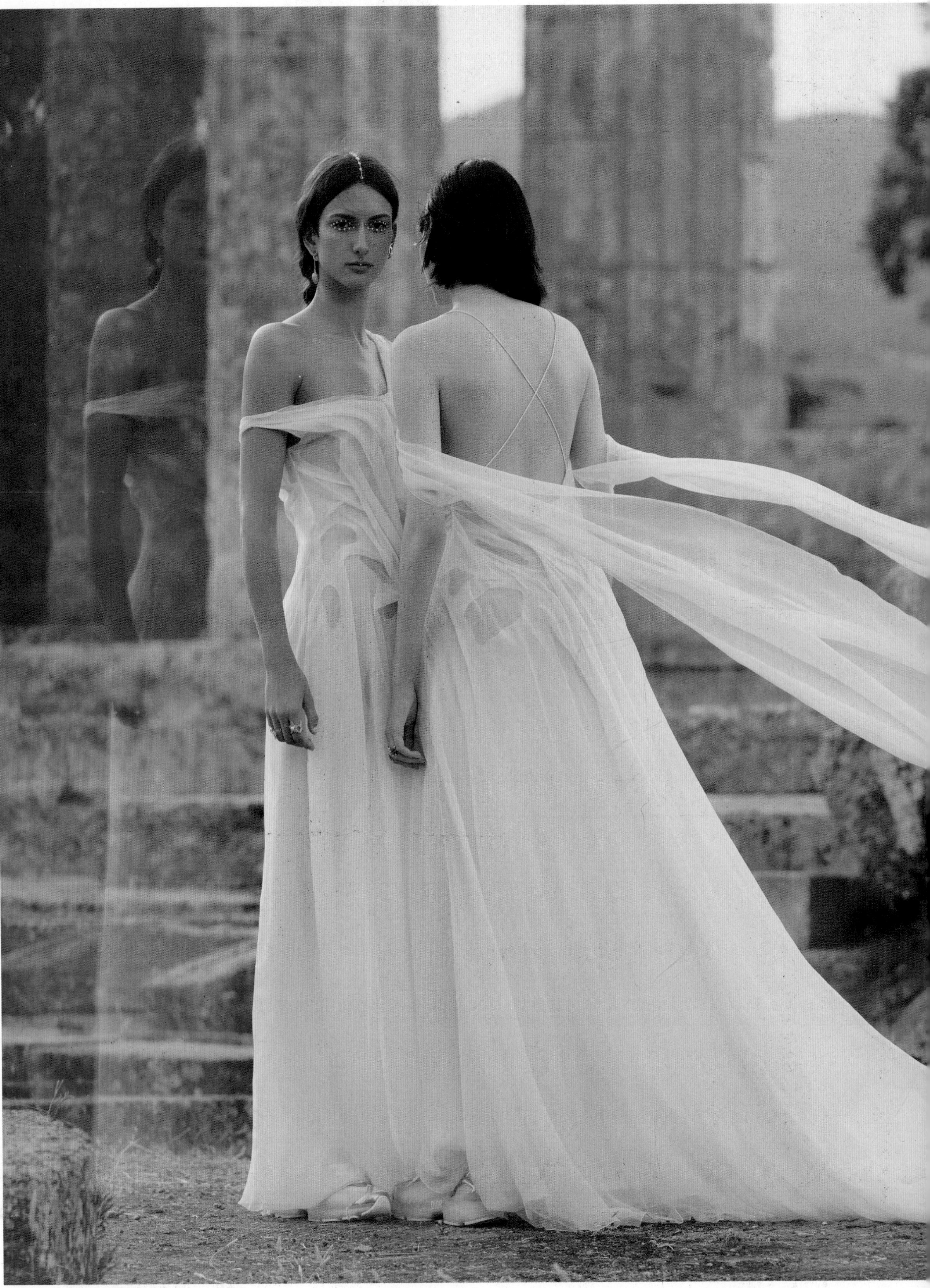

This page: Tumi is wearing a printed Lurex jacket by LOUIS VUITTON X FORNASETTI. Studded velvet shirt by LOUIS VUITTON. Cotton track pants with patch appliqué by LACOSTE. And leather boots by MARSÈLL. Opposite: Lauren is wearing a belted leather biker jacket with ruffle hem by SUPRIYA LELE. Viscose roll-neck jumper with logo detail by RAF SIMONS. Knitted cotton cycling shorts by MISSONI. And trainers as before